The Life and Work of
JOHN NASH
Architect

The Life and Work of

JOHN NASH
Architect

JOHN SUMMERSON

London
GEORGE ALLEN & UNWIN
Boston   Sydney

First published in 1980

GEORGE ALLEN & UNWIN LTD
40 Museum Street, London, WC1A 1LU

© John Summerson, 1980

British Library Cataloguing in Publication Data

Summerson, *Sir* John
  The life and work of John Nash, architect.
  1. Nash, John, b. 1752   2. Architects –
England – Biography
I. Title
720'.92'4   NA997.N3   80–40335

ISBN 0-04-720021-9

Typeset in 11 on 13 point Bembo by Northampton Phototypesetters Ltd
and printed and bound in Great Britain by
William Clowes (Beccles) Limited, Beccles and London

To my three sons:

CHARLES ROBERT   EDWARD JOHN
TIMOTHY JAMES

Contents

List of Illustrations

PLATES

FIGURES

Bibliographical Abbreviations

Bolton	A. T. Bolton, *The Portrait of Sir John Soane, set forth in Letters from his Friends* (1927)
Britton and Pugin	J. Britton and A. Pugin, *Illustrations of the Public Buildings of London*, 2 vols (1825)
C. Life	*Country Life* magazine
Colvin	H. Colvin, *A Biographical Dictionary of British Architects, 1600–1840* (1978)
Cwmgwili MSS	The Cwmgwili Papers in the Carmarthenshire Record Office
Davis (1960)	T. Davis, *The Architecture of John Nash* (1960)
Davis (1966)	T. Davis, *John Nash: The Prince Regent's Architect* (1966)
Elmes	J. Elmes, *London in the Nineteenth Century* (1827)
Farington Typescript	The Diary of Joseph Farington, 1793–1821; typescript copy in the Print Room, British Museum
Gent's Mag.	*Gentleman's Magazine*
HLRO	House of Lords Record Office
King's Works	*The History of the King's Works*, ed. H. M. Colvin, 6 vols (1963, etc.)
Loudon	J. C. Loudon, *The Landscape Gardening and Landscape Architecture of . . . Humphry Repton* (1840)
Neale	J. P. Neale, *Views of the Seats of Noblemen and Gentlemen*, 11 vols (1818–29)
NMR	National Monuments Record
Parl. Deb.	Cobbett and Hansard, *Parliamentary Debates* (1803 onwards)
Porden MS.	The Diary of William Porden; in the possession of Mrs Aileen E. Gell, OBE
PRO	Public Record Office
Pennethorne Papers	Papers in the possession of Peter Laing, Esq., and papers formerly (1935) in the possession of James Pennethorne, Esq., Richmond, Surrey
RC Papers	Regents Canal Papers in the Record Department of the British Waterways Board
RIBA Cat.	Catalogue of the Drawings Collection of the Royal Institute of British Architects
Sale Cat. (1835)	*Catalogue of the valuable architectural and miscellaneous library, prints and drawings, of the late John Nash, Esq.* Sold by Evans of Pall Mall, 15–20 July 1835. Copies in British Museum and Soane Museum.
Shide Ledger	Volume of accounts in the Royal Institute of British Architects Library (see p. 86)
Statement (1829)	J. Nash, *A Statement* (1829). Copy in the possession of Peter Laing, Esq.
Summerson (1935)	J. Summerson, *John Nash: Architect to King George IV* (1935; 2nd ed. 1949)
Windsor, RA	The Royal Archives, Windsor Castle
1st etc. Reports SGLR	*1st to 4th Reports of the Surveyor-General of Land Revenues*, 1797, etc.
1st etc. Reports CWFLR	*1st and subsequent Reports of the Commissioners of Woods, Forests and Land Revenues*, 1812, etc.
1828 Report	*Report from the Select Committee on the Office of Works*, BPP 1828 (446) iv
1829 Report	*Report from the Select Committee on Crown Leases*, BPP 1829 (1), iii
1831 Report	*Second Report of the Select Committee on Windsor Castle and Buckingham Palace*, BPP 1831 (329) iv

The Life and Work of John Nash

Records in the Public Record Office

CRES	Crown Estate Commissioners
LC	Lord Chamberlain's Department
LR	Land Revenue Office
MP, MR, etc.	Maps and Plans
WORKS 4	Minutes of the Board of Works

Preface

Forty-five years ago I wrote a book called *John Nash: Architect to King George the Fourth*. Published in 1935, it was the first biography of him to be attempted and contained many errors and misjudgements. In 1977 I undertook the present work because of a growing reluctance to leave behind me a lame book on a noble subject. 'Revision' was out of the question and this new work stands on its own foundations. Much material has been added and the whole has been reorganised and rewritten. Nevertheless, the approach hardly differs from that of the first book. My aim has been simply to reconstruct the life of John Nash and to combine narrative and architectural description in an intelligible account of the man's life and what he achieved in it.

Since 1935 Nash and his buildings have received attention from several authors. I have benefited from Mr Terence Davis's *The Architecture of John Nash* (1960) and *John Nash: the Prince Regent's Architect* (1966); Dr Anne Saunders' *Regents Park: a Study of the Development* (1969); Miss Hermione Hobhouse's admirably illustrated *History of Regent Street* (1975), an essential companion for that subject; Mr Henry D. Roberts' *History of the Royal Pavilion* (1939) and Mr Clifford Musgrave's *Royal Pavilion: an Episode in the Romantic* (1959). Especially valuable has been Vol. VI of the *History of the King's Works* (ed. H. Colvin), containing Dr Michael Port's historical accounts of royal buildings from 1815 to 1851; while the volumes of the *Survey of London* covering the parish of St James, Piccadilly, have been indispensable.

I owe especial thanks to those friends and colleagues who have brought to my attention sources and documents which I would otherwise have missed: in particular to Professor Pierre Duprey, who directed me to the report of the divorce case of 1787 in the *House of Lords Journals*; to Mr Frank Kelsall who unearthed, among other things, the documents in the case of Liardet v. Adam; to Miss Dorothy Stroud, who picked up the scent of Nash's letter to his banker, which has such a strong bearing on his later financial difficulties; and to Mr Peter Bezodis, who led me to the diary of William Porden, whose owner, Mrs Aileen E. Gell, OBE has kindly allowed me to quote from it. Mr Nigel Temple has most generously shared with me the results of his researches into Nash's cottage architecture, undertaken in connection with his *John Nash and the Village Picturesque* (1979).

To Sir Peter Ashmore, Master of the Queen's Household, I am indebted for an opportunity to study the state rooms at Buckingham Palace. To Dr A. L. Rowse I owe thanks for a memorable visit to Cornwall, with Caerhays Castle as its main objective, and likewise to Mr and Mrs Williams of Caerhays for welcoming me to their house, almost the last survivor of the grander Nash castles. Scarcely less memorable was an Irish excursion, arranged for me by Mr Hugh Dixon when I visited Belfast to give the Fine Art lectures at the Queen's University in 1979. To Sir Sacheverell Sitwell I am grateful for his hospitable response to inquiries about the Glenbervie papers. Among the many who have responded to requests for information I would like to thank especially Mr J. M. A. Dinkel, Keeper of the Brighton Pavilion, Mr C. J. Delaney of the Carmarthen Museum, Miss C. J. Baker of the Royal Albert Memorial Museum, Exeter, Mr W. A. Smart, Mr John Harris and Mr Wilfrid Ward. Quotations from Nash's letter to Vere, Sapt, Banbury and Co. in Chapter 13 are by permission of the Secretary of the National Westminster Bank. Miss Langton, Registrar of the Royal Archives at Windsor, has given me valuable help in checking references.

The list of executed works in Appendix I derives from the list developed by Mr Howard Colvin from my original list of 1935 and printed on pp. 581–5 of his *Biographical Dictionary of British Architects* (1978). I am most grateful to him and to his publisher, Mr John Murray, for permission to use and adapt it to the purposes of this book.

It remains to acknowledge, with due appreciation, the sources from which illustrations have been drawn. Two drawings from the Windsor library are reproduced by gracious permission of Her Majesty the Queen. Major Allan Cameron of Lochiel has allowed me to reproduce the splendid portrait of Nash in his possession, Mr Peter Laing the miniatures of Nash and his wife, inherited from his Pennethorne forbears, and Miss Anne Lloyd-Johnes the watercolour of Hafod before the fire of 1807. Mr Leslie Harcourt kindly supplied me with a photograph of the engraving of the Corsham gallery. I also acknowledge with thanks the permission of the following to reproduce the prints and drawings of which they are the owners or guardians and which are identified as theirs in the captions: the Royal Pavilion, Art Gallery and Museums, Brighton; the Trustees of the British Museum; the Devon and Exeter Institution; the Guildhall Library; the National Monuments Record; the Public Record Office; the Royal Institute of British Architects; the Trustees of Sir John Soane's Museum; the Society of Antiquaries; and the Victoria and Albert Museum.

To my wife, who helped me with the index, I owe the deepest debt of all. Without her, there would have been no book to index.

JOHN SUMMERSON
1 Eton Villas, London, NW3

1

The First Forty Years

John Nash was born in 1752 and two fairly trustworthy sources say that he was born in London. Of his parents we are told nothing except that they were Welsh and that the father was 'an engineer and millwright in Lambeth'.[1] These statements can be amplified, though in a somewhat oblique way. Thus, when Nash was thirty-five, we learn that he had first cousins in Wales. One of these was Thomas Edwards, described in a legal document as 'engineer', living in Neath.[2] We know nothing about him except that he had a brother, John Edwards, who was born in 1738 and who, in 1790, was in business in Southwark. He is identified as 'engineer and pump-maker' in a London directory of that year.[3] In 1794 he moved to Lambeth, where the directories describe him as 'millwright and engine maker', and later as 'millwright and engineer' and 'millwright, pump-maker and pipe borer'. Both brothers were alive when John Edwards made his will in 1814.[4] John died in 1818, aged eighty, and was buried at Lambeth.

The importance of John Edwards is two-fold. First, he was evidently in the same kind of business as John Nash's father, who may have been his brother-in-law, though of that we cannot be sure. Second, he had a son, also John, born in 1772,[5] who was, at least from the age of twenty-four a close friend of his older cousin Nash and for nearly forty years was concerned with him in many of his enterprises.

Members of both these families seem to have settled in Lambeth before the middle of the eighteenth century. The names of Nash and Edwards occur with liberal profusion in the parish registers. Between 1746 and 1756 seven couples of the name of Nash brought fifteen children to the font of St Mary's, and though our John was not among them it is highly probable that here was the Welsh clan to which he belonged. The Edwardses were hardly less fertile.

The engineering business in Lambeth with which John Nash's father was presumably associated was of considerable standing. The premises were in Vine Street, off Belvedere

Road (which still exists in name alongside the County Hall and the Hayward Gallery). John Edwards lived in Belvedere House, styled himself 'esquire' and was able to launch his son on a successful career in the law. If Nash's father was associated with Edwards on anything like a partnership basis it would explain why one of our sources stresses that the Nashs' 'were possessed of some private fortune'.[6]

The most critical event in John Nash's boyhood is recorded by the same source. It is that his father 'died when he had not reached seven years', which is likely to mean 1758 or 1759. Our informant goes on to tell us that in due course the boy was 'articled to Sir Robert Taylor', the architect.[7] Here we are at last on firm ground, though we must be cautious about the expression 'articled', for Taylor did not take premiums; he had young men bound to him by indenture in the old-fashioned way and this may account for a statement made at a late date that Nash worked in Taylor's office in a 'subordinate capacity . . . straining paper, copying letters etc.'[8] Nevertheless, we should very much like to know how the widow of the Lambeth millwright came to seek a place for her son in the most consequential architectural office of the day. There is just the faintest shadow of an answer and it must not be ignored.

In 1746, Robert Taylor, then thirty-two and a monumental sculptor rather than an architect, took premises in Spring Gardens, Westminster.[9] These premises were not in the fashionable part of the gardens, breathing the air of St James's Park, but in a fringe of ordinary houses backing upon those in Charing Cross, occupied mostly by tradesmen. Taylor lived there till 1759 when, having given up sculpture and become a highly successful architect, he built himself a fine house in the new street laid out by Edward Southwell on his Spring Gardens property.[10] However, it was while he was still in the old house, in 1757, that two persons of the name of Nash came to live in two separate houses in the immediate neighbourhood. One of them was called John Nash. His house was next door to the disused French Chapel in the street leading out of Spring Gardens to Charing Cross, obviously very close to Robert Taylor for their names are next but one to each other in the rate books.[11] The other was called Robert Nash and his house is not so easily placed. That two people with this surname should arrive in the same year to be neighbours of Taylor is not especially remarkable. What may excite our interest is that Robert Nash had not been in his new house for much more than a year when he died. He was buried at St Martin-in-the-Fields on 4 August 1758. His widow vacated the house.

Unless coincidence is playing a peculiarly malicious game we may surely suspect that Robert Nash, dying in the year of young John's sixth birthday, was the future architect's father, that the elder John Nash was a relative, and that he was responsible for securing a place for his orphaned namesake in his neighbour's office. The sad thing is that it has proved impossible to identify the status, profession or trade of either John or Robert. If this Robert was indeed the 'engineer and millwright in Lambeth' we should perhaps assume that, like John Edwards, he had prospered and was minded to quit the marshy south bank for a more elevated and wholesome address.

To enter Robert Taylor's office was a privilege and any young man remaining there for five years or more would be marked for life by what he learnt.[12] Nash probably went to Taylor when he was fourteen or fifteen, that is in 1766 or 1767. He was still there in 1774 because a certain John Leach was in the office with him and Leach, born in 1760, could hardly have gone to Taylor before that date. Indentures were usually for seven years so Nash would have been out of his term by about 1774.

Taylor was a man of the toughest fibre. With a beak of a nose and an eagle's eye he ran his practice on highly professional lines. The major part of the business was the production of architectural designs of great thoroughness and boldness of scale and by no means void of personal invention. His father having been a mason and sculptor, he had started in that line himself and went to Rome, executing soon after his return the rather sterile composition which fills the pediment of London's Mansion House. It was not a success and he knew it so he switched from sculpture to architecture. With family connections in the City he soon found patrons with full purses and artistically un-encumbered minds who were happy to employ an artist who belonged to their own circle. For them he built London houses which looked like, and were, places of serious business and country houses which looked like, and were, the retiring places of serious men. He became architect to the Bank of England and surveyor of many estates. He filled the office of Sheriff and received the customary knighthood. He made a great deal of money and left it, inexplicably, for the teaching of foreign languages in the University of Oxford. Out of that bequest the Taylorian Institution was eventually built.

Robert Taylor never wasted time. He had an obsession about early rising, getting up at three or four in the morning and going to bed at eight or nine. If this did not exactly save time it provided an undisturbed period of work when most of the world would be still asleep. The apprentices were not required to keep these hours but were neverthe-less got out of bed at five.[13]

If Nash was in Taylor's office, as seems likely, for most of the decade 1766–75, he would have been in contact with some of the very best buildings of the day, such as Taylor's first additions to the Bank of England. These included the grand sixty-foot rotunda and the four aisled halls surrounding it; halls which were like miniature Gibbs churches but lit from tiny glazed domes inserted in their vaults, the walls being defensively windowless. Later on, he may have had some share in that most splendid of London's boardrooms, The Directors' Court Room, with its triple-arched Corinthian approaches and its walls enlivened with antique delicacies more austerely controlled, but no less fluent, than those of the Adams. At the same time he would have seen at least the commencement of the block of lawyers' chambers at Lincoln's Inn called Stone Buildings, the commission for which Taylor won against Adam, Brettingham and Paine; an exemplary model of the London street formula, in beautiful masonry. Taylor's arrogantly severe brick houses in Lincoln's Inn Fields and Lombard Street Nash would know and he was probably in the office when the stone front of the Bishop of Ely's house in Dover Street was going up. In short, by the time he left he had had the opportunity of absorbing

3

the best in construction, design and decoration that the English practice of architecture could offer.

How much Nash benefited from all this is another matter. In later years he expressed no reverence for Taylor. He said that he could not draw and implied that he was a very ordinary man 'who made shift to get on'.[14] This is unfair. The probable fact is that Nash was, if not an idle apprentice, certainly a mercurial one, with a horror of bookish disciplines. He could work like a demon when he chose and the elder Pugin used to tell a story of how he once humiliated Taylor's clerks by sitting up all night to complete a job which they had insisted on postponing for lack of time.[15] More to the point, perhaps, is Nash's own confession of wild and raffish behaviour which drew from Taylor occasional outbursts of grotesque tantrums, pinching Nash's ears and performing some sort of jig with cries of 'harum-scarum, harum-scarum!'[16]

Other and probably more sober pupils in the Spring Gardens office in Nash's time included, besides Leach, just mentioned, Samuel Pepys Cockerell, Charles Beazley and William Pilkington, all a few years younger than Nash, and C. A. Craig, evidently a little older, as he obtained a post in the Royal Works administration in 1775. Craig was an industrious mediocrity but Cockerell, a man with a good family background, arrived at success a long way ahead of Nash, with whose career his own often collided, sometimes with prickly effect. Beazley and Pilkington stayed in the office till Taylor's death and took over some of his practice. Leach gave up architecture (on Cockerell's advice, it is said), took to the law and reached braver goals than any of the group, becoming in turn Vice-Chancellor and Master of the Rolls.

After these years of pupillage the narration of Nash's career runs into difficulties. The fact is that there are two stories and they cannot both be true. On the one hand there is Nash's own story which he told to two acquaintances on two separate occasions and which is consistent and plausible. But on the other hand there are documents of incontrovertible authority which make nonsense of that story or, at the very least, damage it so much by exposing its omissions as to render it suspect from beginning to end. It is possible that if we had all the facts we might compose a narrative which paid respect to Nash's version while not disputing the documents. But as it is we can only conclude that there are certain passages in our subject's early life which he deliberately suppressed. We must be content to follow such glimmerings of truth as he failed to extinguish.

Nash's own story was told to two people: first to William Porden, the architect, in July 1812 and, nine years later, to Joseph Farington, RA, in November 1821. Porden's record is the more informative, as well as the earlier, so let us consider it first.

Nash, says Porden, was 'a wild, irregular youth'. Then follows the 'harum-scarum' story. He goes on:

> When the term of his Articles expired Nash having a small Property about £150 a year in Wales in or near Carmarthen he retired there and according to his own words led a profligate life for 9 or 10 years but with the

character of a Gentleman keeping the best company of *Bon Vivants* and hunting with the most desperate sportsmen . . . During this time Nash never read a book and followed nothing but his pleasures, till he became weary of such a life, and perhaps was unable to support it any longer, when Mr Cockerill [*sic*] who had been bred with Nash, came into Wales to build for Sir William Paxton. Cockerill who knows as well as any man the advantage of making a figure, entered Carmarthen with some éclat as an Eminent Architect from London. Nash seems to have envied his appearance and reputation and exclaimed "I'll be dam'd if I do not get before this fellow yet". Shortly after, he went to dine with (I think a Mr Vaughan) when the discussion fell on architects and architecture and Mr Vaughan declared his intention of building a Bath and would apply to Cockerill for a design "There is no need to go so far," said Nash, "I will give you a design." "You," said Vaughan. "What do you know about designing?" Nash now informed his friends that he had been regularly bred an Architect. "And," says he, "before tomorrow you shall see my design." In the course of the ensuing morning he produced his design – it was much admired. Vaughan determined to build accordingly and requested Nash would give the necessary directions to the workmen. He consented on condition that it should be a "love-job" and staid two or three days to make the working drawings and set the work forward. On his return home his servant brought him a heavy roll which dropped out of his Port Manteau . . . it proved to be a rouleau of guineas which Vaughan had thrust into his Portmanteau unperceived as payment for his designs.[17]

Farington's record is much shorter but agrees with Porden's on all essential points. It identifies 'Mr Vaughan' as John Vaughan of Golden Grove; it includes a further observation by Nash that Vaughan's guineas were the 'first money he received as a professional man' and that 'within a year he had employment which produced him £500'.[18]

A conflation of the two narratives yields what may be considered, on the face of it, a consistent fragment of autobiography. Both authors were told that Nash went to Wales immediately after leaving Taylor and that he there enjoyed an income of £150. Porden says that the 'profligate life' lasted for nine or ten years, Farington that 'country exercises and amusements', presumably the same thing, engaged him till he was twenty-nine. Thus the period of idleness in Wales is neatly pitched between 1771–2 and 1781. There are, however, some difficulties. The first is that 1772 is too early for the termination of the Taylor period if Nash was in the office with young Leach. A second is that 1781 is too early for S. P. Cockerell to have been building in Wales. The real obstacles, however, to the credibility of Nash's story are of another kind altogether.

In the marshy hinterland of south London lay the still semi-rural parish of St Mary, Newington. It had a little brick church. This was rebuilt in the late eighteenth century, again in the nineteenth and finally demolished in the twentieth, but its registers survive and here we discover that on 28 April 1775 John Nash, of the parish of St Margaret, Westminster, was married by licence to Jane Elizabeth Kerr.[19] She was the daughter of Hugh Kerr, a surgeon practising in Walworth and also at Dorking in Surrey. There were three witnesses to the marriage. One was a 29-year-old Newington woman, Anne Burrowes, of whom we know nothing; another was Abraham Ewings whom we shall meet presently as a business associate of Nash; while the third was a young architect and a very promising one: William Blackburn, silver medallist of the Royal Academy, shortly to become a renowned specialist in the design of gaols.[20]

So it seems that the first thing Nash did on leaving Taylor's office was to marry. The picture of carefree gallivanting in Wales begins to fade and is further dissolved when we discover in the Lambeth register that a son, John, was born to the couple and baptised on 10 June 1776. Of this child nothing more is heard.[21] He may have died, but neither the Lambeth nor the Newington registers record his burial. There may be another explanation, of a somewhat bizarre kind, for his disappearance from Nash's life but that must wait to be stated in its proper context. In any case, if family ties did not detain Nash from a prolonged Welsh vacation something else did. In 1777 he made a most determined and courageous effort to make a place for himself in the London building world.

This concerned a project by Sir John Rushout, a Worcestershire baronet (the future Lord Northwick), to develop a property at the north-west corner of Bloomsbury Square. Sir John had just come into the title and the family estate, of which the property formed part; it comprised the Rushout town mansion and some adjoining land and these the baronet now proposed to develop as an investment. He signed an agreement with Nash which presumably took the form of an assignment to him of building leases, to be exchanged, after the usual 'peppercorn' period, for leases at a substantive ground-rent for which Nash, the builder, would be liable until he had sold the houses and reassigned the leases. To ensure the prompt execution of the agreement, Rushout made Nash enter into a bond in the sum of £2,000 with two sureties to complete the rebuilding of the premises by September 1778. The sureties were Abraham Ewings, who had been one of the witnesses at the wedding, and Richard Heaviside, a timber merchant of Parliament Street, Westminster, a man of considerable affluence. Nash was to have the materials of the old houses on the site, valued at £1,000 or more.[22]

For a man of twenty-five this was a pretty bold adventure, especially as the initial operation had to be carried through within eighteen months under a severe penalty for non-completion. Nash seems to have been successful, however, for rates were laid on the new houses by the local vestry in the critical year. Where he was not so successful was in disposing of the houses. There were eight in all, comprising two large houses built as one block at the corner of Bloomsbury Square and six smaller houses along the south side of Great Russell Street. One of these Nash took for himself but the others in the street remained empty till 1781, while of the two big houses in the square one was empty till 1783 and the other (the largest) till as late as 1800.[23] As a speculative venture the project had failed.

Meanwhile, however, Nash had the satisfaction of completing what must surely have been his very first buildings; and as all the houses still stand (Plate 2A) it is a satisfaction which we can share. They forecast with uncanny accuracy the Nash of forty years later in style, in material and in pretension, to say nothing of the rash association of architectural adventure with a gamble in the estate market.

The bond of 1777 provided that Thomas Leverton, the eminent surveyor and architect of houses in Bedford Square, should either 'delineate describe or approve' the elevations but it is clear that they are pure Nash. The front to the square parades eight Corinthian pilasters with their proper entablature, standing over an arched and rusticated ground floor. Here are none of the Adamesque attenuations of Leverton's work and the design is one which Sir Robert Taylor would have approved, at least in principle (though hardly, perhaps, in detail). Furthermore, the exteriors are finished throughout in stucco, a far from common proceeding at the time. The group must have stood out very proud and bold in the Bloomsbury of the 1770s.

This stucco is, as it happens, of some importance to our story. It was supplied – and, no doubt, applied – by no less a firm of contractors than Robert, James and William Adam: a firm rather better known to history as the most sophisticated and inventive architects of the time. In 1774 the Adams had entered into an agreement with a Swiss clergyman, the Rev. Mr Liardet, to market a kind of oil-bound cement he had invented and patented in the previous year. The priority was immediately challenged and the Adams fought and won a case taken against them.[24] Then in 1781 Liardet, believing the Adams to have been negligent and deceitful in their handling of the business, took a case against them. From the bill of complaint and the defendants' replication emerge some very curious facts. The Adams executed work on the two big houses in Bloomsbury Square to the value of £490. Subsequently, in 1779, they covered five houses in Great Russell Street, bringing the total value to £688. In the same year they actually lent Nash £2,000 on the security of the Bloomsbury Square houses, then just finishing and worth, they said, considerably more than that sum. All they ever had from Nash was a bill at three months for half the earlier sum, £240, which 'firmly believing', as they put it, 'that Nash was a solvent man' they discounted, but which was never honoured.[25]

From 1778 to 1781 Nash was living in Great Russell Street, in the end house, next to Bury Place. In 1782, however, there was a change of occupancy and he must have moved. Reasons for this shortly emerge. Not only did the houses he had built remain mostly empty, not only did he owe a great deal of money, but he was in trouble in another direction – his relations with his wife.

John Nash had not been living with Jane Elizabeth for much more than two years when he decided that he had had enough of her. She was extravagant. She ran up bills of nearly £300 with various milliners, a sum which represented something like a third or even a half of what her husband could expect to earn in a year. On two occasions he was arrested for debts contracted without his knowledge. No remonstrances on his part having the slightest effect, in June 1778 he packed her off to the country. This meant South Wales. She travelled with Nash's cousin, Thomas Edwards, the engineer, who deposited her at the house of his sister, Mrs Morgan, in Aberavon. There she remained, sulking in her fine London clothes.

However, she was not without company for long. Nash took a somewhat ambivalent course of action. He instructed a boyhood acquaintance of his, now a clerk in a coalyard at Neath and unmarried, to call on Jane Elizabeth and to 'ride out with her and show her the Pleasures of the Country'. In no time at all, this young man, whose name was Charles Charles, was not only calling but living at Mrs Morgan's for weeks on end.[26]

The result was predictable. What did Nash expect? He went down to Wales for a short visit at Christmas. Mrs Morgan knew very well what was going on but nothing, apparently, was said until, a few months later, Jane Elizabeth was delivered of a baby girl. This was at Thomas Edwards' house at Neath where she had gone to lie in. Mrs Morgan then declared all she knew. Jane Elizabeth made no bones about the child's paternity but insisted that it should take the name of Nash. In July 1779 she returned to London, travelling at least part of the way with Charles Charles, and took up residence in Great Russell Street. In October, however, she was again dispatched to Wales, leaving behind her unpaid millinery bills to the value of forty pounds.

What were Nash's intentions? As the story unfolds we find that at some point he resolved to shatter the bonds of wedlock by the one legal course open to him – divorce. This enterprise, in the long run, was to fail. The amazing thing is that it was ever started but there is not much doubt that it was in Nash's thoughts soon after he left Great Russell Street in 1781, perhaps even before.

For a man in Nash's situation to contemplate divorce was, to say the least, unusual. Divorce could only mean one thing: an Act of Divorce, passed by the Houses of Lords and Commons. In the whole of the last quarter of the eighteenth century only seventy-five divorce bills became law. To promote such a bill entailed a procedure of tedious complexity and an expense of between £500 and £700; and it might take a very long time. Even before the Lords could be petitioned for leave to bring in a bill there were two other bridges to be crossed. First, it was necessary for a case to be taken in a court of common law against the wife's paramour and a conviction obtained, with damages for criminal conversation. Second, a plea had to be entered in the appropriate ecclesiastical court and a definitive sentence of divorce from bed and board obtained against the wife. These two objectives gained, a bill might be drafted, leave obtained, a sympathetic Peer solicited to introduce the bill, witnesses engaged and, at long last, the bill taken through two readings, passed down to the Commons for their concurrence and, at the third, if all went well, be forwarded for the Royal Assent.[27] By which time it was not unusual for the patience and the purse of the prime mover in the affair to have been totally exhausted.

Nevertheless, in February 1782, Nash set the preliminaries in motion. He took a case against Charles Charles in the court of King's Bench for assaulting, debauching and wounding Jane Elizabeth in Neath on 1 January 1779 (a date, as it happens, when Nash was almost certainly in Neath) and at other times, and for forcibly detaining her from her husband for six months. He asked for £1,000 damages. Charles pleaded not guilty to the charges but the jury found to the contrary and damages were assessed, but at only £20 with costs.

In the light of evidence which came out later in the House of Lords, certain aspects of the case do not seem entirely satisfactory. For one thing it could hardly be said with truth that Charles Charles had detained Jane Elizabeth from her husband; for another, the debauching and wounding of Jane Elizabeth is never again alluded to and was probably a gross exaggeration of what was nothing more than a planned seduction. There must remain a strong suspicion that Charles Charles was acting, from beginning to end, on Nash's orders and, in fact, that his role as defendant was a complaisant one. As Charles was in the Marshalsea at the time of the trial he was obviously incapable of paying any damages whatever, let alone £1,000, and it seems rather more likely that he anticipated some compensation from Nash for services in enabling him to secure the conviction he wanted and which he wanted for one reason only – as one of the two essential passports to a process in the Lords.

In the summer of 1782, Nash's affairs were in a state of crisis. All the Bloomsbury houses except one were still on his hands, there were debts galore to be paid, including the expenses of the case against Charles, the money owing to the Adam brothers and, no doubt, a whole army of milliners in pursuit. Where Nash was living in this year we do not know. But his creditors knew. In 1783 he was declared bankrupt.[28]

A commission of bankruptcy was sealed on 30 September. On 31 December following, the Lord Chancellor allowed a certificate of discharge. The period of three months between these dates is not much more than would be necessary for the statutory procedure to take its course and we may assume that Nash acted ingenuously. The certificate describes him as 'formerly of Lambeth . . . and late of Great Russell Street . . . Carpenter Dealer and Chapman'.[29] This may seem a somewhat anomalous description, but it was not as an architect that he was bankrupted, but as a tradesman. In the eighteenth century and, indeed, up to 1861 bankruptcy facilities were available only to traders. Non-traders, who would include most professional men and any person claiming a rank in society, could only be 'insolvent debtors'. These latter were, at least in theory, never released from their debts until they were paid. The bankrupt on the other hand, having declared all his property, was sold up and discharged. Bankruptcy probably suited Nash and the designation 'carpenter' (the addition of 'dealer and chapman' is a mere legal convention) would have the advantage of diverting attention from his misfortunes. To be gazetted in the bankruptcy lists as 'John Nash, architect' would have been decidedly damaging to his professional prospects.

In any case, we may presume that Nash found himself at the beginning of 1784 stripped of all property but a free man. The next we hear of him is in Carmarthen. Nash, it will be recalled, told Porden that he had a small property there worth £150 a year.

9

If he had this in 1783 the bankruptcy would have swallowed it. Real estate was not exempt. How he found his feet at Carmarthen is a mystery but find them he did. This must be the period of what Porden described as 'keeping the best company of *Bon Vivants* and hunting with the most desperate sportsmen'. It is also the period of the alleged profligacy which Nash illustrated with a couple of not particularly lurid anecdotes. One was about drinking parties which lasted over days in any house which was found to have a cellar of good wine. Another was about a wagering session with a drunken Irishman who stripped Nash (also drunk) of everything from his horse and saddle to his coat and watch but lost everything back when Nash staked his entire bank balance against the lot.[30] All this sounds more like a rakish 20-year-old than a man in his thirties with some rather serious problems on his hands. But nice chronology is the last thing to be looked for in Nash's remodelling of his early life.

If Nash arrived in Camarthen penniless he was soon in business again. He met up with a young architect called Samuel Simon Saxon, who had been in Chambers's office in London but presumably had Welsh connections.[31] In 1785 Nash and Saxon submitted an estimate of six hundred guineas for the construction of a new double roof for St Peter's Church and this was accepted. The roof was built and three years later an extra £45 was authorised for the plaster ceiling. This lasted till 1860 when some of it fell down and the whole roof was reconstructed.[32]

With Saxon, about this time, Nash purchased some woodlands at Taliaris, near Carmarthen: possibly an investment in timber, but we are told that he lost on the transaction.[33] In 1787 he acquired in his own name the lease of a piece of waste corporation land near the Towy with an old lime-kiln on it: again, possibly with the idea of improving his fortune in the building materials market.[34] He is also supposed to have done some building in the town. Spurrell, the Carmarthen historian, instances the former 'Six Bells' tavern near the church but this is a common bricklayer's job.[35] He also mentions 'the house at Green Gardens where he (Nash) resided'. This survives in part and is a building of the lowliest kind. It is hardly conceivable that Nash had anything to do with it. For the strange and inexplicable fact is that, in 1787, Nash the bankrupt, the layabout, the gambler, drinker and boon companion, had aquired sufficient means and social connections to set in train what had been maturing in his mind for these past four or five years – the procurement of an Act of Divorce.

With the conviction of Charles Charles in the court of King's Bench he had taken this process through its first stage. He had also obtained, on 6 January 1787, in the Bishop of London's consistory court, a Definitive Sentence of Divorce from Bed and Board against his wife for adultery with Charles who, incidentally, had since died. He was now able to bring in a Bill to the House of Lords. It was presented by Lord Scarsdale, the 61-year-old builder of Kedleston, and read a first time on 28 February. The second reading was ordered for 20 March and then postponed till 29 March. On that date a Committee of the Lords was summoned and witnesses were called. Thomas Morgan and his wife, her brother, Thomas Edwards, a certain Humphry Edwards,

Samuel Saxon and two others were examined. Mrs Morgan described with due delicacy what she had seen in Charles Charles's bedroom. A Mr Richard Woodings, who had known Nash since his marriage and seems to have been in his service in a superior capacity, confirmed the outrageous extravagances of Mrs Nash while stating his belief that 'Mr Nash's conduct was always that of a very good husband'. The household, he said, had been a simple one. In Lambeth besides the Nashes and himself there were only a man and a maid-servant; in Great Russell Street only a maid-servant and Nash's relations with her were entirely proper. Mrs Nash had had notice of the hearing but did not attend and was not represented. She merely presented a petition praying for maintenance of herself and the child, on the passing of the Act.

But the Act was not passed. On the question being put whether the Bill be read a second time it was resolved by their Lordships in the negative.[36]

The proceedings in the Lords were reported in at least one newspaper, *The World*, where we are told that the Lord Chancellor (Lord Thurlow), in his summing up, did not as he might well have done charge the husband with collusion but showed himself 'clearly adverse to the divorce'. Apart from one or two editorial nudges, the report is accurate but the editor chose to enliven it by inserting in italics a totally extraneous piece of gossip about the defendant:

> *This Mrs. Nash was the dame, of whom a very extraordinary tale was not long ago related in the newspapers. She used to impose upon her husband with a simulation of pregnancy, and actually bought children whom she brought up as her own, to carry on the imposture.*[37]

So improbable a story can hardly be pure invention. What was the truth? A possible interpretation is that Nash was incapable of giving his wife a child and that she, dreading the stigma of infertility in a society of fast breeders, shuffled some Lambeth foundling into the home. The sheer technical difficulty of acting out such a charade militates against such a hypothesis, but an unbalanced woman might perhaps attempt it. As we have seen, a son of John and Jane Nash was registered in June 1776, a year and six weeks after the marriage. If this was part of the deception and was exposed as such it might account for the lack of any further references to the child. Apart from this, *The World's* scandalous little paragraph is of no importance to our narrative and may be left as a marginal curiosity.

The failure of the divorce, after such large expense and care, must have been a stunning blow. How did Nash foot the bill? Was the divorce business underpinned by some family subsidy, perhaps involving the Edwards clan who figured conspicuously among the witnesses? We do not know. Nor do we know what became of Jane Elizabeth and Charles's child. She, poor chattel, had secured an order for maintenance at £10 a quarter in 1785, and we may charitably suppose that Nash continued the remittances. She was still alive in 1795[38] but had presumably died before 1798, the year in which Nash, at forty-six, took a new wife.

Meanwhile, Nash's career reached a crisis of a very different and altogether more promising kind. It seems likely that 1787 was the year of his declaration at John Vaughan's dinner-party that he had been bred an architect, a declaration promptly ratified by the erection of the bath at Golden Grove. Within a year of that event, Nash told Farington, 'he had employment which produced him £500'. What employment this was we may plausibly conjecture.

In April 1787 Richard Jones, a solicitor of some consequence in South Wales, writing to Squire Philipps of Cwmgwili about various personal and local matters, mentioned in passing the failure of the divorce case. 'Mr. Nash met with a sad disappointment', he wrote, adding: 'I verily believe had he succeeded he would immediately have claimed a relationship with me', an observation which we may suppose to mean that Nash had in mind an early marriage with some relative of Mr Jones.[39] However that may be, a letter from Jones to Philipps, dated just a year later, mentions Nash in a different context altogether. Jones was now engaged in drafting a parliamentary bill which would enable the County Borough of Carmarthen to pull down its old gaol and build a new one with, in addition, that other type of punitive institution known as a 'house of correction'. A question of alternative sites had arisen. One party favoured building outside the town; another maintained that the old site offered a less costly solution and one which was perfectly practicable, notwithstanding a difficulty about water supply. This latter party was supported by Jones and 'Mr. Nash', he wrote, 'is willing to depose on oath . . . as to the saving'.[40]

So it seems that, as early as April 1788, Nash was advising on the construction of the new gaol. According to an inscription which survived till the building's demolition, it was begun in 1789 and completed three years later. Nash was the architect. It was his first public work. On its completion in 1792 he entered his forty-first year.

2

The Carmarthen Years:
from Prisons to the Picturesque

The architect of the new gaol had been living in Carmarthen for no more than four years when he undertook the commission. His statement that he had inherited property in the neighbourhood is no doubt true for without some such social and territorial roots he could hardly have made for himself the position he did. It is difficult to reconstruct his mode of life in those years. He lived, as he told Porden, 'with the character of a Gentleman', while acting at various times somewhat outside that character: as contractor for the new church roof and as a speculator in sundry property and building concerns. With the commission for the gaol, however, he emerges as a gentleman-architect, a species not very common anywhere and excessively rare, if not unique, in Wales.

But Nash defied classification. Physically, he was a little man, so conspicuously short that to his contemporaries, old and young, he was 'little Nash', sometimes in amused friendliness and sometimes, among the hostile or jealous, in contempt. Squat but sturdy, he was by no means unprepossessing. The 'round head, snub nose and little eyes' to which he cheerfully confessed in later years,[1] were no hindrance to what an elegant woman, again at a much later period, called 'a very clever, odd, amusing man'.[2] He can hardly have been otherwise than that in his late thirties, making himself agreeable to the South Wales squirearchy, sharing their bucolic humours but climbing imperceptibly to a dignity and sophistication beyond their range.

In the local political arena he attached himself to the Whig faction, led by the richest of the Carmarthenshire magnates, John Vaughan of Golden Grove, Lord Lieutenant of the county and its parliamentary representative from 1779 to 1784.[3] He was not only Nash's first patron but very probably the man behind his engagement as architect for the

13

gaol. A Whig ally of Vaughan's was John George Philipps of Cwmgwili, a youthful and somewhat lethargic follower of Charles James Fox, who filled the Borough seat till, overcome with distaste for Parliamentary life, he quit in 1803.[4] Nash's letters to him among the Cwmgwili papers are racy outpourings which Philipps never seemed to find the energy to answer. But they remained friends long after Nash had left Carmarthen for London. Many other friends and acquaintances flit through the Cwmgwili papers but to none of the names can we attach substance.

The affair of the new gaol had exercised the burgesses of Carmarthen long before Nash's arrival in the town. In common with nearly all county towns of the period, prison conditions at Carmarthen were utterly degrading and filthy. In a society becoming steadily more refined and humane nobody was unaware of this but it took the iron will and analytical brain of John Howard to bring conscience to the point of action. His peregrinations brought him to Carmarthen first in 1774.[5] The gaol, built into the shell of the old castle, was as horrible as most of its kind. There was no water and the well was useless; the cells were miserably small and the condemned cell reeked of damp. Five years later he came again. He found no alteration and this time there was 'a number of idle and profane people playing at tennis'. The gaoler lived far from the gaol, was unsalaried and subsisted, as most gaolers did, on fees and tolls extracted from prisoners and their friends.

The year of Howard's second visit, 1779, was also the year of the Penitentiary Act under which premiums were offered for model plans.[6] The winner of one of these was, as it happened, a man well-known to Nash – William Blackburn, who had stood witness at his wedding. The gaols and houses of correction which Blackburn built between 1786 and his early death in 1790 were the first great Howardian models.[7]

Howard was at Carmarthen yet again in 1788 and on this occasion prickings of conscience aided by scoldings from the judiciary had so far modified local opinion that he was invited to leave recommendations for a new building.[8] Now this was the very year in which we find Nash brought into the business – and Howard's recommendations were presumably the basis of his design. The plans have not survived, however, and the building, after a period of use as a police station, was demolished in 1938.

To the public view, the gaol presented only a restricted frontispiece of dressed masonry (Plate 2B), rather like three bays of one of Sir Robert Taylor's country-house stables but with a narrow rustic doorway in the centre bay surmounted by a balcony which served for public hangings. Rather oddly, the Act authorising the building only reached the statute book in the year in which (according to the inscribed tablet which it bore) the building was finished – 1792.[9]

Nash's success here brought him a commission to design a smaller gaol at Cardigan, where Howard's strictures on the older building – waterless, verminous and filthy – had been no less severe.[10] The building, finished in 1793, has long since vanished but old photographs (Fig. 1) show a plain stone-faced, pedimented fore-building with wings to left and right and a projecting chapel at the rear.

1. Cardigan Gaol, completed in 1793.

Nash designed a third gaol, this time in England – at Hereford. An advertisement in the *Glocester Journal*, 10 September 1792, invited tenders from tradesmen for the new building. They were advised to inspect plans 'at the house of Mr Nash, architect, in Carmarthen' or alternatively 'at the house of Mr Saxon, in Parliament Street, Westminster', from which it appears that Nash maintained an association with his partner in the contract of 1785 for the new roof at Carmarthen church.

Of the Hereford gaol nothing is left, but photographs exist, showing very clearly the Howardian arrangement: long vaulted corridors with galleries (Plate 3A), meeting at a central hall, lit from windows in the angles; cells stacked along the corridors and galleries; stairs at each end. A severe architectural image; but the long vistas of cantilevered galleries were not without effect, an effect which Nash was to find himself happy to elaborate in more than one of his country houses.[11]

The stone frontispiece on the public road at Hereford was much on the lines of Carmarthen but with a pair of columns in the centre bay and, it seems, a garlanding of chains in imitation of Dance's famous device at Newgate.[12] This gaol cost £18,646. Nash, charging a commission of $4\frac{1}{2}$ per cent, took a fee of £720 with, in addition, the rather disproportionate sum of £340 for travelling expenses, the reason being, no doubt, that by the time the building was finished in 1796 he was no longer living in Carmarthen but at a fashionable address in London.

All three of Nash's gaols have gone and they are not, perhaps, any great loss to English architecture. They showed that he could do what would be expected from a pupil of Taylor, that he could handle a set programme successfully and make a stone wall not only grim but eloquently grim.

A more exacting and peculiar problem came his way while the Carmarthen gaol was building. In 1789, the Dean and Chapter of St David's opened a subscription for the repair of their cathedral. The west front was in trouble. It overhung its base and was moving further over every year; if it collapsed, the Norman arcades behind it would start to tumble. The measures which Nash took to forestall disaster were these. First he built a masonry platform on piled foundations against the base of the west front. On this he erected a system of timber shoring to hold the arcades and triforia in place while he took down the upper part of the west wall. He then cased the lower part of the west wall in new masonry with a vertical face, built two buttresses to resist the thrusts of the arcades[13] and extended these westwards across open arches to masonry counterforts with pyramidal summits matching those of the new buttresses. This 'flying-buttress' effect was rather doubtfully assisted by invisible 'flying' arches embedded in the buttresses and counterforts. Finally he rebuilt the upper part of the west wall vertical, with a traceried window of his own invention.

The visual effect (Plate 3B) was certainly striking, and was admitted, even by a mid-Victorian critic, to be 'by no means contemptible'. The workmanship of the local mason was, however, indifferent and movement had started again by 1861, when Sir Gilbert Scott, with his superior expertise in rescue operations of this kind, got rid of all Nash's work and rendered the building back to something like its original form.

While St David's was in progress and the gaols finishing, Nash had public works of another kind in hand – bridges. In 1791 a bridge committee in Monmouthshire accepted his design for a stone bridge consisting of a single segmental arch with a span of no less than 285 feet (85 feet more than the Grosvenor Bridge at Chester, not built till 1832). It was actually begun but discretion soon prevailed and Nash was paid off.[14] In the following year the magistrates of Cardiganshire commissioned a new bridge over the Rheidol at Aberystwyth, a five-arch masonry structure on traditional lines, which lasted till 1886. For the same authority Nash built in 1793 a stone bridge to carry the road from Tregaron to Lampeter over the Teify at Trev-Gevail. Here, the responsible magistrate was Thomas Johnes, whose connection with Nash, of another sort, we shall shortly discover.

It was also in 1793 that a summons came from Abergavenny, whose inhabitants were concerned with a programme of 'improvement' and required Nash's advice. 'Improvement' was a wonderful word. It could mean anything from the laying of sewers to the building of a County Hall. It was to mean, in Nash's future, a great deal more even than that: the building of a huge metropolitan highway connecting parks, waterways and palaces. But that was not for twenty years to come. Meanwhile, Abergavenny wanted to build a new market house and to pave, light and drain the streets. With Nash's advice, an Act of Parliament was sought and obtained and commissioners appointed. Nash was instructed to prepare a plan and estimate for 'Butchers-shops, Shops, Sheds, Stalls, and Shambles, Standings and other conveniences'. Further, he was to estimate for laying down iron water pipes instead of the old lead ones supplying the market and for 'pitching and flagging' the principal streets. The market house was a very modest thing indeed; nothing more, probably, than an enclosure with iron gates (made by a local ironmonger) and orderly rows of shops and stalls. It cost only £810, with a commission of £52 10s. to the architect. Finished in 1795, it lasted for thirty years.[15]

'Improvement' was also in the air at Stafford, and with rather grander intentions. A County Hall was required and in 1794 designs were solicited from several architects, including Nash. He submitted with his plans a perspective drawing of dazzling elaboration (Plate 4A) with over a hundred figures which, if not drawn by Rowlandson, are a very passable imitation of his style.[16] Market day is in full swing and the new building rises majestically in the background. Nash has taken to the new fashion for inset columns and low bald-headed domes. He may have thought that this design, in such a spectacular presentation, would sweep the board, but it did not. The Stafford burgesses preferred a rather tame offering by John Harvey, a pupil of Samuel Wyatt and a man whom Nash was to displace in a very different situation twelve years later.[17]

During the summer of 1795, Nash stayed with a Worcestershire squire, Sir Edward Winnington, at Stanford Court. This was a business visit with social overtones. The business was, once again, bridge-building. The bridge across the Teme at Stanford, cracked by the previous winter's frosts, had collapsed and the little village of Stanford was inconveniently divided into two parts. Sir Edward, acting as a Worcestershire magistrate, wanted not merely a bridge but an iron bridge in one span which would run less risk of being swept away by flood than an old-style stone structure with one leg in the stream. For advice on this audacious project (the building of iron bridges being still rare) he had summoned the architect of the new bridge at Aberystwyth.[18] That, as we have seen, was of stone and of a traditional type but it appears that Nash had some recent experience of iron and had, in fact, been consulted about the famous Wear bridge at Sunderland. According to his own account he had proposed a stone bridge of enormous span but this being condemned as too daring, had followed with a design in iron which was carried out and proved a spectacular success.[19] Nash's claim to have designed the Sunderland bridge is not, however, wholly convincing. When it was finished in 1796 the credit went to one of the local gentry, Rowland Burdon, MP, described as 'engineer, architect and paymaster', Nash, many years later, told Lord Glenbervie that the bridge 'was first projected by himself and the design stolen from him by Mr. Burdon'.[20] That cannot be quite true because the origins of the Sunderland bridge have been shown to be connected with an experimental structure set up by the technological socialist, Tom Paine, at Paddington Green in 1790. Indeed, when that was broken up, Walkers of Rotherham, the founders, used some of the materials for the Sunderland structure.[21]

Whatever the truth of the matter, Nash, when he was staying at Stanford Court, was described by a fellow guest as 'the ingenious architect who had built the famous bridge at Sunderland'. The fellow guest was a Miss Butt, a clergyman's daughter who was later to become Mrs Sherwood and the admired author of the *History of the Fairchild Family*. Miss Butt took a dislike to Nash and found 'the little man . . . pert, impudent and ugly'. She alludes to him as a married man though she was probably ignorant of the attendant circumstances. She resented, in any case, the pains he took to ingratiate himself with the daughter of the house as well as with Sir Edward, his client.

The bridge was built and Miss Butt had to concede that it was 'a most light and elegant thing'. The younger Winnington children romped on it in high glee, only to hear the next morning that it had fallen down flat an hour or two after their visit. A village boy went down with it, but escaped unhurt.

The construction of the bridge was highly curious as may be seen in a drawing (Plate 4B) said to be a copy of one by Nash.[22] The effective 'arch' seems to have consisted of fifteen iron units (like little pendant arches) acting as voussoirs and presumably bolted to each other and to the continuous curved element which supports the roadway. If the balustrade was also iron (which is doubtful) it would have something of the effect of a lattice girder. There is no obvious precedent for the design and its fate discouraged imitation. But it took more than that to discourage Nash. Two years elapsed before there was again a bridge at Stanford, but his second arch survived for more than a century and to this we shall return.

The three gaols, the west front of St David's, the Abergavenny improvements, the two Welsh bridges and the first Stanford bridge, all belonging to the Carmarthen period, represent Nash's first exercises in public architecture. His essays in the domestic field, in the same period, were more numerous. Twelve houses, all in Wales, have been authoritatively assigned to him and there may well be or have been others not yet identified. Only four of the known houses still stand, all in some degree defaced. The whole collection is interesting, not so much for the intrinsic beauty of the houses, though they have a grain or two of originality, as for the evidence they supply of a career promoted in an unpromising countryside by sheer force of personality and social manipulation and arriving in a very short time – six or seven years – at something like national recognition. In 1789 it could almost be said that there were no architects in Wales. By 1796 Nash of Carmarthen was 'eminent' and 'celebrated', mentioned in guidebooks and even in a county history.[23] The personal triumph is, on the whole, rather more impressive than the architectural performance.

The houses were of the 'villa' type – square or oblong blocks of no great size with three or four good rooms on each of two floors, neatly folded round a staircase planned for effect, the stair often climbing up a curved wall. Not to spoil the villa image, the service quarters were in an annexe of discreetly negative character screened by shrubs. Such houses were several degrees more sophisticated than the overblown farmhouse type with Palladian trimmings which was the commonly accepted model for the mansion of a South Wales squire.[24]

Ffynone in Pembrokeshire, built for one of the Colby family, and very much altered in 1904, is a nice example (Plate 5A; Fig. 2). There is still a Taylorian touch about the pedimented entrance front but the scale is smaller and the mouldings are lighter. Llysnewydd, Cardiganshire, for a Col. Lewis (Plate 5B), demolished c.1970, had the same sort of plan but the handling was more original. There was a bold Doric porch and, in

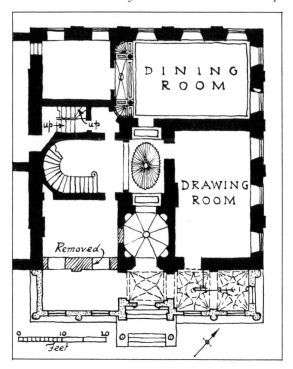

2. Ffynone, Pembrokeshire. Sketch-plan (1933).

the roof, a feature which can hardly be called a dormer and is clearly meant to give a touch of pomp. This feature turns up in several of Nash's later designs where its source becomes recognisable, rather surprisingly, as the attic storey of Sir William Chambers' Strand front of Somerset House. Llanayron, another lost Cardiganshire house with a plan like the last two, was for another Lewis, unrelated to the last. Here Nash departed still further from Taylorian convention.[25] The entrance front had a slightly recessed centre with, left and right, big triple windows with semi-circular heads and radially fluted tympana of the kind which Adam introduced in his Royal Society of Arts building in the Adelphi.[26]

These tentative experiments were to lead, as we shall see in the next chapter, to something much more interesting in the design for Southgate Grove, Middlesex. There we shall find the Llysnewydd 'attic' and the Llanayron windows integrated with real gusto in a beautiful house which was to be one of the foundations of Nash's London reputation.

Of other houses of the Welsh period only two need detain us, and in both cases rather because of the influences exercised by the client on Nash's creative future than for any spectacular innovations in the buildings themselves. These two very special clients were Thomas Johnes of Hafod in Cardiganshire and Sir Uvedale Price of Foxley in Herefordshire.

Thomas Johnes was a man of rare talents, romantic inclinations and very great inherited wealth, most of which he saw fit to invest, at huge risk, in visions of a re-generated peasantry labouring happily in a countryside of incomparable beauty. The vision touched reality only at moments. The beautiful landscape was real and so was the treasure-house of art and letters which Johnes created in it in 1786–8 on the site of the dismal old manor. But the peasantry were real only in their mindless resistance to the new methods and new opportunities in which Johnes solicited their co-operation. If there were moments when Hafod glowed with elysian anticipation, there were others when black gloom descended. And there were moments of disaster.[27]

Johnes's first architect at Hafod was Thomas Baldwin of Bath, who built him a house of which we have, unfortunately, no visual records. When in 1793 Johnes decided to enlarge and enrich the place he brought in Nash, perhaps because Baldwin had run into bankruptcy or perhaps because he hoped for something from Nash closer to his own imaginings than the old City Surveyor could supply. Nash seems to have rebuilt the main front, reordering the windows and adding Gothic pilasters, tracery, cresting and pinnacles in plenty (Plate 6A). Not only that, but at one corner of the house he realised one of Johnes's favourite dreams. This was the library, a self-contained octagon, rather like a chapter-house, with book-lined walls lit from a Gothic lantern in the roof and eight slim Doric columns of variegated marble supporting a gallery for access to the higher shelves. Where the library joined the house, Nash introduced a little rotunda inviting a left turn to the drawing-room. Beyond the library, one side of the octagon opened into a long conservatory.

All this was seen by C. R. Cockerell, S. P. Cockerell's 18-year-old son, touring Wales in 1806. He was not quite as enthusiastic as some of Johnes's visitors. He did not care much for the house, and the library was 'a good room but affected as Nash's things generally are'. One thing that pleased him was the junction of the octagon with the conservatory: 'a good idea'.[28] He was very possibly the last person to cast a professionally critical eye on Hafod, for in March of the following year the house caught fire and was burnt to the ground in a few hours.

The outer walls stood and Johnes, stoically calm, immediately started to rebuild. 'All Nash's buildings are gone', he wrote to his friend, George Cumberland, 'and you will say no loss. But Baldwin's stand firm. I shall employ him again, for he is an able, and I believe, an honest man.'[29] Nash, it seems, had not lived up to expectations.

In the end Hafod was rebuilt within the old walls, perhaps by Baldwin. The octagon rose again and at some date was surmounted by an oriental onion dome. In the middle of the nineteenth century a huge Italian aggrandisement was begun by Salvin (who, incidentally, had been a Nash pupil) but never finished. In the middle of our own century the site was laid flat.

The remodelling of Hafod and the building of the library and conservatory were the most interesting things Nash had done – interesting because they were done for and in close collaboration with a man whose knowledge, taste, curiosity and sense of adventure in the arts was exceptional. Moreover it was in Thomas Johnes's circle of friends that

Nash came to know two men who were of inestimable importance to him; not so much as patrons but because they admitted him to a movement in the philosophy of art which, already in motion in their own minds, was soon to stir the world of landscape-gardening and, beyond that, to project into architecture a new sense of the poetic relationship of buildings to landscape. These two men were Sir Uvedale Price and Richard Payne Knight, the progenitors of 'the Picturesque'. Knight was a cousin of Johnes on his mother's side; Price, a friend since their schooldays at Eton. All three were much of an age, a few years older than Nash who turned forty in 1792. There is no precise evidence that Johnes introduced Nash to either of these two men but the network of acquaintance, kinship and patronage is too close to admit much doubt.

The more immediate association, which is also the better documented, is that of Nash with Sir Uvedale Price. Price, straying from his paternal estate of Foxley, fell in love with the conjunction of seascape and mountainous landscape at Aberystwyth and in or before 1797 decided to build a small house there. He procured a plan from a local carpenter but then heard of Nash, possibly through Johnes. Nash designed for him the little triangular house, subsequently called Castle House, which was pulled down in 1895 and of which the quaintest, if not the most accurate, records are the little china models once sold as souvenirs.[30] A letter from Price to Sir George Beaumont dated 18 March 1798 tells us how this came about and why:

> At first I thought of running up two or three nutshells of rooms, and got a plan from a common Welch carpenter; then Nash was mentioned to me, & he had a mind to build me a larger house indeed, but a square bit of architecture. I told him however, that I must have, not only some of the windows but some of the *rooms* turned to particular points, & that he must arrange it in his best manner; I explained to him the reasons why I built it so close to the rock, showed him the effect of the broken foreground & its varied line, & how by that means the foreground was connected with the rocks in the second ground, all of which would be lost by placing the house further back. He was excessively struck with these reasons, which he said he had never thought of before in the most distant degree, & he has I think contrived the house most admirably for the situation, & the form of it is certainly extremely varied from my having obliged him to turn the rooms to different aspects.[31]

One could not hope for a more precise and circumstantial account of Nash's induction to the mystery of the Picturesque. Price's talk of the 'broken foreground' and the 'second ground' may be somewhat baffling to us who never knew Aberystwyth in its wild days. But it evidently made sense to Nash. Price was using the language of William Gilpin, whose books of *Observations*, in which he analysed natural scenery as a critic might dissect and expound a work of art, would almost certainly be known to Nash; especially the one on the Wye valley, published in 1778. What Nash may not

21

have 'thought of before in the most remote degree' was perhaps the idea of designing a house with an explicit relationship to a particular landscape. Here at Aberystwyth the Picturesque was powerfully present. In one direction there was the ocean breaking on rocks; in another, the jagged ruins of an old castle; in a third, a range of massive cliffs. Price's house was to embody an appreciation of these three scenes, so various in content and mood.

A triangular plan was clearly the answer. Triangular houses were not uncommon, though they were mostly in the nature of follies or conceits, or else theoretical tests of ingenuity. Blaise Castle, near Bristol, is an example of the first; a plan in Batty Langley's *Gothic Architecture* of 1742, of the second. Of Nash's interpretation (Plate 6B) we have, unfortunately, only an outline plan and some very inadequate views,[32] but it was certainly neat. Inside an isosceles triangle with a right-angle at the apex and a base of about 100 ft Nash compacted three octagonal towers, with apartments between them. The main apartment, of which Price gave the dimensions as 20 by 30 ft, probably ran along the base line and overlooked the sea. The three towers rose a little way above the rest of the house giving it a squat castellar silhouette.[33]

If this commission represented Nash's first contact with the philosophy of the Picturesque, as Price seems to imply, he had a great deal more to learn. He must immediately have got hold of Price's classic exposition of the subject, the *Essay on the Picturesque*, first published in 1794. There he would find the theme expanded in larger and more elegant style than Gilpin could command or had ever attempted. Gilpin's perceptions were limited to the discovery of a new enjoyment of natural scenes as if they were works of art, characterising such scenes as 'picturesque'. Price took the word and invested it with new powers and limitations. Gilpin had made no clear distinction between what was picturesque and what was beautiful; Price insisted that 'picturesqueness' (he coined the word) and 'beauty' were absolutely different. Burke had already, in a famous essay, distinguished between the Sublime and the Beautiful; now Price proposed the Picturesque as a third category of aesthetic sensation, distinct from either.

This was no mere academic exercise. One incentive to writing the book was Price's extreme dislike of the so-called 'improvement' of park scenery by Capability Brown and his followers. All over England, parks had been moulded, shorn and replanted on Brown's ideal model. His 'belts' and 'clumps' were seen everywhere; to Price they gave the idea of 'having been made by contract in London, and then sent down in pieces and put together on the spot'.[34] The ideal of 'high polish and flowing lines' embodied in Brown's methods was in fact an abuse of nature. It was the antithesis of the Picturesque whose basis was in variety and intricacy, something which 'time only, and a thousand lucky accidents can mature so as to become the admiration and study of a Ruisdael or a Gainsborough'.[35] The landscapes of Britain had to be rescued from 'improvement' by the heirs of Brown and cultivated on the principles of the Picturesque. To these principles the great landscape painters were the most reliable guide.

If none of this had any very direct concern with architecture it implied a new approach to building in the country. The accepted ideal of a smooth Palladian mansion standing on smooth grassy swards above the smooth waters of a serpentine lake stood condemned. The relationship of a country house to the environing landscape was shown to be an altogether more sensitive problem. It was not merely a matter of style but of siting, shape, scale, aspect and, of course, convenience. The problem of the little house at Aberystwyth, with its triple obligation to the Picturesque, Nash had solved very nicely, but in terms typical of eighteenth-century symmetrical 'nutshell' planning. He perhaps did not know at the time or at least did not fully appreciate that some twenty years before he built Castle House a house had been built in Shropshire which represented a totally new departure and was in fact the first original statement in the architecture of the Picturesque. This was Downton Castle, near Ludlow, and the owner was Richard Payne Knight.[36]

Knight and Price held at this time identical views on the philosophy of the Picturesque. The ideas of each inspired the other. It was Price who prompted Knight's long didactic poem, *The Landscape*, to which Price's *Essay* was the immediate response. Both detested the Brown tradition and made it the starting-point of their search for new attitudes and definitions. Both believed in the unique potency of the Picturesque as an idea and in the relevance of Claude, Poussin, Ruysdael and other landscape masters of the past to its understanding. But only Knight had faced the issue in architectural terms and this was because of his decision to rebuild the family mansion at Downton. This was a challenge to himself on his own ground. The site of the house was superb, overlooking the wooded valley of the Teme, with a wonderful panorama of folding hills beyond; the river itself a resounding chaos of rocks and splashing water. To insert in this scene a primly dressed, porticoed, sash-windowed residence would have been, to Knight, a kind of vandalism. His young rash intelligence (he was still only twenty-four) conjured up something different and it proved to be a gesture of revolution.

Knight built his house as a castle. Not, however, the kind of castle which Robert Adam had been building in Scotland and some of his followers in England – balanced arrangements of towers, turrets, bartizans and battlements – but a castle with the rugged imbalance of Warwick or Goodrich. Downton is not a very big house but it is difficult to describe. One remembers it by its towers: a massive square tower, nearly windowless; an octagon corner tower; then a round tower and behind it another round tower. As an architectural composition it hardly works. It is a random piece. Inside, however, it is very different. Unexpectedly, the square tower encloses a domed dining-room, a miniature Pantheon, and from here a vista is disclosed through two drawing-rooms to a circular room within the octagon tower. All this is classical, somewhat in the style of Henry Holland; and a marble fireplace makes a scholarly reference to one of the temples at Paestum. In short, the interior is the proper setting for a man of taste and learning, a man of consequence in his own county and at Westminster. The exterior shrinks away from commitments of this kind; it is just a grey, massive landmark, evocative indeed but answering no questions.

At what date Nash became acquainted with Downton and its owner we do not know.

He was certainly visiting there by 1799.[37] What is certain is that some years before this the house had made a deep impression on him. This calculated randomness, hidden away in wildest Shropshire, was a revelation. Horace Walpole's Strawberry Hill, to be sure, was random, but that was because it had been built in fits and starts. Wyatt's Lee Priory in Kent, 'a child of Strawberry', was another irregular piece, affecting to be monkish. Downton affected to be a fortress. But it was fortification in the misty undisciplined sense of broken silhouettes and clustering towers as seen in a picture. This elusive image had been brought into focus and translated into actuality without losing its delightful ambiguity, its mobility of form; and in translation had become an elegant and convenient dwelling. The possibilities in this transformation were endless. They were, indeed, to be exploited for a hundred years but it was John Nash who first saw how to play the castle game which the owner of Downton, more philosopher than architect, had put into the architect's hands.

Nash's castles, however, belong later. In the years in which he made acquaintance with the masters of the Picturesque he was still in Carmarthen, his marital troubles receding, cutting a gay figure in Carmarthenshire society, extending his acquaintanceship beyond the border and reaching towards London in a variety of ways about which we are not too well informed. A London address emerges for the first time in 1796 and it is a good one: 30 Duke Street, St James's.[38] He probably had lodgings there. But his business was still chiefly in Wales and throughout 1795 he had plenty to occupy him there, as well as in Hereford for the gaol and in Worcestershire for the Stanford bridge. Of his comings and goings in 1796 we are slightly better informed and the year begins with a social episode of an unexpected kind.

Every winter a troupe of strolling players came, under their manager, Henry Masterman, to play at the little theatre in Carmarthen.[39] They were well received by the gentry who sometimes joined in their productions. One such occasion was on 8 January 1796, when a playbill announced that *The School for Scandal* and *The Farm House* would be given, the first of the two to be acted entirely by amateurs. Nash was billed as Sir Peter Teazle, a Mr Hughes as Charles and a Captain Vaughan as Trip. There was a full house and Nash's performance was remembered as 'admirable' by one of the professionals. He was Charles Mathews, then a very young actor in Masterman's company but to become in due course a stage celebrity and to remain always a friend of Nash. In 1796 he had just deserted a Dublin company in which he was unhappy and was on his way home to a dull career in his father's shop. Happening to see a bill of Masterman's in Swansea he offered his services and was accepted. He played at Swansea, then at Carmarthen, where everything delighted him. 'It is a beautiful Theatre', he wrote, 'and holds £30. The scenery is really capital.'[40]

The excellence of the scenery, one would like to suppose, had something to do with Nash. It may equally have had something to do with a talented young Frenchman who now comes into the picture. Auguste Charles de Pugin was a victim of the French revolution. The story is that, fighting under the Royalist flag, he was injured and left for dead, was thrown into a common grave near the Bastille, climbed out, swam the Seine, made his way to Rouen and embarked on a ship bound for England. Casting about for a livelihood he happened to see a newspaper announcement that a Mr Nash, architect, required a draughtsman and that the services of a foreigner would be preferred. He called on Nash and found in his waiting room a French nobleman of his acquaintance in pursuit of the same object. But it was Pugin who was engaged.[41]

To equip himself for the kind of draughtsmanship Nash required (possibly on the lines of the Stafford County Hall perspective) he obtained admission to the Royal Academy painting school in 1792.[42] As this would keep him in London we must assume that he worked independently, taking instructions from Nash on his periodic visits from Carmarthen. The preference for a foreigner is curious. Nash certainly had a leaning towards French taste, which at that time was the taste of the Prince of Wales's court and of his architect, Henry Holland. There was plenty of talent in London's *emigré* population and it is perhaps worth mentioning that, many years later, Nash took into his office a young man called John Foulon, born in England but the son, it appears, of a Marquis de Foulon, whose situation in the nineties may have been much like Pugin's.[43] Could the Marquis have been the other candidate in the waiting room?

In any case, Pugin was certainly employed by Nash in Wales and was associated with him for many years in various ways. But he made a career of his own, married into the English gentry, acquired some fame as a watercolourist and ran a successful drawing-school where among his pupils was Charles Mathews' son who, after a spell in Nash's office and a false start as a District Surveyor, followed his father on the stage.[44]

Pugin was an energetic, affable man with a rattling store of anecdotes, rendered memorable by their transmission in broken English. He greatly admired Nash, holding him up to his pupils as a model of fortitude and determination. To one of his pupils, Benjamin Ferrey, we owe the account, just given, of his early life, along with some useful sidelights on Nash's. They come in Ferrey's biography of Pugin's famous son, the man whose furious satire on the age of stucco – the *Contrasts in Architecture* – exploded in the year of Nash's death.

Of Nash's other assistants in the Carmarthen years we know only two. One is a Mr George, who assisted on the Carmarthen gaol and eventually made a career for himself in the town.[45] The other is James Morgan who served Nash for more than forty years and survived him by twenty-one.[46] Never for an instant does Morgan emerge as a personality, but he is always there. He is the backroom partner, the *alter ego*, the deputy, the agent, the man of straw, whichever character the master needs at the moment. His usefulness is inexhaustible and we shall meet him constantly, though never face to face.

The year 1796 saw Nash in passage between Carmarthen and London. Mostly, it seems, in London, but in October he was in Carmarthen mustering support for his friend J. G. Philipps in his parliamentary election campaign which, with much prodding and spurring from his friends, he won.[47] In December, Nash was in Scotland but by Christmas again in Carmarthen.[48] A letter of January of this year from Admiral Macbride to J. G. Philipps, dated at Cowes, suggests that he was or lately had been in the Isle of Wight.[49] It may have been his acquaintance with the admiral which first took him to the island, possibly on a professional errand. If so it was an introduction of some consequence both for Nash and for the island, as we shall see later.

After 1796 Nash is once again a Londoner. At this juncture it might be supposed that his social success and professional eminence in the west would pale in the metropolitan glare. Nothing of the kind. His celebrity blazed. He was also more than moderately rich; richer, that is to say, than might be expected even of an uncommonly successful architect in mid-career. This is a matter as puzzling to us as it was to some of his contemporaries. A correspondent of John Soane writing many years later, in no kindly terms, about Nash's way of life, asked: 'whence came the original supplies, I wonder?'[50] We may wonder, too.

Nash's recovery after the crash of 1783 and his subsequent prosperity can hardly be accounted for by his trading and professional activities alone. Of patronage on a grand scale there is no sign and we are driven to the conclusion that, somewhere or other, there were family resources which became available at the moment of crisis and a good way beyond. Ferrey's statement that Nash's parents 'were possessed of some private fortune' assumes significance here but gives us no lead. Enquiries into relatives with the name of Nash have proved fruitless. There is, however, that other family which may have been his mother's and whose fortunes were, it seems, closely linked with his own: the family bearing the not uncommon Welsh patronymic of Edwards.

Of this family something was said in the last chapter. There was the 'first cousin', Thomas Edwards of Neath, engineer, who was involved as a witness in the divorce episode. There were John Edwards of Lambeth and Llyrela and his son John, whom Nash consistently describes as his 'cousin' until in 1830 he calls him, significantly, 'my only relative'. This cousin John played an extremely important part in Nash's life and his life-story must be noticed.

Born in Lambeth in 1772, he was twenty years younger than Nash. The first known mention of their relationship is in a letter from Nash to J. G. Philipps, dated 16 June 1796, recommending Edwards as a London agent in his election campaign. 'If an agent is employed in town,' writes Nash, 'and your interest does not point otherwise, let me recommend my cousin John Edwards, No. 5 New Inn. You know him therefore I need not add any more on that head.'[51]

In 1796 John Edwards was twenty-four and, it seems from his address, already practising the law. Three years later he married the daughter and heiress of a Welsh squire, Thomas Williams of Court Herbert, Glamorganshire, and was then described as 'of the Inner Temple'.[52] In 1807, his wife having died, he married the widow of John Dalton of Russell Square.[53] By her he had a son to whom he gave the names of Nash Vaughan, the names probably of the boy's two sponsors at the font. By 1810 he had taken a partner into his legal business called John Wittit Lyon and the firm of Edwards and Lyon, attorneys, practised at 72 Great Russell Street. Meanwhile Edwards and his wife lived next door, in Bloomsbury Square. These addresses we have met before. They were the two houses forming the large block on the corner of Great Russell Street which Nash had built in 1776 and failed to sell. They were among his few substantial assets at the time of the bankruptcy and would in the normal course of events be seized on behalf of his creditors. How, then, do they come to be in the hands of his cousin John in 1810? Had the Edwards family stepped in at some point to retrieve their cousin's embarrassed situation?[54]

Whatever the answer, young John Edwards was hand-in-glove with his cousin John Nash, at least from 1796. The firm of Edwards and Lyon handled all Nash's legal affairs and were brought in on every enterprise with which he concerned himself. The association was also personal and domestic. When in due course Nash built himself a house in Regent Street it interlocked with the house he built for Edwards; and when, near the end of Nash's life, George IV was minded to reward his architect with a hereditary title, things were to be so ordered that Edwards should inherit it.

Edwards, however, was to die in 1833, two years before his cousin.[55] He had become by that time immensely rich. Not only had he married two rich women but in 1829 he became the residuary legatee of William Vaughan of Lanelay, Glamorgan, whose property in South Wales included coal and iron mines. He then added the name of Vaughan to his own and left a very handsome fortune indeed to his son Nash Vaughan Edwards Vaughan.[56] He sat in Parliament for a couple of years in 1819–20 as Member for Glamorganshire, figuring as a Tory demagogue and setting all the local landowners by the ears.[57] He sat again (as John Edwards Vaughan) in 1831–2 as Member for Wells. He voted, very naturally, against the Reform Bill.

What sort of a relationship was this between these two men? The twenty-year difference in age and Nash's intense anxiety that Edwards should inherit such wealth as he might gather may suggest an irregular kinship. But if Edwards had been a natural son of Nash some hint or rumour would surely have reached us. Besides, Edwards' parentage is well established. A romantic relationship of a homosexual kind is, from what we can gather of the two personalties, wholly improbable. The likeliest answer is quite simply a community of interests and ambitions, social, financial, professional and, indeed, racial. These two Welshmen may have set out from Lambeth but their roots were in Wales – and Wales was perhaps the source of the wealth which made their London adventuring possible. How that wealth was garnered, how distributed and what obligations it created or imposed, are matters totally obscure and must, at least for the present, so remain.

With the ending of the Carmarthen years and a fair prospect opening in London, Nash was by no means indifferent to the fact that there was still no bridge across the Teme at Stanford. He had learnt some important, if elementary, lessons from the dire collapse of 1795 – and exerted himself to devise a method of building an iron arch whose security could be guaranteed. In a new design he adopted a principle in whose originality he had sufficient confidence to take out a patent. This he did in 1797, entrusting the legal process of enrolment to John Edwards.[58] The principle involved was the very simple one of forming an arch out of iron boxes, each box shaped to the curvature of the arch like a stone voussoir and either bolted or stubbed to its neighbours. The boxes were of similar depth to stone voussoirs but much longer, so that five of them might form an arch which would require thirty or forty stones. The boxes could either be left hollow as mere frames or given bottoms and filled with rubble.

On this principle a new bridge was constructed at Stanford. It cost the county £1,200 but the inscription on it struck a personal note:

> To Sir Edward Winnington this bridge, the first under the Patent and cast at Coalbrook Dale, is inscribed by his friend the inventor and patentee John Nash. Finished in September 1797.[59]

The bridge survived till 1905, when the Worcestershire County Council replaced it with a reinforced concrete arch between the old masonry abutments. Some of Nash's iron balustrades, identical in design with the gallery railings in Hereford gaol, may still be seen planted against the wall of the neighbouring inn – a last testimony of the Carmarthen years.

3

Dover Street and Cowes: the Repton Connection

Throughout 1796 Nash was constantly on the move, his spirits high, his energy inexhaustible. A letter he wrote to J. G. Philipps at Cwmgwili on 17 December 1796 reflects his mood and motions in that year.[1] On the cover he puts an outrageously massive 'MP' after Philipps' name, in playful celebration of his election for the borough of Carmarthen. He tells Philipps that he is just back from 'the cursedest journey to Scotland I have ever experienced' (so it was perhaps not the first). He is dining that evening with Admiral Macbride in Holles Street and in a few days will be setting out for Bath, then on to Carmarthen where he expects to dine on Christmas day: he is taking his young cousin 'Jack' Edwards along with him. There is a scrap of war news about Napoleon's latest move against Mantua; there is some gossip about a mutual friend (a Miss Harrison) who, having just married an *emigré*, is now Mrs de Lambert and is going to sell up her London house and live in Geneva. For some reason unknown to us there is 'the devil to pay and no pitch hot!' As to his own domestic arrangements, he writes:

> I am going to commence housekeeper & have partly agreed for a house with a piece of ground adjoining Dover street looking down hay hill over ye Marquiss of Lansdowns gardens. 99 yrs £280 a year but I mean to let the house for £200 a year and build on the adjoining spot so that my house will front you as you come up hay hill.

The ground concerned was that on which stood No. 28 Dover Street with the vacant site for No. 29 next door northwards. Nash moved fast. There was a brief trip to

29

3. 29 Dover Street.

Carmarthen in June 1797[2] but he was in No. 28 by the end of that year and by the following Christmas the new house, No. 29, was built and in occupation.[3]

It is not till December 1798, however, that the real motive behind this building enterprise emerges. There was no hint of it in the correspondence with Philipps; but on the 17th of that month Nash took a new wife. This lady was Mary Anne, daughter of a Mr Bradley, of the firm of John and Robert Bradley, coal merchants, of Abingdon Street, Westminster.[4] The firm had been bankrupt in 1783 (the very year, as it happens, of Nash's own failure) but had evidently recovered.[5] Mr Bradley seems to have had a house at Robertsbridge, Sussex, for it was from there that his elder daughter, Grace, married a Mr Parker of the Tax Office in the following year.[6] The Bradleys were not gentry in the stricter sense and the nature of their business puts them in much the same social class as the Nash and Edwards families. Mary Anne's mother, perhaps slightly better-born than her husband, was a Gregory and one of her aunts by marriage had married a Pennethorne, a name which will come prominently into the story in due course.[7]

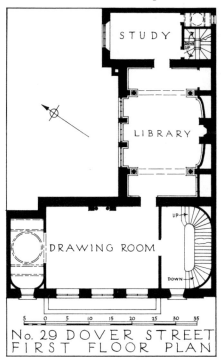

4. 29 Dover Street. First floor plan.

The marriage was at St George's, Hanover Square, and the witnesses were Thomas Fasset and Edward Hyde, names which carry no special significance for us.[8] A miniature of Mary Anne (Plate 7A), probably by the royally-patronised Anne Mee, painted about this time, shows a pretty, dark-eyed girl with a longish nose. A companion likeness of Nash (Plate 7B), though by a different artist, shows him, at forty-five or thereabouts, already bald and with that air of impudence which had so provoked Miss Butt at Stanford a few years earlier.

As for the new house (Figs. 3 and 4), here was impudence in bricks and mortar – and stucco. Wider than most houses in the street, with a three-bay colonnade commanding the slope up Hay Hill, nobody could suppose it the residence of an ordinary citizen; while it certainly had nothing of the perfectionist reticence of the town-houses of the aristocracy. It could only be one thing: the house of an architect and one with an uncommonly strong sense of his importance. James Wyatt's house in Foley Street was, by contrast, discretion itself; John Soane's, in Lincoln's Inn Fields (his first house of 1792), a thing with which any moderately successful lawyer might have been content. Henry Holland's so-called 'pavilion' in Sloane Place was, perhaps, more what Nash was trying to emulate, for the porch with its coupled Ionic columns exactly echoed Holland's frontal colonnade (and, indeed, the colonnade which Holland had raised as a screen before Carlton House).

31

Behind the wide and glossy frontage the plan of the house was conventional enough. It was entered through the right-hand bay of the porch. From the vestibule a stair, curving against the party-wall, led to a drawing room twenty-six feet long across the front, with a little domed cabinet room at the far end. Running back from the drawing room was the library with the fireplace on the right, three fine windows facing north on the left and Corinthian columns on pedestals carrying the main beams as entablatures. Beyond was the study, with a tiny domed closet and a back stair, leading up to the drawing office and down to the dining-room which was under the library. The main bedroom, second floor front, had mahogany drawers and cupboards neatly fitted in the window embrasures. The interior details of the house were not particularly striking and one could believe it was built in a hurry. In 1814, Nash added a conspicuous extra storey in the form of an 'attic' with oval windows and figures in Coade stone representing Geometry, Music, Painting and Poetry.[9] Badly mutilated in the 1930s, the house was damaged by bombs and then pulled down.

A town-house of this calibre might seem to imply the ownership of a country seat of equivalent ostentation and such a house was already building itself in Nash's imagination. He had been familiar with the Isle of Wight since 1793, perhaps through his friendship with Admiral MacBride, and it was somewhere about 1798 that he acquired a property in East Cowes. On it he built, by easy stages, his country retreat and main seat of hospitality, East Cowes Castle. The island was a curious place to choose, one might think, for a country residence in 1798 when the war with France was going badly and invasion no remote possibility. But it was healthy and beautiful and the Southampton mail-coaches accomplished the seventy-six miles with reasonable comfort and expedition, the mail packet to Cowes connecting with the arrival of the night coaches.

The Isle of Wight is cleft on the north by the estuary of the Medina on whose west bank the little town of Cowes crowds down to the water. Opposite is East Cowes where today factories and bungalows make the scene but where until Victorian times there was nothing but woods and fields. The land which Nash bought here was a little way up the estuary, on high ground which dips into a valley, rises and dips again to the river.

There he built his castle. Why a castle? The success of the castellated nutshell on the rocks at Aberystwyth is one possible answer; another is the abiding impression of Downton. But if indoctrination by Price and Knight led him in this direction there was also the circumstance that no less an architect than James Wyatt, the Surveyor-General himself, was either building or preparing to build a castle at Norris, adjoining Nash's property.[10] This was for Lord Henry Seymour, brother of the Marquis of Hertford. Unlike Nash's house, it was finished in one go, and a very splendid piece it is. It is as irregular as Downton but with more energetic movement and even less ornament. Seen from the Solent, it has a spectral beauty and, in the days when ocean liners carried one this way to America, its image of a calm patrician Britain was not soon forgotten.

Nash's castle started modestly. Local tradition has it that it was built, in the first instance,

32

round the stump of an old windmill which Nash reused to contain his staircase. That could be true; the staircase certainly has an odd relationship to the rooms around it. Early representations of the castle show that there was no comparison with Norris. But East Cowes Castle was to grow mightily, as we shall see, with its owner's ascent to higher levels of esteem and affluence.

The year 1798 was a memorable one in Nash's life. It was the year in which he married a new wife, built a new house and started to build a castle. Another event of prophetic significance belongs to that year. In the catalogue of the Royal Academy's exhibition at Somerset House, which opened in the summer of 1798, we find over the name of John Nash an exhibit entitled: 'A Conservatory for His Royal Highness the Prince of Wales'.

Here we must leave Nash's personal life and consider his professional engagements in the years 1795–8, the transitional years during which the celebrated architect of Carmarthen became the even more celebrated architect of Dover Street, London. So far as we know, his first commissions on English soil were the gaol at Hereford and the bridge at Stanford. Nobody called him across the border to build a country house until in 1795 John Scudamore of Kentchurch in Herefordshire enlisted his services. These were required not for an absolutely new house but for the remodelling of an old one. Colonel Scudamore had come into this remote piece of the border country fifty years before but it was only when he was sixty-eight that he made up his mind to modernise. The old house was an irregular patchwork with a fourteenth-century hall, a massive tower of the same century and sixteenth and seventeenth-century additions. Nash pulled much of it down but accepted the irregular plan and built it up again picturesquely in a castellated style. To give the interior modernity and coherence he introduced a long corridor, wide enough to be called a gallery, running right along the house and ending in a flight of steps leading to a space lit by a traceried window, like the east end of a church. This was the first of Nash's country-house galleries. Many more, and grander, were to follow.

Scudamore died while the works at Kentchurch were in progress and Nash's scheme was never completed.[11] Situated where it is in time and place we must think of it as an outlier of the Welsh practice rather than as a breakthrough into the larger world of English country-house building.

The breakthrough was soon to come. In 1796 Paul Cobb Methuen of Corsham Court, Wiltshire, decided to enlarge his house sufficiently to receive such of the family collection of paintings as remained in his London mansion. Elizabethan and proudly symmetrical, Corsham had been enlarged once already at the hands of Capability Brown in 1760. He had extended it by two lateral slabs: one on the east containing a series of five rooms and another, on the west, a library and kitchen quarters. Now Methuen required a further extension, of more stateliness, on the south – and for the design of this he first consulted James Wyatt. He was also interested in extending Brown's improvement of the

33

landscape and so enlisted the help of the man who had succeeded Brown as the leading professor of the landscape art, Humphry Repton. At the same time, he consulted Nash. Wyatt was then, to his great indignation, dismissed and Nash engaged as architect.[12]

Nash was already known to Methuen. Nash and Repton were certainly known to each other. But it was here at Corsham that the two professionals first joined in the simultaneous enhancement of a landscape and transformation of the house within it. From this exercise a partnership emerged which was to bear fruit and be of advantage to both parties while it lasted; which was for four or five years. At the end of that period it exploded, with decisive gains on Nash's side and bitter recrimination on Repton's.

The two men were exactly of an age and the early careers of both had been chequered and unsatisfactory: Repton's, however, unlike Nash's, of transparent respectability, with no dark passages. Repton, like Nash, had a little money behind him but not enough to dispense with ambition and a career. At thirty-six he had achieved nothing. A post with William Windham in his brief tenure of the Chief Secretaryship in Dublin had collapsed with Windham's precipitate resignation. Participating in John Palmer's mail-coach enterprise, he had come off badly and lost money. Then suddenly the idea struck him that his destiny lay in what had been for him a dilettante resource: the study of landscape. About the same year that Nash, pricked by envy of young Cockerell, resolutely turned to architecture, Repton, with no less resolution, turned to landscape. He would be the great 'improver' of his day, the new 'Capability'.[13]

When Nash and Repton came together at Corsham both were well instructed in the Picturesque. Nash, as we have seen, had the confidence of Uvedale Price and was acquainted with Payne Knight. Repton had conversed with both, wandering through the Wye valley with Price and through Hainault forest with Knight. He had entered into controversy with them, defending Brown against their arrogant assaults and reproaching their over-romantic and unpractical devotion to Nature untamed and the cult of sublime rockeries and tangled undergrowth in the paintings of the masters. His book of 1795, *Sketches and Hints on Landscape Gardening*, dedicated to the King, contained his own theory of what he was the first to call 'landscape-gardening'. The theory was not profound but it was consistent and, being the outcome of seven years' assiduous practice, contained a great deal of commonsense. No fewer than fifty-seven Red Books (landscape reports, so-called because mostly bound in red morocco) were listed as the repertory of 'sketches' and 'hints' from which the book took its title.

Repton, unlike Brown, never attempted the role of architect; but architecture and landscape being in so many instances interdependent he needed collaborators – professionals who were sympathetic to his ideas. A landscape was to be seen from the house, the house was to be viewed within the landscape; there were lodges, cottages and outbuildings to be considered; there were questions of style and there was the vital question of siting. His first regular collaborator was William Wilkins, the Norwich architect, father of a more famous son. Between 1789 and 1793 Wilkins had contributed his talents to at least eight of Repton's improvements, and built at one of them,

Donington, Cambridgeshire, a Gothic house of outstanding distinction. At Courteenhall, Northamptonshire, and Buckminster, Leicestershire, he had worked with Samuel Saxon, the man with whom Nash had built the new church roof at Carmarthen. Then, at Corsham, he worked with Nash.[14]

The alterations to the house (Plate 8) were, in this instance, more important than the landscape projects. Nash took a high hand with the Elizabethan carcase. He raked out the old hall and the adjoining rooms (no doubt a great chamber and parlour) and threw the whole space of the main block into one. This 'Grand Hall' as he called it (Plate 9), was 110 ft long with continuous galleries half-way up the walls and a staircase with double returns at each end. With its iron brackets and rails, made at Coalbrookdale, it was curiously like the corridor of Hereford gaol, the main difference being that at Corsham every piece of iron was finically elaborated into Gothic.

Northwards of this Nash built an octagonal saloon which, with a music-room on one side and a dining-room on the other, filled the space between the two Brown wings of 1760. As it was decided that the new north front should be in what Repton liked to call 'Elizabeth's Gothic' the question arose of how the exterior of the octagon should be treated. An appropriate model was found in the eastern part of Henry VII's chapel at Westminster. Though as Repton observed, 'somewhat earlier than Elizabeth', and certainly not octagonal it provided an answer of a sort. The rest of the north and the whole of the east fronts were Tudorised and a highly curious – indeed, unique – composition resulted. A view of it hung in the Royal Academy exhibition of 1797. Repton took some pride in it, insisting in later years that it was a joint creation of himself and Nash and, furthermore, that his son, John Adey, who had specialised in Gothic studies, had participated, though without acknowledgment.[15]

For Nash, the outcome of this commission was far from happy. Even if the house was an artistic success, which is by no means certain, judging by such views of it as exist, everything else went wrong. It was usual at this period for the money for building work to pass through the hands of the architect and to be remitted by him to the contractors in the various trades at appropriate intervals. Nash could be singularly careless in such matters and in 1799, payments to the plasterers were so far behind that Whitford, the contracting plasterer, took an action against him. Sheriff's officers turned up in Dover Street and the plasterers had to be promptly placated. But in March 1800 they were again in revolt. The carpenters, too, were becoming abusive. Walker, the clerk of works, wrote to Nash in despair, threatening to quit. Worse than all this was that dry rot was rampant in the old cellars. Much worse still, dry rot made its appearance in the new ceiling over the music room.

As time passed, defects of construction and design became more horribly manifest and the family retreated to their London house. Continual botching at great expense did nothing to stop the rot. Nash grovelled and said that as 'an upright man' he would take any blame that could be laid at his door. This hardly helped. More rot appeared in 1808, this time in the huge floor and the timbers over the saloon, which had to be expensively replaced in oak. Eventually, in 1816 Paul Cobb Methuen died, leaving to his son, Paul, a cold, damp inconvenient house which set at risk the very paintings which it had been rebuilt to preserve and display. Paul did the only possible thing. In 1840, after years of worry and discomfort, he tore down the whole of Nash's work and brought in the sturdy, competent Thomas Bellamy to rebuild. There is now almost nothing left of Nash at Corsham except the many-gabled 'dairy' on the north front and, inside, the 'Gothic' library, a fireplace and some joinery. All are inexcusably feeble in design. Nash's 'design' for the fireplace survives. It is a hasty scribble on the back of a letter from the unhappy clerk of works.[16]

Corsham, in short, was a disaster. It was not quite the only one in Nash's career. He was one of those architects whose reputation for original genius induced an excess of self-confidence where his obligations as constructor and manager were concerned. The collapsed bridge at Stanford was an instance. Uvedale Price seems to have been aware of this propensity when recommending him to Sir George Beaumont in 1798. 'He is reasonable in his charges,' he wrote, 'but don't trust his estimates but get some other person to execute his designs, and don't say I told you so.'

He was not, perhaps, the ideal workmate for the tidy-minded, punctual and conscientious Repton. Nevertheless the partnership seems to have rolled along smoothly through 1797 and 1798. It was conducted on a business footing. The arrangement was that Nash should pay Repton $2\frac{1}{2}$ per cent on the cost of any work which came through the latter's recommendation. This involved Nash charging Repton's clients 7 per cent, a high fee, keeping $4\frac{1}{2}$ per cent for himself and paying the rest to Repton. His own clients were charged only $4\frac{1}{2}$ or 5 per cent.[17]

To 1797 belong four houses near London, all brought to Nash's hands by Repton. These were Southgate Grove, Middlesex, for Walker Gray; a house called 'Casina' in the village of Dulwich, for Richard Shawe; one called 'Bank Farm' for Major-General St John at Kingston-on-Thames; and Sundridge Park, near Bromley, Kent, for Sir Claude Scott.

The first three of these were what Repton liked to call 'creations', which is to say that they were on sites newly acquired and especially chosen for building.[18] They were also villas, being relatively small, compact and classical, with no agricultural land but ample pleasure grounds around them. The fourth house, Sundridge, was different because it replaced an older mansion and involved compromises in siting and design.

Only Southgate Grove and Sundridge still stand. At Southgate Repton helped Walker Gray to choose the site. It is now a public park and the house is still as Peacock's *Polite Repository* (1798) describes it, 'situated in the midst of a grove of trees beautifully scattered over the lawn, the ground falling gradually to a fine piece of water'. Municipal paths and fences mar the effect but not irrevocably. The house itself (Plate 10A) is a square stucco mass, with an Ionic order in Portland stone doing different things on each of the exposed sides, and an attic storey containing oval windows of the kind we met at Llysnewydd. The ground floor windows have decorative tympana consisting of radial fluting round a shell within the relieving arch – a motif apparently unique to Nash and used over and over again in his later work. The interior is planned round a grand but poorly-detailed staircase, the main rooms being arranged in such a way as to give two continuous vistas through folding or sliding doors: one from the breakfast room through the dining-room and across the drawing-room, the other from a conservatory across the library and through the drawing-room, each vista terminating in a large window looking on to the park. The house is as conscious of its aspects as was the Castle House at Aberystwyth. The little breakfast-room, with a vaulted ceiling, is painted to imitate a birdcage with plants seen through the bars, and in the hall are classical reliefs in *grisaille*.

Among houses of the 1790s, Southgate Grove stands out as one of the most original, less because of its plan, which is on the usual villa pattern, than because of the spirited modelling of the exterior: the play of columns and pilasters in couples, the idiosyncratic 'shell and fan' windows and the attic storey. A drawing of Southgate Grove hung in the Academy of 1797 and the house seems to have been much applauded. It earns a whole paragraph in *Paterson's Roads* and was the only Nash house included by Richardson in his highly selective *New Vitruvius Britannicus* published in parts from 1802.

'Casina', at Dulwich (Plate 10B), was a different thing altogether. This too was seen at the Academy in 1797. It was built for Richard Shawe, a solicitor employed by Warren Hastings in the great trial of 1788–95.[19] There are no satisfactory views of the house, which was demolished in 1906.[20] Nash's point of departure was perhaps the 'Pavilion' which Henry Holland had fashioned out of an older house at Brighton for the Prince of Wales in 1788. The projecting, domed centrepiece and the low wings with Ionic columns *in antis* are much in the Holland style. But this very striking frontal composition contains only four rooms and to make a sizeable house Nash added at the rear a two-storey flat-gabled block which, one feels, may not have composed too happily with the domed centre.

Here again, the site was of Repton's choosing and he proposed the introduction of an ornamental canal which would continue through adjoining estates to the advantage of the whole area. The idea was not taken up but it may have been the germ of Nash's handling of another canal as part of the scenery of Regents Park, thirteen years later.

Of General St John's Bank Farm at Kingston we know very little. It was a small house externally much on the lines of Llanayron.[21] As to the fourth house in the group, Sundridge Park, Nash's participation is rather ambiguous. Repton claimed that the plan was his and he regretted sharing the credit for it.[22] Two views were exhibited in the Academy of 1799 under Nash's name which, of course, was to be expected. Whether the basic idea of a domed *tempietto*, flanked by receding wings, was his or Repton's, it certainly became a useful element in Nash's compositional repertory and recurs very happily, as we shall see, in some of his Regent Street arrangements. Inside the house is a most elegant circular stair, on the axis of the *tempietto*, but it seems that the credit for this should go neither to Nash nor to Repton but to Samuel Wyatt.[23]

Between 1797 and 1800 Repton was ranging round the country, one estate after another submitting to the persuasive interleavings of the Red Books. Where building came under consideration he introduced Nash. Building projects, however, did not always mature quickly and some of these introductions had long-term issues. At Attingham, for instance, where Repton was engaged in 1797, the saloon and circular staircase were added to the existing house only in 1806–7. At Blaise, near Bristol, also visited by Repton in 1797, the famous Hamlet was not built till 1811. A place where house and park did synchronise in conception, so that the future house was portrayed in the Red Book, was Luscombe, near Dawlish. None, perhaps, of the partnership houses had quite so distinct and original a flavour as this.

In 1795 Charles Hoare, the banker, brought his delicate wife to Dawlish for her health. The climate suited her so he bought some land with the intention of building.[24] He summoned Repton who came down in February 1799, completing the Red Book at home by June.[25] In the course of his report, having settled the question of a site, he argues that of 'character'. He pronounced in favour of 'a castle which by blending a chaste correctness of proportion with bold irregularity of outline, its deep recesses and projections producing broad masses of light and shadow, while its roof is enriched by turrets, battlements, corbles, and lofty chimneys, has infinitely more picturesque effect than any other stile of building'. He then introduced the architect. 'By availing himself of these advantages, my ingenious friend, Mr Nash, without losing sight of internal arrangement, disposition, or convenience, has given the house an outline which from its chaste Simplicity must always please the Eye of Taste. Its very Irregularity will give it consequence, while the offices and mere walls which in a modern building it would be essential to conceal, by partaking of the Character of the Castle, will extend its Scite, and make it an apparently considerable pile of building.'

Phrase by phrase, this pretentious nonsense brings out the foibles of its author. Here is the old cliché about 'chaste Simplicity' with the new one about 'irregularity'. Here is the snobbery of 'consequence' and apparent size, along with the obsequious reference to the 'Eye of Taste'. Applied to a design by Nash such language is ludicrous for whatever the faults of his buildings they are never genteel. It may well have irked but more likely amused him to be promoted in this way by his garrulous partner. Anyway, Charles Hoare was sufficiently taken with the designs to go ahead and build.

The site which Repton chose is between two hills; one a steady slope of grassland, the other covered with trees. The background is forest, owing its present density to Repton's planting. A long drive brings the visitor suddenly to a perfect prospect of the house, adroitly pitched in the lap of this landscape.

The house is, as Repton recommended, irregular and battlemented – a toy castle (Plate 11B, Fig. 5). The octagon tower signals its cousinship to Downton, but where Downton is wistfully evocative Luscombe is provocatively quaint. The plan looks very original but is simply an 'explosion' of the kind of small domestic plan which Nash had been using in his Welsh houses of the eighties. One part explodes upwards as a tower;

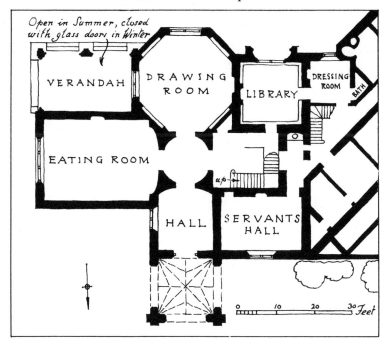

5. Luscombe Castle, Devon. Plan as first built. (Redrawn from an original at Luscombe.)

another part goes down to one-storey height and becomes a 'veranda', with movable glass doors. The entrance hall jumps outwards as a *porte-cochère* and is blown up high enough to seem to be another tower. Given the desire to be 'irregular', 'Gothic' and 'picturesque' while preserving the conventions of a gentleman's residence, this is the obvious way to do it. The interesting thing is, of course, that it was actually done – here, possibly for the first time. The grand originality of Downton has been reduced to an acceptable formula for a middle-sized country dwelling.

Several things are worth noting at Luscombe because they are peculiar to Nash and recur time and again in his later castles. The dominant tower, mostly octagonal but sometimes circular, is a constant; so, very nearly, is the porch treated as a *porte-cochère*; repetitive, too, is the over-simplification of Gothic to the point of crudity in the window tracery and finials. Nash took the minimum of trouble with his Gothic vocabulary. He took, for that matter, little enough trouble with anything involving fine detail. The interior of Luscombe is in the classical taste but, apart from a fireplace with classical reliefs, is singularly lacking in studied ornament.

What did intrigue Nash in the castle business was the free play of architecture once the conventions of style and symmetry were thrown overboard. Today we may tend to see here a straw in the wind of architectural revolution and such perhaps it was. To Nash

39

in his time it was nothing so portentous: simply a new architectural game sanctioned by the spirit of the Picturesque.

Two views of Luscombe were shown at the Academy in 1800 over Nash's name. After that year the partnership is no longer heard of; it had dissolved itself. On what occasion and exactly why we do not know but Repton permitted himself one or two bitter allusions to it in his later writings. One reproach was that Repton's elder son, John Adey, who had been trained as an architect under the elder Wilkins, served in Nash's office and, it seems, collaborated in the design of various houses, including Corsham, had been excluded from any sort of recognition. 'His name,' wrote Repton in the *Theory and Practice of Landscape Gardening* (1803), 'has hitherto been little known as an architect, because it was suppressed in many works begun in that of another person, to whom I freely, unreservedly and confidentially gave my advice and assistance, while my son aided, with his architectural knowledge and his pencil, to form plans and designs, from which we have derived neither fame nor profit; but amongst the melancholy evils to which human life is subject, the most excruciating to a man of sensibility, is the remembrance of disappointed hope from misplaced confidence.'[26]

Nash, it would seem, had used the partnership altogether too ruthlessly for his own personal advancement; a proceeding which the innocent Reptons had not anticipated. Every one of Nash's Royal Academy exhibits between 1797 and 1800 represented a building which had come to his drawing-board on Repton's introduction and in no catalogue entry is the name of Repton mentioned. Of these exhibits one in particular seems to show Nash's thrusting self-interest in a peculiarly cruel light. This is the drawing of 'A Conservatory for H.R.H. the Prince of Wales', shown, as we have already seen, in 1798.

Conservatories are unlikely to be wanted otherwise than with reference to garden plans and improvements. In the year previous to the exhibition of this design, Humphry Repton had been summoned to Brighton by the Prince of Wales to give his advice on the improvement of the gardens at the Pavilion. Between 1797 and 1802 he was paid £264 0s. 6d. for his services.[27] If these improvements involved proposals for building work it would be natural, and indeed obligatory (if the partnership principle was to be honoured), for Repton to bring in Nash. No doubt that is what he did.

In the library at Windsor is an unsigned, undated drawing (Plate 7C) which may very well be the exhibit in question.[28] It is a sectional view of a three-aisled conservatory consisting mostly of iron and glass, unadorned except by flowers, shrubs and climbing plants which almost completely envelop the columns and roof-trusses. As an all-iron construction it is fairly advanced for 1798. Here, it seems, is Nash the engineer, the patentee of the Stanford bridge design, showing off his expertise at the summit of the patronage pyramid. The design was almost certainly not executed. Nor can we argue from it that Nash, at this period, was recognised by the Prince otherwise than as a professional man whose services, among those of many others, were considered for the delight and adornment of his domain at Brighton.

Not for another fourteen years have we any evidence of an association of Nash with the Prince and his court. After 1800 he was on his own. His Royal Academy exhibit of 1801 was in response to an invitation to him and to Repton 'severally' by the President and Fellows of Magdalen College, Oxford, to submit designs for a new quadrangle.[29] Both designs hung in the exhibition, Repton's a modest, well-informed study in domestic Gothic, Nash's a palatial affair, making symmetrical play with ogee-capped turrets. The designs represent the parting of the ways. Nevertheless, for some years Nash continued to reap the advantages of his association with Repton. George Stanley Repton, Humphry's second son, who had joined his office in 1796, was still with him, which seems to indicate that some kindness survived the dissolved partnership. And introductions made between 1797 and 1800 continued to bear fruit. One of the most interesting of these was to Lord Berwick at Attingham in Shropshire.

Repton's first visit to Attingham was in 1797, the Red Book being dated in that year. The first lord had died in 1789, leaving to his successor a huge stone palace standing four-square behind the stiffest and most attenuated of porticos, in flat parkland of indifferent quality. Called in by the second lord, Repton did what he could, mainly by widening the little river Tern and sorting out the wooded area alongside. To Nash fell, in the first instance, the designing of one or more lodges.

Meanwhile, Lord Berwick, who had spent a couple of years in Italy and brought back a collection of paintings, needed a gallery in which to display them. In 1807 he got Nash to fit one into the existing house, occupying the space where its original architect, George Steuart, had proposed but not built a grand circular staircase and two secondary ones.[30] It is a fine room, though the detailing is, as so often, dreadfully feeble and makes a sad show alongside Steuart's brilliant decorations in other parts of the house. The main interest of the gallery is its top-lighting through an iron-and-glass cove.[31] Nash at first proposed a series of glazed ovals in the cove, made up of cast-iron units to be made at Coalbrookdale. This method proving impracticable he resorted to small squares of glass in compartments between the cast-iron ribs which carry the ceiling. The result may not be the height of elegance but the construction of a continuous glazed cove carrying a ceiling was something which had almost certainly never been attempted before. Happily, the experiment succeeded and the cove is still there.

A short distance from Attingham and still on the Berwick property is the small house called Cronkhill, probably the 'House near Shrewsbury' which Nash exhibited at the Royal Academy in 1802 (Plates 11B and 12A). Here is a new departure altogether. The round tower is not a Gothic castle tower but the tower, perhaps, of an old Italian *castello* which has been made into a villa or a farm; and the arcade along the front of the house is so simple that 'loggia' and 'verandah' seem descriptions altogether too exotic. The combination of these elementary forms is the essence of 'picturesqueness'. Cronkhill is apprehended at once as a comment on the landscape in which it stands, a landscape of sweeping fall and rise from the dawdling meadow above which the house stands to the far distant Wrekin. There had been nothing quite like this in English architecture but it

41

is not difficult to account for it. One thinks of Payne Knight's speculations on the architecture appropriate to the Picturesque and his recommendation of 'that mixed style which characterizes the buildings of Claude and the Poussins'. That may indeed be the answer; or part of it.

Cronkhill was built for Francis Walford who is said to have acted as steward to Lord Berwick.[32] He was only about twenty-three when the house was built and it is a fair guess that Lord Berwick, who had brought back some Claudes in his Italian baggage, was, with Nash, the arbiter of the design. Of the plan all that need be said is that none of the rooms is circular and that the exterior roundness of the tower is contrived for a purely pictorial purpose.

If Nash had built Cronkhill and nothing else it would entitle him to a place in the history of the Picturesque. He did not, in fact, build very much in the Cronkhill manner and nothing else in this fashion quite so successfully. The nearest to it is Sandridge, at Stoke Gabriel, Devon, shown at the Royal Academy in 1805, built for the widowed Lady Ashburton, high on the east bank of the Dart, with woods screening it on three sides. A vicarage at Lissan, County Londonderry, built for the Stewart family in 1807 after he had built their castle at Killymoon, is a more modest version of the same theme with an arcade like Cronkhill's. And one may add to the series the unpretentious Southborough Place, Surbiton, built in 1808 for Thomas Langley, with Tuscan eaves and an octagonal porch.

Still in the Attingham neighbourhood, but an entirely separate property, is Longner Hall, the seat of the Burtons. Robert Burton, in 1805 or thereabouts, employed both Repton and Nash but, as by that time the two were not on speaking terms, it was scarcely a happy party. Where the house was concerned there was sharp disagreement. In the Red Book we read of 'another person, with whom (as I had no conference on the subject) I find it impossible to agree, either in the spot proposed for the new house, in the Style of Architecture, or indeed the necessity of a new house at all'.[33] The old house was, in fact, demolished by Nash and the new one built in Tudor Gothic out of deference to its predecessor (Plate 12B). It is, for its time, a most original composition, consisting of gabled wings at right-angles to each other, with a traceried 'veranda' (like Luscombe) tucked into the re-entrant angle. A suburban recollection of Longner will be seen twenty years later in Park Village West and echoes reverberate through Victorian suburbia till the middle of the century. In addition, Longner has one of Nash's most ambitious domestic staircases, fan-vaulted in plaster above and below (Plate 13).

Longner was the last house with which the names of Repton and Nash were associated. Nash was now perfectly well able to look after himself. People were coming to him for the sake of his own original genius and not because he was recommended by the man who was improving their parks. He was cutting a considerable figure in the social life of London, and at the Royal Academy not a year passed without some architectural novelty being displayed over his name. His career as a country-house architect was secure and for a dozen years from the turn of the century it ran a triumphant course.

4

Castles and Cottages: Woods and Forests

In the first twelve years of the nineteenth century Nash built about twenty country houses. He substantially transformed half a dozen more and enlarged or altered many. He built cottages, lodges, park entrances, dairies. His patrons were from here and there. Some were legacies from the Repton partnership; others emerged from the network of Welsh and West Country acquaintances of the nineties, while others again he seems to have picked up in the course of social skirmishing in London. Among thirty-six patrons we find six lords (or lords to be), three baronets and a mixed bag of affluent country gentry: an assemblage of no particular colouring and certainly no political colouring at all. Nash built indifferently for Whig or Tory. Nor in any single instance does this patronage connect with either the old King's twilit court at Windsor or the livelier court of the Prince at Carlton House. It is a clientele typical of any London architect who had made his name.

As to the size, style and quality of these houses there is much to be said and some of it will be said when we come to review them in chronological order. But it may be as well to start by trying to define what direction Nash was taking in the development of country-house design. His classical houses are few; they were influenced mainly by Henry Holland and we may, for the moment, set them aside. For the greater number of houses the clue is perhaps to be found in a comparison of two of the houses discussed in the last chapter – Luscombe and Cronkhill.

Luscombe (Plate 11A) is a 'castle' and we noted there the influence of Payne's Knight's Downton, an influence which was to become even more apparent in later houses in the castle style. Cronkhill (Plate 12A) is not a castle but a free creation drawn from impressions, through paintings and engravings, of the Italian vernacular. What the two houses have in common is purposeful asymmetry. What makes them different from each other is the kind of profiles and arrangements they display; and these are, to a certain extent, interchangeable. If Cronkhill had machicolations on its tower and battlements on top of its arcade it would become, as near as no matter, a 'castle'. With only a little more ingenuity, Luscombe could be dismantled and adjusted to the point of being naively Tuscan. In both houses what really matters is the movement of mass and surface within a broken silhouette. The ornaments give an associational twist to the movement and we shall observe in many of Nash's works that a very little ornament suffices to do that. There is no studied medievalism in any of Nash's works; his 'Gothic' vocabulary was so limited that to call it rudimentary would be an overstatement. Nor did he attempt to elaborate any system of ornament appropriate to the Italian vernacular mood. The effect of his great houses is one of picturesque 'movement' with a rather offhand stylistic characterisation in the direction of Gothic, Tudor or Italian or, indeed, a combination of any two – or three.

As to the plans of the houses, they can be sorted very roughly into two classes. There are those which, like Luscombe, take the conventional villa plan and 'explode' it to produce the desired irregularity of outline and variation of surface. And there are those which depend on a spinal 'gallery' from which the main rooms are entered and which has staircases at one or both ends, the irregularities and variations being arranged round this formal element. The 'gallery' type seems to be unique to Nash. We noted its first appearance, at Kentchurch, in the last chapter. He never abandoned it and its sundry transformations, through twenty-five years, lead eventually to Buckingham Palace.

Luscombe and Cronkhill belong to 1799–1802. In 1802 Nash was commissioned to build a house in Ireland, and it took the castle form. The house, replacing an ancient castle, was Killymoon, near Cookstown, in County Tyrone. Its owner was James Stewart, who sat as the member for that county in the first united Parliament which met at Westminster in 1801. About that date he became a friend of the Prince of Wales. He had obtained plans for a new house incorporating parts of his old one from the Dublin architect, Robert Woodgate. In 1802, however, he replaced him by Nash.[1]

Killymoon stands on an abrupt eminence by the fast-flowing Ballinderry. Contrary to the impression given by George Repton's neat elevational sketch (Plate 14A), it is, in perspective, a disconcertingly wild composition with a number of competing features, the most curious of which is the tall porch with its three enriched 'Norman' arches. From this a narrow vaulted corridor leads up to a vestibule with an almost flat plaster-vaulted ceiling and thence, through the slimmest of pointed arches, into a profoundly gloomy staircase-hall, lit only from tinted glass in a lantern sitting on pendant Gothic arches, picked out in pale blue and gold.[2] To the left of this, the two principal rooms, both classical, open from a barrel-vaulted lobby. The drawing-room has splayed angles, each containing a huge pier-glass so that the room and the company in it are projected and multiplied with engaging effect. Like Luscombe, the plan (Plate 14B) is that of a villa, but expanded and 'exploded'. Nobody could call Killymoon an elegant house but it is certainly original. Nash showed two views of it in the Royal Academy exhibition of 1803.

Nash's next castle was Garnstone,[3] near Leominster, Herefordshire, built about 1806 and demolished in 1958. Samuel Peploe was thirty-one when he inherited the property and started to rebuild. As a Herefordshire squire he would know Nash's work at Hereford and Kentchurch. At Garnstone Nash tried his hand at Tudor Gothic, somewhat in the style of East Barsham, the famous brick house in Norfolk, Garnstone being, however, of green sandstone in seven-inch courses. The stair occupied a massive tower with abbreviated six-light traceried windows at the top. From the staircase hall extended a hall or very wide 'gallery', sandwiched between the front range and a back range containing the principal rooms. Much altered before demolition (the stair entirely rebuilt), it was probably never one of Nash's more interesting creations.

Contemporary with Garnstone was Childwall,[4] near Liverpool, built in 1805–11 and demolished in 1949. It was for Bamber Gascoyne, son of another Bamber who died in 1791 and grandson of an immensely rich Lord Mayor of London, Sir Crisp. The younger Bamber sold the family estate in Essex and was forty-eight when he commissioned Nash to build on his new property near Liverpool, which city he had represented in Parliament from 1780 to 1796. Childwall was a compact castellar mass, built of the local red sandstone, with square and octagon towers as the prominent elements. The octagon tower contained a study on the ground floor, and this was on the axis of a long hall or 'gallery' at the far end of which was the stair, climbing up the walls in three flights. The hall had a flat ceiling panelled diagonally in squares and supported, where it joined the walls, by plaster fan-vaults springing from mural colonettes, which became pendants where the staircase intervened. Something like this, with almost identical detail, may be seen at Longner (Plate 13). The library (whose window is seen on the right in the photograph) and drawing-room ran parallel with the hall, while the dining-room ran across the ends of both.

The next castle, in order of date, takes us again to Ireland. This was Kilwaughter, County Antrim, built in 1807 and now a ruin.[5] It was for Edward Jones Agnew, descended from an ancient family whose castle occupied the site in the twelfth century. So here, as at Killymoon, the castle idea had historic roots and some of their more substantial fibres were absorbed into the new fabric. The new house, built of roughly-dressed basalt blocks with sandstone dressings, was pretty crude. A huge drum of a tower (35 ft in diameter) was the main feature. The plan was simple, much like Cronkhill, though enlarged in every direction and lacking the open arcade. The windows, all rectangular with labels, were filled with wooden tracery; window sills were enriched with carvings of a primitive kind, supplied presumably by a local artist and probably never seen, still less approved, by Nash.

Around 1808 came three monster castles: Ravensworth in County Durham; Aqualate in Staffordshire; and Caerhays in Cornwall. Of these, only Caerhays survives,

Aqualate having been burnt down in 1910 and Ravensworth demolished in 1952. All three have or had a plan of the 'gallery' type.

Taking each of these houses in turn, Ravensworth seems to have been the first to be begun. It was built for Sir Thomas Liddell, Bart, created Lord Ravensworth in 1821, a man of ancient family, great industrial wealth and, among other things, a patron of George Stephenson. He represented Durham in the Tory interest in 1806–7 but then retired at the age of thirty-two to concentrate on the development of his coalmines and the building of his new house.[6] Nash was up north, probably visiting Ravensworth, in 1807[7] and the old house was demolished in the following year. To that date or thereabouts we may assign the earliest of the plans at the RIBA (Fig. 6)[8]. It shows a house with a gallery 20 ft wide and 100 ft long, consisting of five bays, domed in the classical manner, leading to a lobby and thus to a cylindrical tower containing the principal stair. The lobby brings us also (right) to the drawing-room and (left) to the library, the latter connecting with the main suite of living rooms running alongside the gallery.

But if the house was begun like this it was finished very differently. It seems that, about 1822, radical changes were made, still under Nash but with the participation of Lord Ravensworth's eldest son. At that time the stair was brought into the gallery and the gallery itself transformed and given a timber roof on the model of Eltham Palace (which, significantly, A. C. Pugin had just illustrated in his *Specimens of Gothic Architecture*). It was said to be still unfinished in 1834 and building continued in the forties, long after Nash's death.[9]

For us the early plan is more important than the achieved building and it connects at once with the plan of another house, built at nearly the same time as Ravensworth. Aqualate Hall[10] in Staffordshire was built between 1806 and 1812; it was burnt down in 1910. The builder was John Fenton Fletcher who inherited this and other properties in a very roundabout way from a nephew of his great-grandmother. He took the name of Boughey in 1805 and was made a baronet. Aqualate has some pretensions to be 'Tudor' because here the towers are capped by huge ogee roofs (Plate 15A). Nevertheless battlements and machicolations draw it into the 'castle' class and its plan (Plate 15B) is, in principle, that of Ravensworth and, as we shall see, of Caerhays and Shanbally. Of its interior neither records nor memories survive.

Caerhays[11] is on the Cornish coast at Veryan Bay, but the house stands away from the sea, from which it was completely hidden till the Victorian love of seascape induced one of its owners to shift some of the intervening soil. It was built for John Trevanion Purnell Bettesworth, who assumed the surname of Trevanion in 1801. He was a cousin and acquaintance of Lord Byron; he was Sheriff of Cornwall in 1804 and elected Whig Member for Penryn in 1807, the year before he started to build. The house has a noble military stance (Plate 16) with a defensive terrace and cylindrical watchtower towards the coast and a richly-wooded hill behind. It is built of squared rubble and the detail is bluntly simple. As at Ravensworth, the main apartment is a long wide gallery, with a stair rising

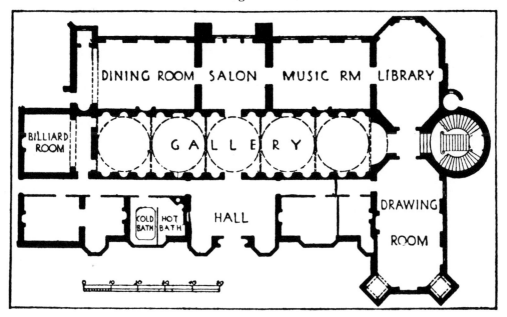

6. Ravensworth Castle, Co. Durham, begun in 1808. An early plan, not as executed, with a gallery of five domed bays. (Redrawn from an original in the RIBA.)

and returning in two flights at one end; at the other end a lobby gives access to a little circular closet and (left and right) the library and a circular drawing-room, the latter connecting (as does the library in Nash's Ravensworth plan) with a suite of rooms parallel with the gallery. The gallery rises to the roof and in the roof are long skylights, while round the walls of the gallery runs an iron-railed balcony, duplicating an inner upstairs corridor. Ornament is sparse but where the gallery joins the walls is a typical Nash arrangement of miniature groins springing originally from mural colonettes (now removed).

Now come some rather smaller pieces in the series. In Sussex, about 1809, Nash built two castles for two brothers, sons of the Sussex historian, Sir William Burrell. Both were in their thirties. For the elder of the two, Sir Charles, he built Knepp Castle; for the younger, Walter Burrell, West Grinstead Park. Knepp was seriously damaged by fire in 1904 but still stands. West Grinstead is in ruins. Both have round towers. At Knepp[12] the tower contains the stair and connects through a square lobby with the inner hall, saloon and dining-room: exactly the arrangement of one end of Nash's first plan for Ravensworth. At West Grinstead (Plate 17B)[13] the tower contains a circular dining-room and the plan recalls Cronkhill, especially as an open arcade extends across the front. This dining-room at West Grinstead was one of Nash's more thoughtfully-decorated interiors. There was a cornice of tiny groins connecting at each springing with wall-ribs descending to the dado and terminating in reversed tracery. There were curved recesses,

47

with side-tables under four-centred arches, mirrors with Gothic frames, a marble Gothic fireplace with Gothic grate and, on the doors, pierced brass Gothic finger-plates. With the purpose-made Wilton carpet of Persian design the room had a very complete air of Strawberry Hill prettiness.

The last two castles on the list were both in Ireland. Lough Cutra Castle, in County Galway, was built for Charles Vereker, later the second Viscount Gort. Born in 1768, Vereker had a distinguished military career and was badly wounded while opposing the attempted French invasion of Ireland at Calloney in 1797. He represented County Limerick in the Irish Parliament from 1794 to 1800 and, though opposed to the Union, at Westminster from 1802 to 1812.[14] It was in 1811 that he decided to build on his Irish estate. He had seen Nash's castle at East Cowes, was impressed, and wanted one like it. Nash was by this time far too busy in London to visit sites in Galway, but he made a design and put the execution of it into the hands of two of his former pupils, James and George Richard Pain.[15]

Lough Cutra Castle, built on a terrace blasted out of the rocky banks of the lough, does indeed bear a resemblance to Nash's vanished castle. The great octagon tower is the octagon tower at Cowes massively increased in girth. The plan of the house, however, is different – a compacted version of Ravensworth. It falls into the 'gallery' class but only just, the 'gallery' being simply a longish Gothic hall with the main entrance in the middle of one side. From this hall there is access to a round turret containing (as at Cowes) a circular staircase. Alongside the hall is the saloon or drawing-room. This enters, at one end, the great octagon tower and, at the other, a room of flattened octagon shape giving a bay-window effect towards the lough. On the axis of this room is a second octagon tower (on the landward side) and this is overtopped by its own circular stair-turret, so that the silhouette of Lough Cutra is more amply towered and turreted for its size than any house in the Nash series.

The third Viscount Gort, drifting towards bankruptcy in the 1850s, sold the house and, at the age of seventy-one, married a rich widow. She, a Mrs Tudor, was, as luck would have it, the owner of East Cowes Castle and there is a pleasant story of the shattering effect on the elderly Viscount when his new wife introduced him to what seemed to be a simulacrum of his old home.

Last of all there is – or, alas, was – Shanbally in County Tipperary, already mentioned because of the close association of its plan with Ravensworth, Aqualate and Caerhays. Shanbally was built for Cornelius O'Callaghan, created Viscount Lismore in 1806 and aged about forty-three when he obtained from Nash plans for his house. The plans, developed in full detail (Plates 18A and B), were executed in exemplary fashion by one of the Hargrave family of mason-contractors who had emigrated to Ireland in the previous century. As it stood before neglect and demolition overtook it, the house was a radiant example of its kind, built of beautifully-cut stone ready to defy the centuries.[17] It was blown up by demolition contractors in March 1960. The plan is a brilliant coalition of ideas we have already met at Ravensworth, Aqualate and Caerhays; but here the gallery, 19 ft wide, is only 45 ft long. It had a Gothic fan-vault with details more conventionally 'correct' than in earlier houses (Pugin's hand, perhaps) and flat traceried lights in the crown of each bay.

Shanbally was the last of the 'castle' series and the most accomplished of them all in plan and detail. Outside the series but also in Ireland, was one great classical house, the only complete classical house of any consequence Nash ever built after the early essays at Southgate, Dulwich and Sundridge. This was Rockingham, County Roscommon,[18] built for Robert Edward King, first Viscount Lorton of Boyle. As a young man King had distinguished himself in the amphibious operations against the French in the West Indies. Returning to Ireland he entered the House of Commons, but in 1798 was tried for killing a man who had eloped with his sister. He was acquitted, and represented Boyle in the Irish Parliament from 1798 till the Union. He married in 1799 and was created Baron Erris of Boyle in the following year.[19] The Viscountcy followed in 1806 and in 1809 he was discussing plans and estimates with Nash on the site. He was then thirty-six. He spoilt the house eventually by nearly doubling its height in 1822.[20] It was completely destroyed by fire in 1957.

The main theme at Rockingham (Plate 19A) was the one Nash had used at the Dulwich Casina – the 'pavilion' idea introduced by Holland at Brighton. The plan, however, was very different. Behind the three main rooms in the grand facade (drawing-room, library and parlour) was a gallery of three domed bays and beyond the central bay a grand staircase, while at one end of the gallery was the entrance hall and at the other a music-room.

Far more pretentious than Rockingham, though not a completely new house, was Nash's reconstruction of Witley Court, Worcestershire, for the third Baron Foley.[21] Foley had inherited at the age of thirteen an estate recklessly squandered by his father and loaded with debts. Restoring his position by marriage to a daughter of the Duke of Leinster in 1806 and being not without a touch of extravagance himself, he started to transform the family house at Witley into a palace. For him Nash recast the old Palladian plan, built a new wing and added gigantic Ionic porticos front and back. The back (garden) portico is eight columns wide and two deep at the sides, probably the biggest portico of any country-house in Britain (Plate 19B). The other portico, only six columns wide, fills the space between two towers originally of a Palladian kind but redressed by Nash in a more vernacular spirit, with pitched roofs and deep eaves. Nash seems to have been trying to combine the severe antique (the porticos) with casual Italian of the Cronkhill sort. C. R. Cockerell, who visited the house in or about 1825, saw some effectiveness in this but found it badly done: the porticos carelessly detailed and not in command of the composition. He was scathing about what he called the *vario-symmetry* of Nash's new wing, balancing the canted bay of the dining-room against the square bay of Lord Foley's room at either end of the library. Nor did he find anything to commend in the interior where Nash inserted a gloomy 80-ft gallery of his usual kind with a continuous balcony for access to the bedrooms and a stair at one end, as at Caerhays.[22]

The Victorian reconstruction of Witley disposed of nearly everything that was amusing and characteristic about Nash's design and gave little of any value in exchange. Today it lies in ruin. No doubt Cockerell was right in his criticisms of the house; they were of a kind which might be directed against nearly all Nash's big houses: superficiality and carelessness in the working out of ideas in themselves original and striking. Few things are or were more bleak and unsympathetic than the interiors of Nash castles and that, no doubt, is one reason why so few have survived.

Of Nash's domestic interiors in the classical style, few survive. The library at Barnsley Park, Gloucestershire (c. 1810), with delicate paintings in the Percier manner in the wall-space over the book-shelves is unexceptionable. More questionable is the library at Caledon, Co. Roscommon (1808–13) where a shallow dome, subdivided into hundreds of little coffers, hangs menacingly over the middle part. At Caledon Nash again introduced the Percier style, in an attempt to intensify the effect of Thomas Cooley's beautiful oval drawing-room. His new rooms at Witley seem to have had paintings in this style though on a more ambitious scale with, according to Cockerell, 'large Etruscan heros, chariots etc.' The name of the painter (surely a Frenchman) has not been found.

Of the score or so of houses which Nash was brought in simply to remodel, three are worth mentioning because of the stylistic aptness of the new exteriors. At Helmingham, Suffolk, for Lord Dysart (1800) his additions to the late Gothic house are discreet and sympathetic; at Hale, near Liverpool, for John Blackburne (1806) he gave the old house a new 'Jacobean' front which was a modest and plausible counterpart to the old; similarly at Lord Talbot's house at Ingestre, Staffordshire (1808–13) his 'Elizabethan' was loyal in spirit and detail. He had a surprisingly nice eye for 'period' when an old house appealed to him.

This feeling for the old and venerable descended into the rural vernacular, and here is a curious thing. If Nash would take too little trouble in developing and refining the design of a huge castle, he would take no end of trouble in detailing a cottage. This brings us to an altogether different aspect of his country work.

Nash's country-house practice was in one respect peculiar. Growing as it did out of a partnership with a landscape gardener it was rather more concerned than it might otherwise have been with the peripheral building needs of a country estate. Repton had taken an architectural partner because he wanted professional help with these things – the little, necessary things which could so easily mar the scene but, if sensitively handled, help to make it: conservatories, lodges and gates, stables, farmhouses and farmyards, barns, granaries, but most of all, cottages – cottages for gatekeepers and other estate servants, for pensioners or even, on somewhat more ample lines, for an agent or a curate. At such things Nash proved singularly adept; indeed, it could be said that for sheer architectural skill they are among his happiest works. If it was Repton who set the questions it is obvious that in answering them Nash found a personal and intimate delight and long after he and Repton had parted he went on producing them for his own clients and friends. He even had, by 1804, a set scale of charges: for cottages 3 guineas each, for a farmhouse 7 guineas, for a farmhouse and farmyard 15 guineas, for lodges 10 guineas.[23]

These buildings have proved perishable but records of them kept by George Repton in three immaculate little sketch-books, extending roughly over the years 1802 to 1818, give us much of the information we need.[24] In these books are plans, elevations and sections of between twenty and thirty cottages, some traceable to existing buildings, some not. The smallest cottages comprise one room up and one down; the largest are of modest farmhouse size. No two are exactly alike but all are stamped with the same character and give the impression of having been evolved on a strict and consistent principle. This is certainly the case and it is worth elaborating.

The cottage as an object of visual and not merely economic or comically grotesque interest came into its own in the last decade of the eighteenth century. Previously it had been an architectural nothing, an accidental fabric of no fixed date or purpose, botched and converted for the use of the poorest of the community; or, if it were a new cottage, a mere box of brick, rubble or rough-cast; or, if quantity and sightliness were required, one of a number spaced in a simple pattern, as in the famous instances of Houghton, Lowther and Milton Abbas. But this rational and often creditable attitude to the cottage missed something out and this was in due course discovered to be the very soul and nature of the cottage. The peasant cottage was, to be sure, an accidental creation. But so were rocks and ruins and so was the whole furnishing of the picturesque landscape. So the cottage came to life, along with a special kind of happiness attributed, without their permission, to its inmates. Gainsborough painted it, merging cottage and cottagers in the landscape of which they seemed a natural part. His friend, Uvedale Price, saw the cottage in the same way:

> A cottage of a quiet colour, half concealed among trees, with its bit of garden, its pales and orchard, is one of the most tranquil and soothing of all rural objects, and as the sun strikes upon it and discovers a number of lively picturesque circumstances, one of the most cheerful; but if cleared and whitened, its modest retired character is gone and succeeded by a perpetual glare.[25]

This is a painterly vision of the cottage, seeing it as indigenous, natural and as much part of landscape as trees and water or as the hovels in Dutch paintings. A new cottage could hardly evoke these sentiments – unless, indeed, it could be so contrived as to embody the 'lively, picturesque circumstances', the accidentals, of the old, without being absurd or extravagant. Could this be done?

The first writer to translate Gainsborough's or Price's feeling for the cottage into terms appropriate to architectural invention was James Malton. He was a younger brother of the far better-known Thomas Malton and, like him, was a topographical artist rather than an architect. His *Essay on British Cottage Architecture* first appeared in 1795, with the intriguing subtitle: *an attempt to perpetuate on Principle, that peculiar mode of Building which was originally the effect of Chance*. It contained fourteen designs, 'graduated from a simple hut to a habitation of a gentleman of fortune'.

The cottage principle, said Malton, combined a number of 'describable somethings'. These he listed as follows:

> A porch at entrance; irregular breaks in the direction of the walls; one part higher than another; various roofing of different materials, thatch particularly, boldly projecting; fronts partly built of walls of brick, partly weatherboarded, and partly brick-noggin dashed; casement window lights.

Malton pays tribute to Price's theory of the Picturesque (it confirmed views formed from his own experience) and quotes a passage from Knight's *The Landscape*. He is a true disciple of the movement and for him the preservation and perpetuation of the British cottage is a part of it. Old cottages, he says, are disappearing. Their principles must be extracted and incorporated in the new.

When we turn from Malton to Nash we find a distinct community of feeling in their designs. Nash may or may not have derived something from Malton. He must certainly have found him sympathetic.

It is difficult to give a date for the first cottage designs by Nash. Early among them are likely to have been a set of seven shown in small panel paintings preserved at Attingham Park, Salop. One of these is inscribed 'Cottages and Village belonging to the Rt. Hon. Lord Berwick at Attingham. John Nash, 28 Dover Street'.[26] The address dates the panels at approximately 1798, the year after Repton had delivered his Red Book on Attingham to Lord Berwick. The cottages are shown as part of a scattered group composing, presumably, the 'village', and one panel shows a uniform row of cottages. This latter may possibly be represented by a row still standing at Atcham on a site opposite the gates of Attingham Park. Otherwise there is no evidence that the cottages were ever built. In the sale of Nash's drawings (1835) was one entitled 'Inn at Addingham' (*sic*). If a 'village' was really contemplated, this design would have belonged to the set.

The Attingham designs are evidently part of a project to create a picturesque hamlet on Lord Berwick's estate, for reasons as to which we have no information. A few years later a rather similar project was envisaged and at least partly executed at another estate where Repton carried out improvements and where Nash was involved. This was at High Lee, near Knutsford, in Cheshire.

John George Lee succeeded to the property of East Hall, High Lee, in 1791, when he was twenty-two. The old family house had been burnt down nine years earlier and rebuilt by his father who had, just before his death, called in Repton to improve the park. On

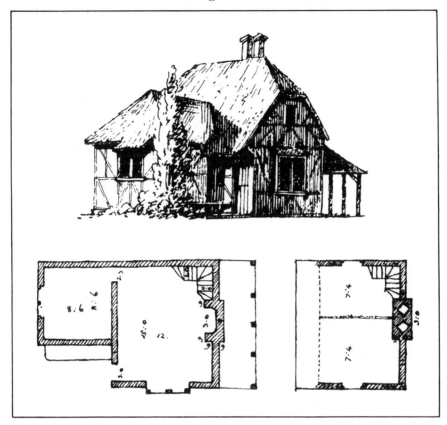

7. Cottage for Uvedale Price. Drawing in G. S. Repton's sketch-book (RIBA).

Repton's suggestion the main road was diverted to remove it further from the house and this involved the demolition of the village inn and some other buildings. John George Lee fancied the idea of creating a new 'village' and corresponded on this subject with Repton and Nash in 1797–8.[27] The project does not seem to have got very far but in 1810 Nash was still in touch with Lee and designed a village school which (now a private dwelling) still stands. Nash also provided designs for two cottages, a gateway and lodge and a blacksmith's shop and cottage, as well as making some internal improvements to the mansion house and adding a conservatory. Here, as at Attingham, the idea of a 'village' group was in the air and on paper if not on the ground. Nash was to carry it forward and realise it on a different scale in his Park Villages at Regents Park of the late 1820s.

Meanwhile, cottage designs were produced for a variety of occasions and locations. In one of Repton's books is a design marked 'Sir U. Price' (Fig. 7), presumably for Foxley, Herefordshire, a peculiar study in half-timbering which suggests that it was an experiment on lines proposed by Price himself. There are designs for Henry Vernon

(Hilton Park, Staffordshire), Lord Thanet (Hothfield Place, Kent), Sir Charles Taylor (Liphook, Hampshire), Lord Macclesfield (Shirburn, Oxfordshire), Dr Matthews (Belmont, Herefordshire) and others. How many of Nash's cottage designs were executed we do not know; how many of those executed still survive would require a rigorous exploration of all the estates where Nash was employed. Among the known survivors are two at Moccas, Herefordshire,[28] built in 1804, and in this instance we have a letter from Nash to his client, Sir George Cornwall, which well illustrates the care he took with these things. The letter concerns the detailing of certain projections over the windows. Their construction is carefully explained and Nash continues:

> I am very glad you have written to me on the subject for I have the mortification daily to see these minutiae of cottages misunderstood and very much of their good effect depends on the right understanding of their details. They are meant to be essential parts of the construction and growing out of the necessity of the things themselves. When this principle is lost sight of they become pretensious and mere appliqués, than which nothing is more disgusting.[29]

So perceptive a plea for honesty of construction is unlooked-for at this date, more especially in an architect not notable for fastidious detailing.

A moral incentive in cottage-building for the poor or the aged was nothing extraordinary but rarely did it extend to the architectual forms which the cottages might take. It did so, however, in a group which Nash designed for John Scandrett Harford, the Quaker banker of Bristol, on his estate at Blaise Castle near that city. Harford had aquired the estate, with the castellated folly which gave it its name, in 1789. He had built himself a plain stone house, designed by Paty of Bristol. Repton had added a Tudor-style lodge and gateway.[30] An octagon dairy, thatched, built in 1804, is almost certainly by Nash who likewise added a curved conservatory to the house. Then, in 1810, Harford negotiated with Nash to build accommodation for pensioners on his estate.

If Harford had in mind the usual formal row of almshouses, he was to be diverted to something very different. According to C. R. Cockerell, it was Nash who suggested to him that a more humane way of providing for old people was to give each his own separate cottage and to group the cottages in a secluded spot, in no way advertising the philanthropy of the proprietor.[31] This would be entirely characteristic of Nash, who had a strong sense of humanity and justice where the unfortunate or under-privileged were concerned. Such a group could, moreover, be a beautiful thing in itself. Harford entered into the spirit of this interpretation and Nash pegged out the sites of the proposed cottages in a field. In August 1810 he was in Ireland and it was there that he made the designs for at least some of the cottages, sending his sketches to George Repton to be drawn out in the office and submitted to Harford. By October, the cottages were nearly finished and Nash, back from Ireland, made a rigorous inspection of them.[32]

The cottages (Plates 20 and 21), known collectively as Blaise Hamlet, are cottages for cottagers, with all the appurtenances and accretions of the typical peasant home, from the improvised pigeon-house in the gable to the attached privy or pantry at the side. They are built of rubble masonry with some plaster and weatherboarding and tall brick chimneys. There are four types of roof – pyramidal, hipped, gabled and hip-gabled. The cottages also differ from each other in the shape and placing of the porches and bay-windows. What brings them all into accord while at the same time making each a curiosity in itself is the device of the continuous penthouse. This is an area of thatch or tile which sits above the ground-floor windows and continues round the house to cover the porch, bay-window or whatever else projects; or else it is merely bracketed or coved to make an embrasure or to shelter a seat. These features are rarely found in Nash's earlier cottage work. At Blaise, the penthouses are the making of the scene, a levelling against the undulations of the site and a counterweight to the soaring Elizabethan chimneys. The latter Nash considered one of the great features of the design, recommending Harford to have bricks specially moulded to patterns sent to him by Repton.[33]

Harford reckoned to spend £2,000 on these cottages but in the end they cost him £3,800, partly, no doubt, because of his architect's loving insistence on quality and correctness of finish.[34] Blaise Hamlet earned high and continuous favour with the public and with artists. The inexhaustibly inquisitive Prince Pückler-Muskau visited it in 1828 and was enchanted.[35] It was much illustrated. A splendid series of lithographs by J. D. Harding[36] and a smaller series by Joseph Horner, illustrated here, appeared about 1860 and in the Bristol Art Gallery is a touchingly beautiful watercolour view by John Linnell. Victorian taste could not repudiate this honest endeavour to combine picturesque effect with humanity and true constructive skill. The Victorians were themselves great cottage builders, building often with more pretension but never, surely, with more sincerity than John Nash.

A column stands on the green at Blaise recording Nash's authorship and the date of completion, 1811. This, his sixtieth year, was the last in a stretch of some dozen years during which he had enjoyed uninterrupted success as a domestic architect. From near obscurity he had come level with Soane and almost with Wyatt. He commanded the heights of his profession – or very nearly. There was, indeed, one height which he had not scaled: he was not a Royal Academician. Why he was not is a matter for speculation. From 1797 to 1803 he exhibited regularly in the annual exhibition at Somerset House, showing never fewer than two and in one year (1798) as many as six drawings. In 1804 he did not exhibit. In 1805 he had only one drawing on the walls and thereafter none. It looks as if, in the first seven years, he was making a determined effort to display his talents acceptably at Somerset House but then either from indifference or discouragement ceased to trouble himself or the Academy further.

Discouragement might well come from within the narrow circle of the academicians themselves and from one academician in particular. In the exhibition of 1796, James

Wyatt had shown his design for enlarging Corsham. In the very next year Nash exhibited, either with or just possibly without malicious intent, *his* proposals, thus exposing to the world the fact that Wyatt had been unseated and his own design preferred. This may not have mattered very much at the time but in 1805 the President of the Academy, Benjamin West, took it into his head to resign and his place was taken by – James Wyatt. Benjamin West was friendly to Nash; James Wyatt, after the Corsham dismissal and what must have seemed to him the deliberate humiliation in the exhibition of 1797, understandably hostile. Furthermore the other architect-academicians consisting of Dance, Yenn and Soane are most unlikely to have wished to admit Nash to their circle; Soane, in particular, would have opposed such a proposal. Just what rumblings of intrigue and jealousy there may have been in 1804–5 we do not know but, although Wyatt's presidency lasted less than a year, West being re-elected in December 1806, Nash's association with the Academy was at an end.

Far more important than any titular honour which Nash may or may not have desired or sought was an appointment to a post in the government service which he accepted in 1806. The post offered, on the face of it, little in the way of prestige or profit; but the ultimate outcome of Nash's tenure was of such superlative significance that it is necessary to consider the appointment and the circumstances attending it with some care.

The Office of Woods and Forests, responsible for the protection, maintenance and management of the forests of the Crown, had a history going back to James I. At the head of it was the Surveyor-General of His Majesty's Woods and Forests, usually a politician of no great consequence. Among the functions of the office was the care of various forest lodges and other structures, the property of the Crown, and in 1795 it was thought to be in the public interest that an experienced architect should be placed in charge of this work.[37] The post of Deputy Surveyor-General was therefore created. It was given, in the first instance, to Soane who enjoyed the patronage of the prime minister, Pitt. Soane held it for four years, at the end of which he found himself unable to discharge the duties 'with satisfaction to himself' and resigned.[38] The job was then given to Wyatt, a truly extraordinary appointment, considering that, as Surveyor-General of Works, he already had more than enough to do and was failing lamentably to do it. He lasted, however, till 1805 when the office of Deputy Surveyor-General was dropped and a relatively unknown architect, John Harvey, who built the County Hall at Stafford, was engaged in the simple capacity of 'architect in the Office of Woods and Forests'.[39]

The appointment was in the hands of the Treasury, but the Surveyor-General in office would certainly have the nomination of officers in his department. The Surveyor-General from 1803 was Lord Glenbervie and it was he, no doubt, who got rid of Wyatt and introduced Harvey. However, with the change of government consequent upon Pitt's death in February 1806, Glenbervie resigned. There followed the coalition known as the 'ministry of all the talents', with Grenville as First Lord of the Treasury and Charles James Fox as Foreign Secretary. With Fox in the government, places had to be found for his friends and to one of these, Lord Robert Spencer, second son of the Duke of

Marlborough, went the surveyorship of Woods and Forests. Lord Robert dismissed Harvey and appointed in his place John Nash.

Lord Robert – 'comical Bob' to his friends – was no great politician but for nearly forty years had been a devoted friend and follower of Fox. In the wild gambling days of 1780 he had lost a fortune, but got a new one when Fox, Fitzpatrick and he opened a faro bank at Brooks's. Out of this he bought himself an estate at Woolbeding in Sussex where Fox and the Foxite Whigs were always welcome.[40]

Why Lord Spencer replaced Harvey by Nash is explained in a statement made some twenty years later by Charles Arbuthnot who, as the holder of an office equivalent to Lord Robert's and as Nash's principal employer, made it his business to find out.[41] It appears that a bridge in Hyde Park, carrying the 'King's Road' (Rotten Row) across a stream trickling south from the Serpentine, required widening. Lord Robert gave orders, presumably to Harvey, for this to be done. The result was so very unsatisfactory that Lord Robert called in an independent adviser, and the independent adviser was Nash. Nash having made a favourable impression Harvey was sent packing and Nash installed.

Arbuthnot's story, obtained at second or third hand, is very dry and leaves us speculating. Why did Lord Robert Spencer choose Nash as his adviser and was his acquaintance with him limited to the executive requirements of the Woods and Forests? The presence of a design for an octagonal rustic cow-house in one of George Repton's notebooks[42] marked 'Lord Robert Spencer' suggests otherwise. Its likely destination would be Lord Robert's estate at Woolbeding.

Moreover, there is evidence that Nash made the acquaintance of Charles James Fox. A letter written to him by Fox was sold with his copy of Fox's posthumously-published *History of James II* in 1835.[43] If they met, Woolbeding would be a likely place, though if Nash's connection with Lord Robert only started in 1806 it would have to be in the very short period before Fox's death in September of that year. Arguably, therefore, Nash may have been known to Lord Robert before 1806.

Whatever the case, the patronage of Lord Robert was of enormous consequence. From the mending of a bad design for a wooden bridge it led to all the things with which the remainder of this book is concerned.

5

Marylebone Park

Marylebone or Marybone Park was that part of the manor of Tyburn which Henry VIII enclosed as a royal hunting-ground. It was a curious shape – very roughly circular, with no natural boundaries – so that one could suppose it to have resulted from a perfectly arbitrary enclosing exercise on the part of Henry's surveyors. As a royal park, stocked with deer, it remained till the Commonwealth when it was put up for sale in lots to the highest bidders. Much of the timber was felled by Parliament and the rest sold by the new owners for quick profit. The deer were evacuated to St James's Park and the naked ground was then used for grazing cattle. Restored to the Crown in 1660 it passed through the hands of two favoured noblemen and then of a group of moneyed men among whose descendants the holding was split into two leaseholds. One of these reverted to the Crown in 1803. The other was extended to 1811, by which date it was in the hands of the fourth Duke of Portland, whose father had bought the remainder of the extended lease at auction in 1789.[1]

The third Duke had inherited through his wife the entire manor of Tyburn which included, most notably, the building enterprises of his father-in-law, the second Earl of Oxford: Cavendish Square and the streets adjoining, Harley, Wimpole and Welbeck Streets, stretching north nearly to the New Road (Marylebone Road); to which the Duke himself had added Portland Place. Another part of the manor lay to the north-west of the Park at Barrow Hill. The Duke might well have hoped, by taking up the last twenty-two years of the lease of the Park, to make some further arrangement with the Crown by which he and his successors could continue their developments across the New Road, into the Park and onwards to Barrow Hill, thus creating what would certainly have been the biggest property interest in the capital.

However, the Duke was not the only one to see a fabulous aurora on the Park's horizon. The whole question of the control and profitability of Crown lands was wide open. In 1786 a statutory commission had been set up to collect information and to devise and execute a rational administration of these widely-dispersed and often ill-defined properties. Marylebone Park came under review in the commission's first report, as a result of which the rents, found grossly out of proportion to the value of the land, were raised. Sixteen more reports followed, covering all the Crown lands throughout England and Wales. In the seventeenth and last report (1793) it was recommended that, in principle, all Crown estates should be retained by the Crown and controlled by a board of three commissioners acting under the Treasury.[2]

This recommendation was accepted by the government but did not immediately take effect. Instead, a new appointment was made. A 58-year-old Scotsman, John Fordyce, who had been one of the three commissioners under the Act of 1786, was constituted Surveyor-General of Land Revenues. This was an office of some antiquity which had once had a working relationship with the Office of Woods and Forests but had declined into a mere sinecure, denuded of records and without even a proper address. Its last incumbent had been the pleasantly witty and notoriously idle George Augustus Selwyn and it suited him. He died, however, in 1791 and the office remained vacant for two years. In 1793, however, it was given to Fordyce. In the following year an Act was passed, the substance of which was founded on the work of the commission of 1786. Its effect was to put the management of the whole land revenue of the Crown firmly into the hands of the new Surveyor-General. He was to issue a triennial report to the Treasury.[3]

It is clear from everything he wrote that Fordyce was a man of imagination and ability, though at his death little was recorded of him except that he married a sister of the Duchess of Gordon.[4] In fact, he had held a land revenue appointment in Scotland, was an active farmer on his own estate near Berwick and had in his younger days stood, though unsuccessfully, for Parliament.[5] The four reports he sent to the Treasury as Surveyor-General of Land Revenue were the crown of his career. Where Marylebone Park was concerned, it was his realistic projection of its future which made possible everything which followed.

No sooner was he installed in office (he had two new houses built in Whitehall Place, one for official business and one for himself) than a Marylebone problem of challenging aspect presented itself. In June 1793 the Duke of Portland, obstinately reluctant to surrender all interest in the Park, made an offer. He would exchange some of his own property in Barrow Hill for an acre-and-a-half of Crown land next to the New Road, on a site somewhat to the east of where Madame Tussaud's now stands. Here he intended to build a church for the parish of St Marylebone. At the same time he would surrender his right of way across the Park in exchange for a narrow strip, nearly a mile long, on which to form a public road leading to a new burial ground. This was a fine and handsome gesture, for Marylebone was in great need of a capacious church to supersede the little old brick box in the High Street. But Fordyce saw objections. One was that the so-called acre-and-a-half was found to be much more like five acres. The other, more serious, was that the direction proposed for the new road would strike obliquely across any northward extension of existing roads such as a new layout would almost certainly require. He thought, besides, that a *via dolorosa* leading to a cemetery might be an inauspicious beginning to an enterprise dependent for its success on rising land values.[6]

On 27 June 1793 he wrote to the Treasury explaining his attitude and, in the same letter, made the Duke's proposals a text for a general warning against temptations to erode the integrity of the property:

> I must . . . humbly recommend, that before agreeing to this or any other Proposal for the alteration or disposal of any part of Marybone Park, a general plan should be formed for the Improvement of the whole of it, lest such partial alteration should afterwards be found inconsistent with what should, on full consideration, and the best advice be deemed most for the benefit of the Crown.[7]

Here, for the first time, is expressed the idea of developing Marylebone Park as a comprehensive and consistent unit, doing so, moreover, with 'the best advice'. Fordyce then seeks permission to employ a surveyor to bring an existing map of the Park up to date, to have it engraved and a copy given to 'every architect of eminence in London'. Finally, he proposes that 'a considerable reward should be given to the person who should produce such a Plan . . . as, having been laid before His Majesty and your Lordships, should be adopted . . . The whole being the plan of one Architect, the parts would be consistent with each other . . . ornament as well as convenience would be attended to'.

After a delay of nearly three months the Treasury replied, approving all Fordyce's ideas and authorising a 'reward' of anything up to £1,000.

All this was in 1793, when Nash was in Carmarthen and still a long way from being an 'architect of eminence in London'. He would certainly know all about it but thirteen years were to pass before his appointment to the Office of Woods and there is no reason to suppose that in that hectically ascendant period of his life the future of Marylebone Park was of much concern to him. Indeed it was not of much concern to the profession generally and the grand offer of £1,000 seems to have been shrugged off by the architectural eminences as one of those traps for the unwary where reputation was set at risk for very dubious rewards.

Three plans were, indeed, submitted to Fordyce but they were all by one man, John White, who, as the Duke of Portland's surveyor, made it clear that he was not putting in bids for the 'reward'. The plans were simply a demonstration of his noble patron's continued interest in the soil. One of the plans was, in due course, published by his son and it is not without merit; its main feature was a huge crescent of houses facing the New Road and providing, in its grounds, the site for a monumental church.[8]

Fordyce's first report, published in 1797, contained an account of the events just recited. His second report came in 1802 and his third in 1806 but in neither was

Marylebone Park mentioned. Then, in 1809, came his fourth and, as it turned out, his last report. There is very little in the main text about the Park. What there is concerns the urgency of increasing its value as building land, a benefit which, he believed, could only be attained by the cutting of a great thoroughfare between the Park and Charing Cross, thus giving future Park-dwellers reasonably expeditious access to the Law Courts and the Houses of Parliament.[9] A not unimportant statement, on which we shall have occasion to expand at large.

What the fourth report does contain relative to the Park is a memorandum by Fordyce outlining his own vision of what Marylebone Park should become. He was now in his mid-seventies and the memorandum reads rather like an *envoi* to the next generation. Underlying the whole document is a wonderfully clear perception of the Park as a social, architectural and, as we might say, organic totality. He begins by stressing that the architect must think broadly of the estate's relationship to the growing metropolis and not be deterred by seeming obstacles which, he says, Parliament could remove. Water supply must be the first consideration. Primrose Hill or Hampstead or possibly the river Brent or the Grand Junction Canal would probably be the answer. Then he shows a nice flair for the particular within the general:

> In the choice of situations for Markets, the saving of the time of the servants attending them should be considered, with which view those for Butchers Meat, Poultry, Game, Fish and Vegetables, with Fruit of every Kind, foreign and domestic, should be in one quarter, with no great intervening distances; and more space should be allotted to houses for back courts, or curtilages, and stables, than in the heart of the Town can be had, allowing more room for washing, for poultry, and for coals, which are known to be much dearer in Winter than in Summer, or for any other articles that can with advantage be kept in store.[10]

Sewerage is important and will require 'more consideration than may at first be supposed'. Fordyce deplored the waste of good manure by sending it all into the Thames. Anxious for a better precedent, he asked John Barrow, who had been to China with Lord Macartney's embassy and published his experiences, what practices prevailed there. Barrow was not encouraging. He explained that the same carts which took the sewage away at night brought the vegetables to town in the morning. Undeterred, Fordyce recommended a disposition of deep-dug 'basons' from which the 'surface water' should 'run off', while the 'manure' subsided, to be subsequently transported for agricultural use.

Street-lighting was to be considered, along with stands for Hackney coaches, stations for watchmen, patrols, firemen and fire-engines. And, of course, churches. These should be conspicuously sited and there might be a case for a monumental building of a more or less analogous kind:

If any conspicuous spot should appear particularly proper for the erection of some great Public Edifice in which, as has been often proposed, Statues or Monuments may be placed in honour of persons who have distinguished themselves in the service of the Country, it may be right to suggest it, and to give a Plan of the Building; and as no reason can exist against its being a place also of Public Worship, it may serve as one, and probably the most splendid, of the Churches.[11]

Fordyce no doubt had in mind the conversion of Soufflot's church of Ste Geneviève in Paris into the Panthéon in 1791, though as this had been the gesture of a revolutionary government it was hardly a precedent to be quoted by name in an official document. Nash was to refer to the project, a few years later, as a 'Valhalla', a curious anticipation of the word's application to the spectacular temple for a similar purpose which Ludwig I of Bavaria built near Regensburg in 1830–42.

Early determination of the whole plan Fordyce considered especially important, ingeniously arguing that a sense of isolation in houses built in the early stages could be offset by attaching to them ample grounds on short lease, making them in effect 'country houses', *pro tem*. When the tide of building closed in the lease would be surrendered and they would become 'town houses'.

The memorandum ends on a note of optimism. 'It is to be hoped from the known talents of some of the persons who have agreed to give their attention to this great National object, that this opportunity will not be lost, and that something will be produced that will do credit not only to themselves but to the country.' We may be confident that one of the persons of 'known talents' was John Nash.

Fordyce's memorandum was dated 6 April 1809. In August he died. No new Surveyor-General was appointed and the recommendation of 1793 to place the whole responsibility for Crown property in the hands of a board of three was now put into effect.[12] In 1810 the Office of Woods and Forests and the Office of Land Revenues were merged and the two surveyorships put into commission. The three commissioners were Lord Glenbervie, William Dacres Adams and Henry Dawkins. As first commissioner, with a higher salary than the other two, Glenbervie carried the parliamentary responsibility. Born in 1743, he had graduated in medicine at Leyden but switched to the law and picked up influential connections, including Lord North, one of whose daughters he married. He moved amiably through society, meeting all the right people from Marie Antoinette to Edward Gibbon and collecting anecdotes about them, filled a number of political appointments under Pitt, was made a peer in 1800 and in 1803 was Surveyor-General of Woods and Forests, a post from which, as we have seen, he resigned on Pitt's death three years later.

As a civil servant Glenbervie was conscientious and prudent but had none of the initiative and geniality of Fordyce. The Office of Woods, Forests and Land Revenues was not much to his taste. The first commissioner's task was 'thankless' but it had to be done and he did it to the best of his ability which was not inconsiderable.[13]

In 1810 the newly-constituted commission faced the urgent fact that the Portland lease of Marylebone Park would terminate in the following January. The ground would be at the commission's disposal and Parliament and the public would expect measures for its future to be well in hand. As the 'reward' of £1,000 had now been on offer for eighteen years without bringing in a single plan (other than John White's) the offer was suspended and an altogether new direction taken.

Both the Office of Woods and Forests and the Office of Land Revenues had, for some years before the amalgamation, retained professional architects. When Nash was appointed to the Office of Woods in 1806 he had brought in James Morgan as his partner.[14] In Land Revenues was another partnership, in post only since 1809, consisting of Thomas Leverton and Thomas Chawner. Leverton had been in the service of Land Revenues for many years and had been given the principal appointment on the death of a senior man, Marquand, in 1809, It had long been a principle of the Office that two surveyors should be retained, 'to form a check on each other', as Fordyce put it; so young Thomas Chawner was brought in to make a second.[15] The salaries of the two partnerships were identical, Nash and Morgan receiving £200 a year jointly as *architects* and Leverton and Chawner £100 each as *surveyors*, which amounted to the same thing, though with a rather sensitive denominational difference. It was now proposed that these two pairs of professionals, presently in the service of the amalgamated Offices, should each prepare and submit plans and reports on the development of the Park.

Here comes an ironic twist. Leverton, it will be recalled, was the man whom Sir John Rushout had retained in 1777 to check young Nash's design for the houses in Bloomsbury Square and Great Russell Street. Now, thirty-three years later, he finds himself placed by his masters opposite the former bankrupt 'carpenter' in an affair which is not only more or less competitive but into which the bankrupt carpenter enters as one of the most applauded and best-connected architects of the day.

Instructions were delivered to the two pairs of architects on 8 October 1810 and it seems that they were allowed six months in which to study them and shape up their answers. Drafts of the instructions survive in the Crown estate records.[16] The architects' first concern was to be with the methods of development to be adopted, bearing in mind that profitability must go along with beauty, health and convenience. Sewers and drains, the suitability of the soil for brick-making and the problem of water-supply came next. Detailed plans were to be supplied, both for the Park and for a new street connecting it to Charing Cross, with estimates related to both. The types of development proceeding on the adjacent Bedford, Portland, Camden, Southampton and Portman estates were to be critically examined; Edinburgh and Bath were to be consulted as possible models. Relationships with adjoining estates were to be studied. A site had to be allocated to a cavalry barracks. Finally, attention was to be paid to Fordyce's suggestions in his report of 1809. The last sentence of the letter indicated that the architects could, if they thought fit, regard themselves as candidates for the award of £1,000.

The first we hear of the architects' reports is in a letter from Glenbervie to his fellow commissioner, William Dacres Adams, dated 10 March 1811. The papers had lately come into his hands and, being pressed for time in London, he had carried them down with him to his country home, The Pheasantry at Bushey (a rural retreat inherited from his father-in-law, Lord North) to peruse at leisure.[17]

The documents which Glenbervie now had before him were not the report eventually forwarded to the Treasury but drafts, subject to modification by the commissioners in further consultation with the architects. As we have no copies of these drafts it is necessary, for the moment, to follow the commissioners' thoughts and proceedings without knowing exactly what material they had in their hands.

Glenbervie's letter to Adams communicates his first thoughts on the two schemes. It is carefully worded and the writer is clearly at pains to avoid any trace of personal liking for either of the parties. He feels bound, nevertheless, to pronounce Nash's scheme the more weighty of the two:

> There is in Nash's Report a great deal of good reasoning, and his consideration
> of the subject is more enlarged than that of Leverton and Chawner.

On the other hand Nash had not done as he was told. He had given no figures for the capital expenditure required for the preparation of the site nor for the returns which might be anticipated from development in succeeding years. Nor had he answered, point by point, the various questions to which, in the official instructions, his attention had been directed. This, Glenbervie wrote, was 'very inconvenient'. Furthermore, he had most improperly made the report exclusively his own, writing it in the first person singular, over his own signature, ignoring the fact that, in official eyes, he was in partnership with Morgan.[18]

Leverton and Chawner had submitted two reports, more obediently framed but disappointing in their forecasts of revenue. Glenbervie wonders if it might not be expedient to adopt Nash's plan but to employ both sets of architects in its execution: Nash and Morgan for the general form and layout and Leverton for the supervision of individual buildings. He proposes to Adams that he and the third commissioner, Dawkins, should interview each pair of architects in turn, preferably on the site, in order to resolve any doubtful points in their reports. The reports would then be remitted to the architects for recasting and final submission. The suggestion was doubtless followed and it was not till July that the revised reports were handed in. They were transmitted to the Treasury on 7 August, with a covering letter in which the commissioners expressed the view that Nash's plan 'appeared to embrace such a comprehensive, yet, generally speaking, rational and practicable scheme of public improvement . . . as will call for the mature consideration of His Majesty's government'.[19]

The two reports, in the form in which they reached the Treasury in August 1811, were printed as appendices to the commissioners' First Report in the following year and these texts enable us to understand what Glenbervie and his two colleagues had been brooding over since March.

The proposals of Leverton and Chawner are given first. They are understandable at a glance. Leverton and Chawner proposed quite simply to carry the rectangular criss-cross of the Portland estate across two-thirds of the Park. The first third was to consist of streets and squares on the traditional pattern; the second, of sites for villas of assorted sizes, some semi-detached; the third (on the north) was a shapeless residue sliced into eight plots for villas with very ample grounds. Leverton and Chawner declared themselves against 'circular or octangular figures' as being expensive and inconvenient, though they did propose a couple of very shallow and ineffective crescents. Their plan, had it reached execution, would not have disgraced London; it would have been a second Bloomsbury, dispersing into villadom as it proceeded northwards. But one thing it would no longer have been was a Park. As for the new street, Leverton and Chawner merely referred the commissioners to the plan which they had put forward in 1808. Nor did they envisage the developed estate as a gold-mine for the government. An outlay of £8,200 on preparatory works would, they predicted, produce an eventual income from ground-rents of £23,000 – hardly a spectacular yield from five hundred acres of urban land.[20]

Nash's report was overwhelmingly different. In its printed form it occupies ten pages against Leverton's and Chawner's four. If Glenbervie was able to find fault with the draft of March 1811 for casualness and inattention to formalities, he can have found no such blemishes in the final state of the document. It is thorough, shrewdly analytical and written with a sort of *bravura* which renders it immediately convincing.

Nash begins by establishing the relationships of the Park with the adjoining estates. 'In contemplating Marylebone Park it will be proper to consider it as enclosed on three sides by buildings.' On the south contact is, fortunately, with the best-built parts of Marylebone. Portland Place is 'the most magnificent street in London' and that street, with Devonshire Place and Baker Street, he designates as the lines of communication between the old London and the new. The Southampton estate and Somers Town on the east are less welcome neighbours. They have been developed on the bad principle of letting off land by the acre to builders who cram as much street-frontage as they can onto the ground and then look for a profit on the sale of improved ground-rents.

The evils of the leasehold system Nash then chastises in a vivid paragraph:

> The artificial causes of the extension of the Town are the speculations of Builders, encouraged and promoted by Merchants dealing in the materials of Building, and Attorneys with monied Clients facilitating, and indeed, putting in motion, the whole system, by disposing of their Client's Money in premature Mortgages, the sale of improved Ground-Rents, and by numerous other devices, by which their Clients make an advantageous use of their money, and the Attorneys create to themselves, a lucrative business from the Agreements, Assignments, Leases, Mortgages, Bonds, and other instruments of

Law, which become necessary throughout such complicated and intricate transactions. It is not necessary for the present purpose to enumerate the bad consequences and pernicious effects which arise from such an unnatural and forced enlargement of the Town, further than to observe, that it is the interest of those concerned in such Buildings that they should be of as little cost as possible, preserving an attractive exterior, which Parker's Stucco, coloured Bricks, and Balconies, accomplish; and a fashionable arrangement of rooms on the principal floors embellished by the Paper-hanger, and a few flimsy marble chimney-pieces, are the attractions of the interior. These are sufficient allurements to the Public, and ensure the sale of the Houses, which is the ultimate object of the Builders, and to this finery every thing out of sight is sacrificed, or is no further an object of attention, than that no defects in the constructive and substantial parts shall make their appearance while the Houses are on Sale; and it is to be feared, that for want of those essentials, which constitute the strength and permanency of Houses, a very few years will exhibit cracked walls, swagged floors, bulged fronts, crooked roofs, leaky gutters, inadequate drains, and other ills of an originally bad constitution; and it is quite certain, without a renovation equal to re-building, that all those Houses long, very long, before the expiration of the Leases, will cease to exist, and the reversionary Estate the Proprietors look for will never be realized, as it is not till the end of the Builder's term that the Proprietor of the Fee will be entitled to the additional Ground-Rents laid on by the Builder. It is evidently, therefore, not the interest of the Crown, that Mary-le-bone Park should be covered with Buildings of that description. . . .

Nash then draws attention to the fact that wealthy landowners infinitely prefer living near an open space, however dusty and noisy, to living in quiet and unpolluted streets and squares in the built-up part of the town. A park where there were opportunities for riding, driving and walking was, he believed, an irresistible magnet.

Then he brings our attention to bear on the actual lines of his plan. These are shown in an engraving published with the report (Plate 32A). Here, however, we must pause, because the engraved plan is *not* the plan described in the report but a drastically-revised alternative submitted after Nash had been called for an interview with the Prime Minister, Spencer Perceval, some time in August 1811.[21]

This interview was a fateful one for the Park. Perceval took a strong interest in the scheme, perhaps because he had been a suburban dweller himself. For some years up to 1807 he had occupied Belsize House and was accustomed to ride every day to Westminster through the countryside now being transformed.[22] Some semblance of rurality he thought should be retained and he therefore 'recommended' Nash 'to form another [plan] with fewer buildings and a larger extent of Park, to be submitted with those [he] had already presented'. Nash obeyed and sent his revised plan to the commissioners on 29 August. It was forwarded by them to the Treasury on the following day.[23]

That plan is the one engraved in the printed Report. So where is the plan originally submitted to the Treasury? It is nowhere to be found. However, by some fortunate accident there does survive among the Crown estate papers a plan (Plate 22) of earlier date than this and being, in fact, the solitary survivor of the set which Nash delivered with his draft report to the commissioners in March 1811 (which date it bears). Here Nash's original ideas are most cogently and completely expressed and it is from this plan that any account of the development of the Park must take its departure.[24]

The first thing we notice about this plan is the very substantial area of ground allocated to building compared with what we see in the engraved plan. The park is virtually a 'built-up area'. The second thing we notice is that the pattern and distribution of the plan has a close affinity with the planning of Bath by the elder and younger John Wood from 1727 onwards. This is natural enough. Bath was the classic original to which any English architect would turn for ideas. It was at Bath that the circus and the crescent had first been introduced in a flexible relationship to streets and squares.

In London, as early as 1767, George Dance had laid out a miniature triad of square, crescent and circus on a site near Tower Hill. His later plans, all to some extent Bathonian, include a spendidly original composition of the same elements for the Camden estate, never executed.[25] Nash may have known this. He would certainly know a plan for the Eyre estate, adjoining Marylebone Park on the west, designed by an unknown architect, engraved in 1794 and circulated by a firm of auctioneers with an address in the City. This comprised a square, a crescent and a circus, cleverly accommodated on a site of highly-irregular outline. This, again, was not executed, though the circus, surprisingly, survived as a project in isolation till as late as 1807 when it is shown as the 'Proposed British Circus' on Edward Mogg's map of London. In this version it was to be a double circus of $1\frac{1}{4}$ miles diameter with a circular road between two rings of houses. It was, of course, never built. But we need look no further for a prototype of the great double circus which forms the most striking single feature in Nash's plan of March 1811.[26]

In this plan Nash's circus was not to be isolated. Three arms project from it and connect it with an inner rectangle of streets. At the base (south) of this rectangle are a crescent and a square. On the east are three narrow squares while on the north is a long rectangle containing a 'bason' or reservoir to supply the houses with water. The two main streets lying east and west of the Circus are prolongations respectively of Baker Street and Portland Place, the junction of the latter with its northward counterpart being interrupted by another circus whose east-west diameter is on the line of the New Road.

Outside the rectangle which frames the double circus is a marginal area of varying depth. Within this, on the east, is a crescent. On the north is a site for the cavalry barracks, which the architects had been instructed to provide for. In the south-east corner are two sites for markets.

Accustomed as we are to thinking of Regents Park as an open space it is difficult at first to grasp the urban character of Nash's first intentions. All the dotted areas on the

'March 1811' plan are designated for building. Not only that, but the areas of parkland which intervene are by no means unoccupied, being divided into sites for an indeterminate number of villas, each with its own pleasure-grounds and a screen of trees to isolate it from its neighbours.

Along with this plan (and the others which are lost) Nash submitted two panoramic views (Plates 23A and B) illustrating the landscape element in his design.[27] They are in monochrome watercolour and were finished in a hurry. One, sixteen feet long, shows the Park as seen by someone moving round the double circus. The other, seventeen feet long, is a series of merging impressions of the Park as seen from the outer drive, looking inwards. The purpose of these two drawings seems to be to show that, notwithstanding the large amount of ground to be covered by building, the Park would still remain park-like, an essentially Picturesque conception. With an ingenuity verging on the fraudulent, Nash suppressed the urban aspects which he himself clearly valued. Streets, terraces and crescents vanish among the trees. The great double circus, which was to be the dominant feature of the whole, is not seen at all.

A conspicuous feature of the panoramas is the 'ornamental water' snaking through the landscape in a decorative arabesque. The plan shows that this water has its source in a canal, identified as 'course of the grand junction canal', which comes in on the west side, proceeds through the Park and makes its exit on the north. Just before the exit is a straight-sided branch following the eastern boundary of the estate and terminating in a basin. On the plan it is marked 'commercial canal'. The system of waterways is obviously of great importance in the design and, before we go further, its origin must be explained.

The Grand Junction Canal, between Braunston in Northamptonshire and Brentford in Middlesex, was opened in 1793 and was one of the great engineering feats of the day. In 1795 this canal was continued from Brentford to Paddington where a large basin was formed. The success of these undertakings encouraged a third: the further continuation of the canal through London to the docks, eliminating the expensive carriage of goods by road between the docks and Paddington. This project was the brainchild of a certain Thomas Homer, and Rennie prepared a design. It proved extravagantly costly and was dropped. Nevertheless, Homer held fast to the idea and early in 1810 brought it up again, this time proposing that it should go round, instead of through, the town. In September the sanction of the Grand Junction Company was obtained and notices of application to Parliament were published. In October Nash received his instructions for the Park. Homer, hearing of this, got in touch with him and was soon being assured that 'there was every probability of the Crown's being favourably inclined to the projected canal going through the Park'. Nash 'requested Mr. Homer to furnish him with such information as he could maturely weigh and, if approved of, submit to such friends as might be induced to promote the undertaking'.[28]

So, in the 'March 1811' plan, the canal was incorporated. Leverton and Chawner, it appears, had also heard of the canal scheme but took the convenient view that it had been 'entirely abandoned'.

At this point we may return to the printed report and the engraved plan (Plate 32A). The canal is there, but instead of pursuing a leisurely course through the Park it is made to turn sharply northwards, then along the barracks site, north again and out. The ornamental water is there, if a trifle less snaky. The 'commercial canal' is there. But what has happened to the design as a whole? It has been ravaged. A whole complex of streets, squares and crescents has been torn out of it. If the double circus dominates, it does so in isolation, approached by two roads instead of three, with no houses on them. All other buildings have been pushed back towards the perimeter of the Park, except the villas. These are still distributed over the ground but from an uncountable number have been reduced to fifty.

This, of course, is mostly Spencer Perceval's doing, though the relegation of the canal to the north-west corner was ordered by the commissioners at an earlier stage on their own account. Nevertheless, we must not make the mistake of seeing the new plan as merely the disintegrated residue of the old. It is far from that. Although Nash had been seriously concerned, at first, at losing the density – the 'Bathonian' density, one might say – of his first conception, he was soon taking an exactly opposite view. 'I have the pleasure to say,' he wrote to the commissioners when forwarding the revised plan, 'that by the disposition of the villas in the new Plan which are proposed to occupy the Park, and the Terraces, Circuses, Crescents and Squares which surround and overlook the whole, I have been able to form a Combination perfectly to my satisfaction.' And he proceeds to an enthusiastic projection of the Park's new image:

> It is humbly submitted, that the double Circus on the Apex of the ground in the middle of the Park, the river-like lake of water in the Valley which will surround it, the stateliness of the ornamental Canal [meaning here the formal 'basin' or reservoir], with its slopes, terraces, balustrades and fountain, now proposed on the summit of the eastern side of the Park, the range of handsome houses that will overlook it, the two ample Crescents open to the Park on its Northern boundary, the extensive line of houses on the Southern boundary, will all be objects of grandeur, suited to the great extent of the Park which they will surround; and when combined with the rural and picturesque scenery of the Park itself, formed by the intermixture of Trees, Lawn and Water (provided that in the grouping of them a general unity of Park-like character be preserved), as great a variety of beautiful forms, comprehended in one magnificent whole, will be produced, as the mind can conceive.[29]

There is here not the least sense of frustration but an almost rapturous sense of having discovered something. Challenge and response have brought about an unlooked-for but entirely felicitous situation. The Bathonian density of the first plan has been exploded and a new 'general unity' on a new scale has revealed itself.

One sacrifice perhaps there was – the suppression of the canal as an element in the scene.

Nash had thought of it as 'a grand and novel feature of the Metropolis' and had supposed that 'many persons would consider the circumstance of Boats and Barges passing along the canal as enlivening the Scenery, provided the Bargemen or People from the Boats were prevented landing in the Parks' – an opinion entirely in accord with the spirit of the Picturesque.[30] But the commissioners thought bargees better kept out of royal parks whether they landed or not.

The printed report and the engraved plan of 1812 have a good deal more to tell us. The plan, for instance, shows certain public buildings not marked on the 'March 1811' plan. One is a circular church, placed in the circus at the junction of Portland Place and the New Road, evidently intended as the new parish church for Marylebone. Another, also circular, stands in the middle of the double circus in the Park; this we may take to be the temple of British worthies which Fordyce had originally suggested, or some monumental equivalent whose character the future might determine. Whatever its purpose Nash envisaged it as 'the grandest apex possible to the whole scenery'.

The siting of each villa is clearly marked, with groves of trees planted in such a way 'that no villa should see any other, but each should appear to possess the whole of the Park' – a nice application of the Picturesque doctrine of 'apparent extent'. One villa arouses curiosity by its shape and size which are those of a big country house or even a small palace. It stands on the cross axis of the formal 'bason' (now resited on the east side of the park) and might seem to be intended for some person of peculiarly lofty status. The Report makes no allusion to this building and the first indication we have of its purpose comes in the scornful review of Nash's plan contained in a pamphlet published by John White, son of the Duke of Portland's agent of the same name, already mentioned, and published in 1815.[31] White informs us that the building 'has been ill-naturedly said to be intended as a cangette for his Royal Highness'. 'Cangette' was White's equivalent of 'guinguette', the word by which the building is indentified on later plans. The guinguettes of Paris were duty-free tea-gardens or places of entertainment in the outer suburbs. Such a building was indeed intended by the Prince, though presumably for his own rather than for public relaxation. An innocent enough intention, surely. The ill-nature was Mr White's.

The market areas in the south-east corner of the Park are fully articulated on the engraved plan and explain the purpose of that arm of the canal marked 'commercial canal' in the earlier plan. This canal ends half-way down the east side of the Park in a circular basin. Immediately to the south is a 'Hay and Straw Market', leading to a 'Vegetable Market' and then to a 'Butchers Market'. This is the shopping area where Fordyce was so insistent that servants' time should be saved, and it is to be served by the canal folk directly from the country side.

Finally, there are the financial forecasts. The figures given in the printed report seem to refer to the 'March 1811' plan. Nash calculated that preparatory work on the site would cost £12,115. With the Park completely built up according to his plan there would be an annual income from ground-rents of £59,429 while the capital valuation when the ninety-nine year leaseholds terminated would be £187,724. He was insistent that these figures were dependent on the Crown becoming immediate lessors of the builders of the houses and the total exclusion of 'adventuring builders'. He had fixed his ground-rents half-way between what such builders would give the Crown and what they would exact from their undertenants. The revised design of August 1811 inevitably showed a dramatic reduction of revenue. Instead of £59,429, the income from ground-rents would be £45,268 15s. This did not perturb the Treasury however. It was still nearly double Leverton's and Chawner's figure of £23,000.[32]

On 22 October 1811 the commissioners received from the Treasury a rather long-winded and ambiguous minute. It began by stating that 'their Lordships could not approve the plan submitted by Messrs. Leverton and Chawner, for appropriating so much of the Estate to building'. With regard to Nash's scheme they were scarcely more forthcoming. They were 'not at present prepared to form any judgment as to the full extent of the appropriation of Marylebone Park in sites for Streets, Squares, Circuses and Villas, with ornamental Water and Plantations so disposed as to impart a high value to the Buildings so erected'. However, they were ready to agree with the commissioners and with Nash that it would be proper to form without delay a drive round the perimeter of the Park and, moreover, to adopt Nash's suggestion of planting trees on areas marked (on Nash's plan) as building sites so that, whether the areas were used for building or not, the Park would begin to present an air of cultivated amenity. The trees could be disposed of as the sites came to be required for building. While not stated in so many words, it was evident that Nash's was the accepted plan.[33]

At this stage, few outside the Office of Woods and Board of Treasury had seen the plans, but one who had was the personage who, since February, had been Prince Regent of England. Lord Glenbervie had been summoned to Carlton House early in September to explain them to his Royal Highness. The entry (a long one) in his journal describing the interview is unhappily lost, but it seems that the Regent was enchanted.[34] Tom Moore, writing to James Corry on 24 October, reported that he was 'so pleased with this magnificent plan that he has been heard to say "it will quite eclipse Napoleon"', whose architectural tributes to the *Grande Armée* were already among the architectural spectacles of Europe.[35] It was, of course, not only the plan for the Park but the project for a great new thoroughfare which stirred the Regent's enthusiasm.

Meanwhile Nash threw himself into the canal project. Although figuring prominently in the plan of March 1811 it was not till 3 May that a group of interested parties met at the Percy Street Coffee House to discuss the canal as a practical proposition. Nash, in company with Homer, Morgan and an engineer called Tate, then went over the proposed line, Nash producing an enthusiastic report in which he affirmed that the line selected by Homer was not only practical but 'the best course the canal can take'. The estimated cost was £280,000, the expected revenue £43,000: a return of something over 15 per cent. At a meeting at the City of London Tavern on 17 July it was resolved to open a preliminary subscription of £250,000 in £100 shares. A committee was appointed, consisting of Nash, Sir Thomas Bernard, Thomas King, Edward Gray and George Ward and his son (neighbours of Nash in the Isle of Wight, whom we shall meet later). Homer was made secretary.

In August Nash was able to announce to a meeting of subscribers that the Prince had approved the undertaking and graciously condescended to let it be known as the Regent's Canal. In December the subscription list was closed at £220,000. By this time Nash had pushed John Edwards and his young partner Lyon into the post of solicitors to the company. In August 1812 James Morgan, whose experience of canal construction was negligible, was appointed the company's engineer. Nash held all the reins.[36]

In June 1812 the first report of the Commissioners of Woods, Forests and Land Revenues appeared and Londoners at last had a chance of judging for themselves what the Marylebone improvements would amount to. There was some regret for the loss of the familiar rural scene but no serious opposition, except indeed from the younger John White who was so embittered about the whole procedure that he went into print about it. His snide allusion to the 'guinguette' has already been noted. His indignation knew no bounds. His father's design for the development of the Park had been set aside and his own house on the New Road was now to be swept away. Nash, through some diabolical agency, had got everything into his hands. What was behind this? 'We would by no means suppose,' wrote White, 'that any sinister motives have led to the preference of Mr. Nash's plan; and still less can we allow the suspicion that an undue favouritism existed.'[37] Which was a roundabout way of saying the exact opposite. What did White know that we do not? What did he suspect? He probably knew nothing. What he suspected was the hidden hand of Carlton House. On that point we cannot prove him wrong. But a study of the official records leaves little room for proving him right.

When the canal bill was introduced in the Commons in July, Thomas Creevey, always ready to embarrass the government, attacked Lord Glenbervie for not having produced a triennial report (it was, in fact, in the press) and both Glenbervie and Nash for having a financial interest in the canal. He proposed an amendment. Wharton of the Treasury rose to the defence and the amendment was negatived by a majority of 34.[38] Outside the House, opposition came from all the obvious quarters. The wharfingers at the Paddington basin, who saw themselves being bypassed, clamoured for compensation. There were complaints that springs would be robbed and drainage interrupted, that certain steam-engines to be installed at Paddington would be a nuisance, the receptacles for manure on the wharves a worse nuisance and, finally, that three hundred acres of stagnant water would threaten the health of the metropolis. These and other points, printed in an anonymous pamphlet, *Brief Remarks on the Proposed Regent's Canal*, were easily dealt with or ignored. The real trouble came when landowners began to object to having the canal in their grounds. Mr Portman would not hear of such a thing and delayed matters by obtaining an injunction in Parliament. Mr Agar, whose estate lay just east of Camden Town was equally violent and started a fierce opposition, which was not withdrawn till the canal was finished.[39]

When plans of the first new streets became available applications for sites began to come in. Two public-house proprietors, already settled on the property and anxious to take advantage of their licences in an area soon to be invaded by thirsty bricklayers, leased corner sites in the proposed continuation of Great Portland Street (eventually Albany Street). They were totally commonplace brick houses and, to contemporary eyes, far from prepossessing outposts of the new Marylebone.[40]

A better start (or so it seemed) was made when the southern half of the proposed circus on the New Road was taken on building lease by Charles Mayor, an unknown builder with £20,000 behind him. The plantations, only a few months old, were removed and houses began to rise at once. Unhappily, neither Mayor's resources nor his abilities were equal to the undertaking. In 1814 he asked, with Nash's support, for a government loan but it was declined and in 1815 he became bankrupt. For a time the fiasco scared away other speculators.[41] It was not till 1819, when John Farquhar, the millionaire East India gunpowder contractor and financial wizard, took an interest in the speculation, that the intended circus began to go forward again in other hands.

The end of 1812 saw part of the canal excavated and work begun on the Maida Vale Tunnel, the latter being designed by Morgan after an abortive competition.[42] Morgan was drawing a salary of £1,000 as full-time engineer to the canal but managing, simultaneously, the planting, digging and road-making in the Park. He also looked after the reports, estimates and drawings required in the course of the partnership's routine obligations in respect of the woods and forests of the Crown.

For their work in the Park neither Nash nor Morgan had anything but their joint retainer of £200, and in November 1812 Nash took the liberty of reminding the commissioners that a premium of £1,000 had been offered for the 'best design' for the Park, now, by its acceptance, conclusively shown to be his. The commissioners boggled and tried to salve their consciences in several directions at once by suggesting a division of the premium into three gratuities – £600 for Nash, £300 for Leverton and Chawner and £100 for John White, leaving Morgan out in the cold. Eventually the Treasury awarded £600 to Nash and £400 to Morgan.

A basis of further remuneration for work on the Park and the New Street was established after consultation with S. P. Cockerell and given authority by a Treasury minute of 14 December 1813. Meanwhile the Treasury had authorised a further payment of £1,000 for work on both Park and Street. In 1814 a contract of employment was drawn up and signed by Nash and the commissioners. This, clarified by an 'explanatory agreement' in 1818, remained in force till the completion of the work.[43]

As for Nash's private practice, commissions had abruptly dried up in 1810; doubtless they had been declined. The only work undertaken by him in 1812 outside his official capacity seems to have been a rescue operation for the Highgate Archway Company who had undertaken to form a new north exit from London through Highgate Hill. This involved a tunnel 765 ft long. When 130 ft of it was built it collapsed. On Nash's advice the tunnel was abandoned and a cutting substituted with a viaduct to carry

Highgate Lane across it. Nash's viaduct, with its lofty arch and three low arches above to carry the lane, was in Roman aqueduct style, unadorned except for a balustrade. It survived till 1901.[44]

The Park was now the centre of his endeavours. 'The completion of the design,' he wrote on 22 December 1813, 'is an object nearest my heart and occupies all my thoughts.'[45]

There was also, however, the Street.

6

The New Street

Just how urgent was the need for a new highway through north-west London may be imagined by anybody who walks through Soho today with the object of proceeding consistently and with reasonable expedition in a given direction. Hardly a street goes anywhere except into another street which crosses it and enforces a left or right turn. Only one street, Wardour Street (in origin a medieval field track), goes all the way through from north to south; and no street goes all the way through from east to west. It is wonderfully frustrating and before the coming of Regent Street this barrage of frustration extended a good deal further west. Between Wardour Street and Bond Street there was only one street going from Piccadilly to Oxford Street without a break. That was Swallow Street, the Piccadilly stub-end of which freakishly survives. You can cross it in five strides. This narrow channel, called on the old maps Little Swallow Street, widened towards the north and, as Great Swallow Street, reached Oxford Street in something not wholly unlike a straight line. All other routes were constricted zigzags.

This stultifying pattern was a legacy of the seventeenth century and its origins are to be found in a history of petty building enterprises on small or subdivided estates; enterprises in which continuity and sense of direction played no part and in which, very often, the builder's sole object was to get something on to the ground and sell it before an interfering officer of the Crown could challenge him with disobedience to some long-forgotten Proclamation.[1]

The need for ways through this clenched overgrowth was sharply seen by John Gwynn, whose recension of the London map, published with a critical text in 1766, was the first declaration of revolt against the capital's disordered increment.[2] He proposed two things. One was a northward extension of the Haymarket, forcing a way through Soho to Oxford Street. The other, somewhat less disruptive, was the widening of the Swallow

75

Streets. There was not, in his time, the slightest possibility of such operations being undertaken and it was not till a generation later, in 1794, that the first actual move towards improvement was made. This was on the recommendation of John Fordyce and consisted in the widening of a little street called Tichborne Street (*alias* Shug Lane and now non-existent) which wriggled north-westwards from the north end of the Haymarket and, as Glasshouse Street (still with us), joined Swallow Street. The widening reduced the wriggle to an acceptable short cut and that was all.[3]

A plan, said to have been made by James Wyatt a few years later, proposed a street starting opposite Carlton House in Pall Mall, going through Golden Square and finishing at the south end of Great Portland Street.[4] A plan on similar lines was made in 1808 by Leverton and Chawner of the Land Revenue Office, presumably at the behest of their chief, Fordyce, who in his Report of the following year made the final and irresistible plea for the new street; irresistible because without it the development of Marylebone Park by the government could hardly be considered feasible. As anyone could see, the chief obstacle to the successful development of the Park was its distance from the Houses of Parliament – 'distance', as Fordyce observed, 'being best computed by time'.[5] He believed that a new highway from Charing Cross to a central part of the Park would reduce travelling time (presumably by carriage) by one-third. He quoted the achievements of Dublin's Wide Street Commission of 1756, sketched out a possible course for the new street and estimated its cost. He did not envisage it as a profitable enterprise but neither did he foresee expenditure of a prohibitive order. He thought a street from Piccadilly to Oxford Street would cost £290,000 but the sale of building sites (not, observe, the leasing) and of old materials would reduce this to a mere £54,000.

Fordyce dying in 1810, his successors, the Commissioners of Woods, Forests and Land Revenues, took over. They, as we saw in the last chapter, delivered instructions to the architects of the newly-united departments of Land Revenues and of Woods and Forests to prepare plans for the development of Marylebone Park, embodying in these the preparation of plans for a new street. Leverton and Chawner, the Land Revenues partnership, contented themselves, excusably, with a reference to the plan they had already submitted two years earlier. John Nash, exerting himself to the full, took the problem to pieces and put together a solution in a report which is a masterpiece of insight and commonsense.[6]

Nash developed his report under three headings: first, *Utility to the Public*; second, *Beauty of the Metropolis*; third, *Practicability*. Under the first head he showed how far from adequate were the plans of his predecessors to the load of traffic which the new Marylebone would bring. They were drawn too far to the east. They would do nothing to relieve the overcrowding of Bond Street or the bottleneck at Cockspur Street. Furthermore they took no account of the social differentiations of the map. This, to Nash, was the most vital factor, the logical clue. All the way from north to south it was possible to trace a distinction between the areas of upper-class living and those of tradesmen and work-people. In the north was the still almost-isolated Portland Place, a fashionable street of great width (125 ft) with good streets leading westward from it but, on the east, streets going a few yards into Great Portland Street and then into an area of shopkeepers and craftsmen. Similarly between Oxford Street and Piccadilly there was a readily discernible line between the Soho tangle on the east and the broad criss-cross of eighteenth-century estate planning on the west. This line was represented by the Swallow Streets which therefore became, for most of their length, the guideline for the new street. But somehow the street had to get itself to Charing Cross and this was not so easy. A swerve to the east was necessary to avoid penetrating the fashionable streets of the St James's Square area and, no less important, to bring the new street down near the east end of Pall Mall, which was to be opened up to resolve the Cockspur bottleneck. Here the appropriate division was represented by St James's Market and St Albans Street which entered Pall Mall directly opposite Carlton House.

By following this line of social cleavage, Nash's object was to provide 'a boundary and complete separation between the Streets and Squares occupied by the Nobility and Gentry, and the narrow streets and meaner Houses occupied by mechanics and the trading part of the community'. 'My purpose,' he wrote when the street was finished, 'was that the new street should cross the eastern entrance to all the streets occupied by the higher classes and to leave out to the east all the bad streets, and as a sailor would express himself, to hug all the avenues that went to good streets.'[7] This policy had two enormous advantages. First, it ensured that the new street should be quite distinctly a west-end street, attracting high rents, and not a mere traffic artery, of indifferent character. Second, it avoided the destruction of modern well-built property and kept the bill for compensation to a minimum by purchasing, so far as possible, in the run-down areas of the tradesmen and mechanics.

The first design for the new street which we have is the one engraved for the printed report of the Commissioners, published in 1812 (Plate 24). It shows Portland Place continued south to Oxford Street where it enters a circus, introduced here, as further north in the Regents Park plan, to defeat by its visual impartiality the 'fashionable objection' to residence beyond a certain zone. The circus also serves here to neutralise a change of direction. The street proceeds south-south-east, avoiding Golden Square and reaching a large new square, almost filled by a public building. Entering the square on the north-west, the street leaves it on the south-east and immediately enters another circus. Here there is again a slight change of direction, so that the lower stretch of the street, terminating in another square, is plumb on the axis of Carlton House.

A spectacular feature of this design is the continuous colonnade proceeding without intermission from (and including) Oxford Circus to the square before Carlton House. Its purpose was not only architectural but social, Nash's idea being that

> those who have daily intercourse with the Public Establishments in Westminster, may go two-thirds of the way on foot under cover, and those who have nothing to do but walk about and amuse themselves may do so

every day in the week, instead of being frequently confined many days together to their Houses by rain; and such a covered Colonnade would be of peculiar convenience to those who require daily exercise. The Balustrades over the Colonnades will form Balconies to the Lodging-rooms over the Shops, from which the Occupiers of the Lodgings can see and converse with those passing in the Carriages underneath, and which will add to the gaiety of the scene, and induce single men, and others, who only visit Town occasionally, to give a preference to such Lodgings.[8]

These colonnades greatly upset Lord Glenbervie who thought them 'pretty on paper' but 'such a repository for Damp, Obscurity, Filth and Indecency as no Regulation or Police will be able to prevent'.[9] He expressed these views to Nash who, though sympathetic, remained unconvinced. Nash saw the colonnades as adding gaiety rather than gloom to the London scene; his picture of ogling provincial bachelors showing themselves off all along Regent Street is pure Rowlandson. Such characters, as well as the pedestrian clerks and the more fortunate citizens who 'have nothing to do but walk about and amuse themselves' are recognisable constituents of Regency London.

One obvious objection to the colonnades was that the shop-windows would be darkened. Nash met this difficulty by proposing skylights to admit light on the *inner* side of the windows, the latter projecting a little to make this possible. As to 'indecency', if it were suspected that the lower orders would make free with the columns in an offensive manner Nash had the ready reply that their 'receding form . . . will preclude any shelter to those who may be disposed to commit nuisances against them'.

Under the second head in this report, *Beauty of the Metropolis*, Nash contented himself with a few descriptive paragraphs which might mean anything or nothing but which, to Londoners of 1810, would certainly evoke the image of a capital city which really *looked* like a capital city and not just a huge huddle of brick houses with a steepled skyline.

The beauty of the Town, it is presumed, would be advanced by a street of such magnificent dimensions; by the Colonnades and Balustrades which will adorn its sides; by the insulating the public building of the Opera; by the effect of the Monuments in the centre of the crossing streets; by the Vista between Carlton House and Piccadilly, terminated by a public monument at one end, and by the Palace of Carlton House at the other; every length of Street would be terminated by a façade of beautiful architecture; and to add to the beauty of the approach from Westminster to Charing-cross, a Square or Crescent, open to and looking down Parliament-street, might be built round the Equestrian Statue at Charing-cross . . .[10]

Monuments at key points were an idea entertained for some time and in part achieved. As late as 1825 Nash was talking about a Doric Temple (circular, presumably) in memory of Shakespeare in Piccadilly Circus;[11] and a fine drawing exists showing a design for a Wellington column opposite Carlton House with a spiral frieze like its Roman prototypes and the Duke on the top of it.[12] This latter must date from about 1816, when the space there was officially named 'Waterloo Place', probably in anticipation of the entire street becoming 'Waterloo Street'. It foreshadowed, of course, the Duke of York's column built in 1831–4 when Carlton House had been demolished. The square round the Charles I statue at Charing Cross was, again, an adumbration of the square which Nash was to lay out there and which in due course would be named Trafalgar. This square, Nash proposed, should be devoted to buildings for the learned societies – the Royal Society, the Royal Academy of Arts and the Antiquarian Society. And there would be statues of George III and George IV.

On the *Practicability of the Measure* Nash's main contention was that as one-third of the property along the line of his street between Charing Cross and Oxford Circus already belonged to the Crown and as the remaining two-thirds consisted of property of the meanest kind, the cost in terms of purchase and compensation would be moderate. In an appendix to his report he hazarded a preliminary estimate. The total amount required for purchase and compensation would, he thought, be £399,803. Against this the annual income accruing from ground-rents would be £28,734: a return of 7.3 per cent.[13]

Lastly, there was the question of drainage. Of the thirteen sewers which at this period carried London's refuse to the Thames, two started within Regents Park; they were the Hartshorn Lane Sewer (formed 1720, beginning near the top of Great Portland Street and issuing near Charing Cross) and the King's Scholars Pond Sewer (formed 1724, beginning in Regents Park, going through Pimlico, and issuing a little to the west of Vauxhall Bridge).[14] The latter, the longest sewer of all, was already seriously overburdened, and John Rennie had been making suggestions for relieving it some years before Nash came upon the scene.[15] Rennie recommended a new sewer, which was to cost £70,000, but Nash pointed out that the line of the new street made a shorter and less obstructed route possible and that the sewer would in this case cost only £54,000, with a proportionately smaller outlay on cross-cuts. After some criticism and discussion Nash carried his point.

Soon after the issuing of this report, the Commissioners of Woods, Forests and Land Revenues gave notice of their intention to apply to Parliament to bring in a bill, at the same time requiring Nash to revise and elaborate his proposals and submit alternative plans and estimates. This he did and the results were forwarded by the Commissioners to the Treasury on 8 March 1813.[16] There were now three plans from which to choose. Plan No. 1 has already been described. Plan No. 2 eliminated the square containing a public building and, to effect the necessary change of direction in the same area, introduced what the commissioners described as 'a bending street, resembling in that respect the High-street at Oxford'. This is the first mention of what was to be the Quadrant, an architectural conception which, in the event, could harldly less resemble the Oxonian prototype. Plan No. 3 contained a square between Piccadilly and Jermyn Street.

The commissioners' choice fell on No. 2, partly because they liked the 'bending street' but mostly because, while cheaper than No. 1, it promised the largest revenue of the three in relation to expenditure. The cost of Plan No. 1 Nash had now revised from £399,803 to £462,527. Plan No. 2 he estimated would cost £380,754. The respective revenues from ground-rents would be £36,831 and £31,999, Plan No. 1 showing a return of nearly 8 per cent and the cheaper No. 2 a return of 9½ per cent.[17] Plan No. 3 was dismissed.

Confronted with such dazzling optimism, the Treasury insisted that Nash's figures should be professionally checked. The commissioners accordingly sent them to Leverton and Chawner, who by this time could be relied upon to prick any Nash bubble within reach. Predictably, they came back with a statement that Plan No. 1, the one estimated at £462,527 would in fact cost £948,522.[18] The Treasury, through the commissioners, invited Nash to comment. He did, crushingly. Leverton and Chawner, he said, had worked on an illogical principle. They did not appreciate the nature of freehold. 'Building,' he contended, 'is not in its nature freehold; nothing is properly freehold but the ground.' Buildings decay from day to day; ground does not, yet Leverton and Chawner had valued all the properties whose acquisition would be required by the plan, ground and buildings together, on a flat rate of twenty years purchase at an estimated ground-rent. Whatever the practice in the day-to-day bargaining of the property market, in the acquisition of properties for public improvements this was indefensible. A severer logic must prevail. Nash took the view that in the case of most of the properties involved in his plan ten or twelve years purchase would represent a fair assessment. Moreover, Leverton and Chawner had suggested a price of 30s. 5d. per foot frontage of the new building sites. To this Nash replied that even the cheapest frontages (north of Oxford Circus where there would be no shops) were worth two guineas. He himself, as it happened, had already (for reasons we shall see) both bought and sold in that area and he knew.[19]

The Treasury agreed that Leverton and Chawner had failed to invalidate Nash's estimate. They ·confirmed the commissioners' choice of Plan No. 2 and directed the preparation of a bill to go before Parliament. This, inevitably, was the signal for opposition to stir. The most plausible representations were made by the vestrymen of St James's who maintained that their shopkeepers would be injured by trade being drawn eastward to the new street. The objection was overruled without much argument. It proved not altogether groundless but Bond Street survived.

The Bill contained eighty-seven sections, beginning with the appointment of commissioners for carrying the Act into effect. They were the three commissioners for Woods, Forests and Land Revenues, in other words, Lord Glenbervie, W. Dacres Adams and Henry Dawkins. Other sections dealt with procedures for compensation and the borrowing of funds. The Commissioners were empowered to borrow £500,00 for the street and an additional £100,000 for the new sewer and its tributaries. The exact line of the street was not defined but provision was made for the protection of one building standing on the site: the church of St Thomas in King (now Kingly) Street. It is still there.

Introduced by Richard Wharton, Junior Secretary of the Treasury, the Bill was debated in Parliament on 15 June 1813.[20] It was opposed by John Calcraft, the Whig member for Rochester, somewhat irrationally, on the ground of expense as if it were a public monument rather than a property investment that was in question. He asserted that the circuses would be 'a great nuisance'. He did not say why but may perhaps have imagined that they would have fenced enclosures as at Bath. He did not at all understand Nash's theory of the binding properties of circuses and said that he must 'stand up for Oxford Street, even against the opinion of Mr. Nash, and say that he did not think so fine a street ought to be spoiled, merely to avoid the sensation of crossing it'. Mr P. Moore, another Whig, scented a danger of Nash seeking to make a fortune at the public expense; he should be made to enter into a contract and not be paid 5 per cent (no figure had been mentioned, in the Bill or elsewhere). In further debate, seven members pressed the indictment of extravagance but the Bill was passed by a substantial majority and received the Royal assent on 10 July 1813.

The New Street Commissioners met for the first time ten days later.[21] They met in the former Woods and Forests house in Whitehall but arranged to move to a smaller house in Whitehall Place as soon as possible. Their first action was to appoint staff. Alexander Milne and James Pillar were appointed joint secretaries; John Marshall and Thomas Davidson, clerks. To Nash, who was to act as an independent professional, they conveyed their confidence in his skill and judgement.

At the second meeting on 23 July finance was the main item.[22] Nash's opinion was that as the public was unlikely to want to invest in the new street the likeliest lenders were the big insurance offices. Already in December 1812 he had been in touch with Sir Theophilus Metcalfe of the Globe and a figure of £300,000 had been mentioned. The Globe, however, when it came to the point, stipulated that the loan should consist of 3 per cent stock. The Treasury did not care to shoulder the risks of fluctuation, so negotiations were begun with another company, the Royal Exchange, who expressed themselves willing to advance a direct loan of £300,000 at 5 per cent per annum. This was accepted. Of this loan, £140,000 was at once paid into the Bank of England, all but £20,000 for current needs being invested in exchequer bills to be sold from time to time as occasion required.[23]

On the line of the new street (Plate 25), 741 houses required to be demolished and of these 386 (mostly south of Piccadilly) were Crown property. The procedure was first to acquire the fee simple of all the houses not owned by the Crown and then to purchase sub-interests of all properties as opportunity allowed, meanwhile stopping all extensions of leases. The business of valuation was enormously complex and S. P. Cockerell was called in to share this burden with Nash.[24] Nash was in his element. He had a magical flair for valuation and very rarely indeed did arbitration find him at fault. Where he was not so successful was in the assessment of goodwill and compensation, factors which, in the long run, extended the costs of the enterprise far beyond his original estimates – or even those of Leverton and Chawner.

By the end of June 1814 notices of compulsory acquisition had been sent to most of the occupiers south of Piccadilly, where the great symmetrical space opposite Carlton House was planned. It was here that the compensation troubles began. This area of prosperous tradesmen and shopkeepers, living and working within the precinct of a royal palace, did not want to be disturbed. But if it had to be disturbed the disturbance must be rendered as advantageous as possible. Appeals against the commissioners' assessments were frequent. Six small tenants in St James's Market, offered a lump sum of £270, went to arbitration and got £2,800. An individual who was offered £600 took his case to court and was awarded £2,400 by a jury.[25] Mr. Illingworth, a wine and brandy dealer with a huge stock of wines in his Pall Mall cellars, declined the commissioners' offer of £3,800; a jury awarded him £5,117 with costs.[26] A certain Colonel Stanley, on the other hand, was content to surrender his Pall Mall house if the government would build him an equivalent house at the north end of the street, as near as possible to Portland Place. His offer was accepted and Nash built the house for £4,590, but this was almost the only transaction of the kind. The general rule was compensation in cash.[27]

In 1815 enquiries for building sites began to come in. James Burton, the great Bloomsbury builder, makes his first appearance in that year, when he began taking sites in the quadrangle which, from 1816, was called Waterloo Place.[28] In December 1815 came a letter from Samuel Baxter, offering to take the four corner sites on which Oxford Circus would be built.[29] This was unexpected because the Commissioners, discouraged perhaps by what had been said in the House of Commons, had told Nash to leave the Circus out. Baxter's offer, however, restored their confidence and he was granted his leases. In 1816 a builder made proposals for the southern half of Piccadilly Circus and Nash was ordered to prepare designs without delay.[30]

Nash, meanwhile, had conducted a remarkable deal of his own. This concerned Foley House, the London mansion of his client at Witley Court. Foley House stood at the south end of Portland Place (the site of what used to be the Langham Hotel). It had been built by Lord Foley's great-grandfather on the Duke of Portland's land and the third Duke had made a gift of the freehold to the next Lord Foley on condition of being allowed to build Portland Place immediately to the north of it. If Portland Place was to become an integral part of the new highway from Marylebone to Charing Cross, Foley House would have to go.

In 1810, before any official plan for the new street was on the horizon, Lord Foley, finding himself short of money to pay for the building works at Witley, had bargained with his architect for a loan of £24,000, on the security of Foley House. In July of the following year, however, this arrangement was modified; £10,000 of the loan was repaid and Nash undertook to pull the house down and develop the site for building.[31] In the interval (October 1810) Nash had received instructions from his masters, the commissioners of Woods, Forests and Land Revenue, to submit proposals for a new street. By March he had come up with the daring notion of forcibly adopting Portland Place as the street's northern outlet. If this could be brought off, one thing was obvious:

the Foley property would become a promising investment for his client and himself. Hence, no doubt, the switch in the mortgage arrangements of July 1811. It presaged that interpenetration of aesthetic and economic advantage for which Nash had so magical a touch.

Nash kept his ideas well under cover and so, apparently, did the commissioners and it was only with the publication of their first report in June 1812 that the New Street plan, with all its implications, burst upon the public. There were howls of dismay at the desecration of Portland Place and when the plan went before Parliament the Duke of Portland himself came forward with an offer of £42,000 to take Foley's property off his hands. If Foley accepted, the plan was dished. Nash took the greatest risk of his career and rushed in with a massively increased offer – allegedly £70,000 – which Foley accepted. It was a staggering price to pay, but 'the new street', wrote Nash in allusion to this episode many years later, 'was an object very near my heart'.[32]

Nash sold the part of the land required for the new street to the Crown in 1814 at a cautious valuation, by S. P. Cockerell, of £10,184.[33] Previous to that, he had sold another part to a Northamptonshire baronet, Sir James Langham MP, who proposed to build a detached house in line with the west side of Portland Place. It was a condition of the sale that Nash should be the architect. This transaction had an important sequel.

While the house was going up a drastic alteration in the line of the new street was forced upon Nash. The influential residents on the west side of Cavendish Square complained that their back premises would be shorn off by the street. The line was therefore shifted some hundred yards to the east, necessitating a sudden sweep to the north-west to join Portland Place. This curving line created new building sites and some of them would inevitably run back to within a few yards of Langham's windows. Langham had no option but to negotiate with Nash for the purchase of the land between his house and the street and to lay it out as a garden. What he paid Nash is unknown but the transaction is said to have been embittered by a furious row between Langham and his architect arising from structural defects in the half-finished house.[34] The baronet came off badly. Nash benefited; and the street benefited from a charming stretch of garden exactly opposite the site which Nash had already designated for a church and where All Souls, Langham Place, was eventually to stand.

Through 1815, 1816 and 1817 the pressure of business at the New Street office was heavy and there were meetings of the commissioners nearly every other day. The chief commissioner, Lord Glenbervie, had stopped attending in April 1814 and had taken himself abroad with his invalid wife. The Prime Minister, Lord Liverpool, made this an excuse for getting rid of him and putting a younger and more robust politician, William Huskisson, in his place.[35] Huskisson was first commissioner till 1823 and bore the brunt of the critical years.

These were the years when the public first became conscious of what was happening. Familiar streets were blocked, house after house was left derelict, then torn down, clouds of dust from builders' rubbish got into eyes and noses, Swallow Street was a scene of desolation and ruin from end to end. Nothing like it had ever been seen and the obvious conclusion to be drawn was that some kind of disaster had overtaken London. For this somebody was to blame and, since it is always more satisfactory to blame individuals than governments, the man to blame was Nash. Nash himself, looking back on these years, recalled how 'the scheme was proclaimed to be impracticable, destructive of the interests of the Crown, and ruinous to all who should engage in it'. Among architects it was 'a common subject for laughter'.[36] Lord Glenbervie, smarting under his dismissal from office, wrote in his journal in 1816 that 'the project of the new street seems to be in a deplorable way and Nash . . . is held in universal abhorrence, except by his royal master and dupe'.[37]

The state of affairs was, indeed, somewhat alarming. Costs were rising steeply, chiefly because of Nash's under-estimate of the awards for compensation and goodwill. Juries, it seemed, were always on the side of the dispossessed. In 1816 the commissioners were obliged to borrow to the full extent allowed by Parliament, namely £600,000 (including £100,000 for the sewer). The Royal Exchange office was approached once more but declined to consider a further loan and it was only after prolonged discussion that the Governor and directors of the Bank of England 'signified their readiness to accommodate the Public Service'. Even so, the Bank found itself unable by its constitution to lend on the security offered by the New Street Act (i.e. the credit of the land revenues of the Crown) and further legislation had to be sought.[38]

The new sewer, in progress under a section of the 1813 Act, with Nash as engineer, was a cause of some anxiety. Allegations of its incapacity and inefficiency were put forward in 1816 and the commissioners asked Rennie, in consultation with two other engineers, to investigate and give an opinion. Rennie's report was favourable, on the whole, though he pointed to several defects which ought to be put right. Nash, meanwhile, as a measure of self-protection, obtained an independent opinion from Telford, and the contractors procured, for the same reason, three separate reports from experienced surveyors. Telford pronounced the sewer to be 'upon the whole very substantially constructed', while William Braham, reporting for the contractors, declared himself ready to verify upon oath that the structure was 'as complete a Sewer, the whole length, as can be executed by the hands of man'.[39]

Not everybody was willing to endorse Mr Braham's opinion unreservedly, but Nash had no doubt that it was 'as perfect a work of its kind as has ever been performed', and, when certain deficiencies had been corrected, Rennie himself was able to confirm that all was well. Nash had originally intended to relieve both the King's Scholars Pond sewer and the Hartshorn Lane sewer by cross-cutting them into the new sewer; but on Rennie's suggestion Hartshorn Lane sewer was let alone and King's Scholars Pond sewer relieved only in its upper length, north of Brook Street.

One major anxiety, because of its totally unpredictable nature, was the letting of sites. In 1815 sites were advertised in the press but this practice was soon discontinued. In one case and one only (Nos 106–54), competitive tenders were invited, James Burton being the successful bidder. Elsewhere the procedure was for Nash to fix the price per foot frontage and for builders to make such informal inquiries as they felt inclined. Substantial and reliable builders could thus be encouraged and the shadier kind of speculator choked off.[40]

Two builders made an outstanding contribution to the success of the Street. One was Samuel Baxter who, as we have seen, rescued Oxford Circus from limbo and brought it to a satisfactory conclusion; he also built the northern half of Piccadilly Circus. The other was James Burton. He was in a different class and certainly the greatest London developer of his time. He had started on the Foundling estate in the 1790s, and then from 1800 proceeded to develop Bloomsbury northwards from Bloomsbury Square.[41] His involvement with Regent Street was very extensive indeed. From 1815 he was building Waterloo Place. In 1817 he took a block of five houses at the corner of Jermyn Street; in 1818, the five houses called Carlton Chambers on the east side of Lower Regent Street; in 1820, the long block of eighteen houses between Leicester Street (now part of Heddon Street) and New Burlington Street; and, in the same year, the block of twelve houses on the opposite side of the street, between Leicester Street (now Regent Place) and Beak Street; in 1821, a block of five houses going northward from Leicester (Heddon) Street on the east; in 1822, a block of thirteen houses between New Burlington and Conduit Streets; in 1823, the block of twelve houses north of Glasshouse Street; and in 1824, a block of four houses on the west side, above Oxford Circus. A total of 74 houses, all in formal groups behind facades designed or approved by Nash; altogether about one-quarter of the houses in the Street.

One incentive to this continuous participation was that, having plunged heavily in Waterloo Place, Burton saw himself losing out badly if the whole Street was not opened up. Nash confessed that without Burton's help the Street might not have pulled through. Whenever there was a site awkwardly hanging fire, Burton was there, ready to step in and treat for it.[42] Only in the Quadrant did his courage and faith in the new street fail him.

The Quadrant was the 'bending street', swinging the line of the main street round to enter Piccadilly on the axis of Carlton House. It consisted of five uniform concentric blocks of building, two on the east side of the Street and three on the west, containing sixty-one houses in all. Being built on a curve these blocks could not be built house by house as the sites were disposed of. Each block had to be built as a single structure. Since neither Burton nor any other builder would take on any of these blocks, Nash took every plot in the Quadrant himself, at the price at which it was being offered, and built the whole thing himself as a personal undertaking. As he afterwards said: 'I do not think the Quadrant would ever have been carried into execution but in that way.'[43]

To say that Nash built the Quadrant himself is putting the matter a little too baldly. The procedure in this formidable speculation was far from simple. In the first instance, in 1818, he agreed with the Crown to take every plot in his own name at a peppercorn rent for the first three years, half rent for the fourth and full rent thereafter.[44] Simultaneously, he persuaded a group of building tradesmen ('a set of builders', he called them) to become his nominees for as many houses as they would take, ninety-nine year Crown leases being granted to them as each house was covered in and the front stuccoed. These tradesmen were men he knew well and who were working for him in several of his other undertakings. Some of them took one house, some two, one as many as eight. Nash was the 'builder' of these houses in the sense that he contracted with each trade to supply materials and labour at agreed prices. The tradesmen were not, however, paid in cash. The value of each tradesman's work was set against the value of the house or houses of which he had undertaken to become lessee. To the cost of the house Nash added a commission of 5 per cent for himself. The value of materials and labour thus accounted for was not necessarily confined to work in the Quadrant but might include work executed in or materials supplied to other buildings for which Nash was responsible.

The main feature of this 'work against work' system of accounting, not uncommon in Georgian London, was that very little cash changed hands. Nevertheless, periodic cash advances had to be made to keep the tradesmen solvent and these loans, Nash claimed, he administered 'to the tune of £60,000'.[45]

The success of the system depended on many things and one of these was accurate book-keeping. Nash's office records have disappeared, with one solitary and fortunate exception: a ledger, handsomely bound in green leather, which somehow got left in a cupboard in a house occupied by one of the Pennethorne family at Shide Hill, Isle of Wight, and is now in the RIBA Library. The Shide Ledger contains accounts with many of the tradesmen who participated in Nash's scheme. The biggest taker was the firm of Want and Richardson, the bricklayers who were building the sewer. They took eight houses. Baxter, the builder of Oxford Circus, took four. Others were Depree, pavior (4 houses); May and Morritt, ironmongers (4 houses); Brindley, lime merchant (2 houses); Prigg, plumber (2 houses); Francis and White, cement merchants (2 houses); Brine, statuary mason, and Brown, plasterer (1 house each). Another participant was William Slark, who made the iron staircases for the Pavilion. The 'work against work' system extended to other tradesmen who did not take houses but were actively employed in other parts of Nash's building empire.

Nash took all the plots in the Quadrant at a ground-rent of £2 12s. 6d. per foot frontage (irrespective of the very variable depths). This, by arrangement with the Crown, he 'improved' by an additional ground-rent of £1 1s. 0d. per foot, which he sold to the Crown, at sixteen years purchase, as the buildings went up. He applied for the money in five instalments in respect of each house on the certificate of an independent surveyor (who happened, it must be said, to be Charles Beazley, a fellow-pupil at Sir Robert Taylor's). With a sum for the redemption of land tax added, the total rent reflected in the leases was £4 4s. 0d. per foot frontage, or about £60 per annum per house.[46] The cost of a typical house in the Quadrant was about £2,500. Lack of documentation precludes accurate computation of the whole but it would be of the order of £150,000.

The success of the Quadrant as a speculation may perhaps best be measured by the fact that, so far as we know, nobody went bankrupt. Nobody pretended it was a roaring financial success either and John Shaw, the surveyor, who would certainly know, said that 'it turned out ill'.[47] The great thing was that it got built. The Street was saved, and that, from Nash's point of view, was all that really mattered.

With the Quadrant in hand, the prospects for the Street began to brighten. In January 1819 it got its name and Nash was instructed to have REGENT STREET painted on appropriate buildings.[48] Gas mains had begun to be laid in the previous year and Nash made various experimental designs for lamp-irons with a view to evolving an economical casting.[49] In the late summer of 1819 the Street was opened, without ceremony, as far as Piccadilly. Oxford Circus, with its long north and south extensions, was complete and, between the Circuses, Burton's handsome blocks had begun to fill up the desolate spaces.

Expenditure, it is true, rose monstrously but with completion well in sight the Treasury remained calm and shouldered the additional burdens without protest, £100,000 being voted in the supplies for 1820 and a similar sum in those for 1821. In 1824 the Treasury advanced £400,000 to the commissioners to enable them to pay off the loans by the Royal Exchange Insurance office and the Bank of England, the balance of £200,000 being found by the commissioners out of sales of Crown lands and quit-rents invested in the 3 per cent funds, *plus* a smallish sum out of current revenue.[50]

The New Street account was finally closed on 5 July 1826. On the expenditure side the figures were as follows:

Paid for property and compensation, legal charges and payments to architects, surveyors and other officers, auditors and incidentals		£1,408,447
Paid in interest on borrowed money	£239,876	
Less rents from the New Street, dividends from invested funds, sale of old materials etc.	173,354	
	66,522	
Cost of new sewer	60,719	
	127,241	127,241
		£1,535,688

The probable revenue from ground-rents and sewer-rates was assessed, at this date, at £35,000. Setting aside the sewer-rates, this was very close indeed to Nash's estimate of 1813 (£31,999). The yield on the outlay was a pathetic 2 per cent instead of Nash's promised 9½ per cent. It was the compensation factor which had proved totally unpredictable, and no wonder. Never in London's history had compulsory aquisition on a comparable scale been exercised. Neither Nash nor anybody else could have forecast how Londoners would react to a situation of the kind imposed on them by the Act of 1813. They reacted, of course, almost to a man, with a virulent combination of resentment and greed.[51]

If we ask how Nash himself was rewarded for his twelve years' toil on the new street, we have his own answer: 'very badly'.[52] For his work on Marylebone Park and the Street up to the end of 1814 he received a lump sum of £1,000. For the sewer a maximum remuneration of £2,500 was stipulated. On all public buildings, houses not yielding rent, on railings, open spaces and lodges he received 5 per cent on the money laid out and for works of this kind designed but not executed 1½ per cent on the estimate. For valuations, whether for purchase or sale, he received ¼ per cent, with 1¼ per cent on resales and more if the resale price exceeded the original by 10 per cent or more.

For letting each plot (i.e. the site of each house) he received one half-year's ground-rent and for this he had to measure and value the ground, design and superintend the building, negotiate with the builders and tenants, give his opinion regarding the necessary covenants and draw the plans in them.

A calculation submitted by Charles Arbuthnot in evidence before a Select Committee in 1828 showed that Nash's total remuneration in respect of Regent Street (including the £1,000 which covered also the preliminary works for the Park) was £30,599; for Marylebone Park £11,182 8s. Considering that all this work was carried on at his own premises with his own staff nobody could say that he was overpaid.[53]

If Regent Street is accounted, as it surely must be, a triumphant success, a notable circumstance is that from conception to completion it was conducted by a very small number of people. Nash himself was architect, surveyor, valuer, estate agent, engineer and financial adviser. But he was acting outside the civil establishment, as a professional man. Within the establishment it was Alexander Milne, joint secretary to the commissioners from 1810 and sole secretary after 1822, who carried most responsibility. He seems an obscure figure now but it was he who ran the New Street office, minuted the commissioners' meetings and conducted with impeccable precision an enormous correspondence with Nash and everybody else engaged in the Street. He worked early and late, often on Sundays, at a salary of £1,000 a year.[54] Nash and Milne were the men who, in the day-to-day business, really mattered. The three commissioners attended with exemplary regularity and the first commissioner had parliamentary responsibilities which could be difficult and embarrassing. Nash had his trusty Morgan and George Repton. Outside that group and leaving aside the complementary initiatives of the building world, there are few names which count for much. Nash was the genius of the group but not its leader. He took his orders from the commissioners through Milne and carried blame for their not infrequently delayed execution. It was all perfectly bureaucratic but on a scale which still admitted a sense of personal responsibility to the task, to Parliament and to the Crown. In Nash's case, most especially to the Crown.

7

The Regent's Architect

The Regency began in the year (almost in the very month) in which Marylebone Park returned into the possession of the Crown. George, Prince of Wales, was installed as Regent in February 1811. In March John Nash signed his first plan for the Park. It might seem that the Prince, entering upon his inheritance, summoned by a wave of the delegated sceptre the architect of his choice. The truth is less simple. Nash came to his seat of opportunity by no royal road of patronage. Lord Robert Spencer's appointment of him to a somewhat underpaid post in the old Office of Woods and Forests in 1806 may indeed have been an act of foresight, but it was also one of common administrative sense. No great penetration of mind would be required to see that whoever took the job in that year would probably be the man to whom, four or five years later, the government would turn for designs for developing the Park. To appoint a man of fifty-four, of widely recognised ability, was prudent and subsequent procedure was perfectly regular. John White's dark hints about 'sinister motives' and 'undue favouritism' may be discounted as the mumblings of a frustrated outsider; and there is no reason to suppose that Glenbervie and his colleagues or the Lords of the Treasury, still less the Prime Minister, were under any sort of pressure to promote Nash's interests.

Nevertheless, an interesting question does issue from behind the scenes. By 1812 it is certain that Nash occupied a position of confidentiality at Carlton House, not merely as a favoured architect but as a servant of the Prince who could be relied upon to act in any sphere where the latter's interests might benefit through his agency. Sir Samuel Romilly, the Attorney-General, noted in his diary for 8 March 1813, that 'Mr Nash . . . ever since his projected improvements of Marylebone Park has been in great favour with the Prince', adding that Nash lived 'in constant habits of intimacy with Lord Yarmouth'.[1] Here is an unexpected association. Lord Yarmouth was the only son of the second Marquis, the Lord Hertford whose wife had been, since 1807, the chief lady in the life of the Prince. The

Hertford circle was the paramount source of influence throughout the years of the Regency. Yarmouth, then in his mid-thirties, was the man who, in his later years, over-exercised his rakish propensities to the extent of making himself the prototype of Thackeray's Marquis of Steyne. That Nash in 1812 should be on familiar terms with him suggests a deeper penetration into court society than could be achieved simply as a consequence of having made an acceptable design for the development of a royal estate. How had this come about?

It will be recalled that as far back as 1798 Nash had exhibited 'a conservatory for his Royal Highness the Prince of Wales' at Somerset House. This in itself may not signify much. Many an artist and many a shopkeeper could claim the acceptance of some trifle as an act of royal patronage. It was also in 1798, however, that Nash started to build his castle in the Isle of Wight. Very close to Nash's property was Norris Castle, built at nearly the same time by Lord Henry Seymour. Lord Henry was the Marquis of Hertford's brother and the uncle of Lord Yarmouth. Neighbourliness among castellated landlords in the island could hardly fail to offer social opportunities of a kind which, with charm and tact, Nash would manipulate to his advantage. Social manoeuvres of this kind must remain a matter of speculation, however, and the fact is that for twelve years after 1800 Nash's architecture is better-documented than his life. But in 1812 we find him involved in a situation where, by his own account, he was proposing to act as one of the Prince's parliamentary pawns.

The political scene which Nash contemplated entering may be outlined as follows.[2] As Prince of Wales, the Regent had surrounded himself with friends of a Whig persuasion whose politics, strongly coloured by the opinions of Charles James Fox, confronted those of the Tories under the leadership of Pitt. With Fox's death in 1806, the Prince's political enthusiasms relaxed somewhat and in 1807 he was declaring himself to be 'not a party man'. The Whigs, however, continued to fix upon his person all their hopes of some day regaining the power and patronage which they had lost in 1784. In 1810 George III's mental condition became such that a regency might, at no distant period, become a necessity. Whig hopes began to run high, for it was believed that, once vested with sovereign powers, the Prince would gather his old friends round him and restore them triumphantly to office. This did not happen. For the first year of the Regency Parliament awarded the Prince only limited powers. The King's recovery was still within the bounds of possibility and the Prince himself declared that a change in the administration would be so much a matter of distress to his revered father that it could not be contemplated. Spencer Perceval therefore was retained in office.

In July 1811 the King's insanity was at last admitted to be incurable. In February 1812 the limitations on the Regency were removed; the Prince was now King in all but name. More earnestly than ever the Whigs looked to him as their saviour. But again they were disappointed. With the full weight of sovereignty on his shoulders the Regent withdrew more and more from party conflicts. The nation was at war and the conduct of the war demanded stability and continuity. If a new administration was looked for it should, he believed, be a coalition. With this in view he made approaches to some of the Whig leaders but with no satisfactory results. Then in May Spencer Perceval was murdered. After further fruitless negotiations, the Prince surrendered to circumstances and sent for Lord Liverpool, whose exclusively Tory administration was to last for fifteen years.

The attachment of the Whigs to the Prince now began to turn extremely sour. They had been betrayed, ignored, sacrificed to expediency and left to roam in the wilderness. Loyal servants of the Prince saw his erstwhile friends drifting by ones and twos into hostile groups and alien camps and felt their own public reputations bruised by the contemptuous abuse which now descended on their master. One of these loyal servants was John Nash.

Nash was a natural politician. He had followed with enthusiasm the political comings and goings of his friends in South Wales. Now, at the centre of political life and with a sufficiency of wealth if not over-much leisure he saw and welcomed an opportunity of entering the House of Commons. In the Isle of Wight the rotten borough of Yarmouth returned two members, both seats being in the gift of Sir Leonard Holmes, one of the principal hereditary landowners in the island. Nash knew Holmes, understood him to support the Whig interest and understood, furthermore, that he might expect an invitation to be nominated for one of the two seats. But in this he was to be disappointed. In a letter to the Prince Regent's secretary, McMahon, dated 2 October 1812, he explained the circumstances. 'Holmes,' he wrote, 'has embraced the Marquiss Wellesley's politics and returns two of his [Wellesley's] friends.' Wellesley was the leading Tory who, after a long and brilliant career in India, had been foreign secretary in Spencer Perceval's administration, from which he resigned in 1812. His views were on the liberal side and he was exactly the sort of leader to whom Whigs, revolting from Carlton House politics, would turn. Nash, however, found Holmes's desertion 'unintelligible'. He asked McMahon to make his disappointment known to the Prince. 'I have no object in Parliament but the Prince,' he wrote, adding a hint that if some other parliamentary opening presented itself he would go as far as £3,000 to meet the expenses.[3]

Nash never entered Parliament. But he did undertake at least one diplomatic mission on behalf of the Prince, a mission of considerable delicacy. The occasion was as follows.

In 1813 the sad business of the Regent's relations with his wife reached one of its periodic crises. It was now eighteen years since they had married and seven since the Delicate Investigation, conducted by four members of the Government, had confirmed her as a silly, irresponsible woman if not positively an adulteress. She was also, it had been admitted, unfortunate. Married to a husband who could not bear the sight of her, her position in English society was unenviable, and to many she presented an object of compassion. Most especially compassionate and active in her defence were those who saw that by taking her side in every controversy which arose the Prince, her husband, was brought further and further into contempt. His treatment of his wife, no less than his treatment of his former friends, put him in the black books of the Whigs and his popularity sank to new depths.

In February a letter from the Princess to her husband, pleading for more generous access to her young daughter, Charlotte, had been returned to her unopened. Her friends handed the text to one of the Whig newspapers, who published it. This instigated a new debate in Parliament, in the course of which the legality of some of the proceedings at the Delicate Investigation was called in question. The Prince and his party were gratified, if a little surprised, when Sir Samuel Romilly, the Solicitor-General, whom they were not accustomed to regard as an ally, rose to justify the proceedings. Romilly was the most admired lawyer of the day and it was seen that if his sympathy with the Prince's side of the case could be maintained great advantages would accrue. So an envoy was sent by Carlton House to talk to him and the chosen envoy was Nash.

On 8 March (the very day, as it happened, that the plans and estimates for the New Street went to the Treasury) Nash called on Romilly. They were already on friendly terms and dined from time to time in each others' houses. Nash started off by saying what a good impression had been made at Carlton House by the 'manly part' Romilly had taken in the debate. He went on to explain that 'though he did not come with any express message . . . yet he knew with certainty that the Regent was very desirous of seeing and consulting' him on the subject of the Princess.[4]

But Romilly objected. He expressed the view that it was unconstitutional for the sovereign to consult with any but his ministers on matters of state.

A few days later Nash called again and referred to a long conversation he had had with the Prince, in the course of which the latter had claimed the right to consult Romilly as his counsel, saying that he was retained for that purpose. Romilly countered with the opinion that the Prince's quarrel with the Princess was not merely the affair of the Prince but 'as much a matter of public concern as the war with Spain or with America', and therefore outside the sphere of the Prince's private advisers. Then, to Romilly's amazement, Nash produced a letter from Lord Yarmouth in which it was suggested that Romilly should be told 'that his advice had been followed with all the attention and respect that any suggestion of his deserves'. What advice? What suggestion? It seems that in his first conversation with Nash, Romilly had hinted that, so much of the evidence taken at the Delicate Investigation having already leaked out, it might be to the Prince's advantage to release the lot (and thus destroy the Princess's reputation absolutely). Nash had reported this to Carlton House. Carlton House had acted accordingly, as became evident when, a few days later, the *Herald* and the *Post*, partisans of the Prince, came out with a catalogue of details of the kind called unsavoury and which could come from nowhere else but the evidence aforementioned.[5]

Nash, at his second visit to Romilly had, however, a more important object than to flatter him with indications of the Prince's eagerness to act on his personal guidance. Hinting broadly at the possibility of a change of administration he asked Romilly if he would 'think it a duty to refuse the Great Seal' unless all his political friends were in the Government. Romilly parried the question but left Nash in little doubt that the answer to the implied invitation would be 'no'.

Four days later Nash called yet again, this time on his own initiative. He said he had had a long private conversation with the Prince and was 'extremely anxious' for Romilly to meet him; that the Prince 'had no person who would speak honestly and openly to him' but that in Romilly he had expressed 'great confidence'.

The following Sunday (21 March), the Romillys dined at 29 Dover Street. Lord Yarmouth was there, apparently for the first time. The other guests were two members of Parliament, the Principal of Jesus College (Dr Hughes) and two of Nash's pupils. Politics were hardly touched upon but at the beginning of the evening Nash took Romilly aside and told him that 'everything was in confusion at Carlton House' and that he and others looked to Romilly as 'the link by which the Prince might be united with his old political friends'. The Solicitor-General stated firmly and finally that such a thing was out of the question.[6]

Most striking in this narrative is the confident familiarity with which Nash plays the role of intermediary between the heir apparent and the legal officer of the Crown. He is no mere messenger but an elder courtier exercising his own goodwill in trying to bring about a reconciliation. With some difficulty we remind ourselves that his actual status in the hierarchy of government at this time was still the exceedingly obscure one of joint architect in the Office of Woods, Forests and Land Revenues. He was certainly very much more than that, both professionally and socially, but how much more it is hard to measure, especially where his relationship with the Prince was concerned. It was not the Prince who had commissioned him to plan the new Marylebone Park, nor set him in charge of the New Street. Indeed, since the conservatory design of 1798 there is no reason to suppose that he had rendered to the Prince any architectural services whatever. Henry Holland was the Prince's architect till his death in 1806, and after him Thomas Hopper. However, in 1813 a commission was placed in Nash's hands which might well seem to be of an entirely personal character and to reflect the kind of relationship which clearly subsisted between Prince and architect. This was the reconstruction of the Lower Lodge in Windsor Park as a 'cottage' for the Prince's occasional use. Here again, however, we have only to glance at the documents to find that Nash, while acting on the instructions of the Prince, was accountable to his official masters, the Commissioners of Woods, Forests and Land Revenues.

In 1812 the Regent had found himself ill-equipped with residences suited to his new rank. The town-house – Carlton House in Pall Mall – was adequate if not overwhelmingly impressive; but country house and park he had none – 'nothing but a house in a sea-bathing town', as Lord Yarmouth put it, the long low domed building on the Steyne at Brighton called the Pavilion.[7] What the Prince needed was a sizeable mansion, not too far from London on the one hand or from Windsor, where the old King was detained, on the other. It devolved upon the Commissioners of Woods to find such a mansion.[8]

In the Great Park at Windsor stood and still stands a big brick house called Cumberland Lodge. The Duke of Cumberland, George III's brother, had lived there and his widow

94

died there in 1809. This house, repaired and improved, would, it was thought, make a very adequate royal residence, pending the day when the Prince would occupy Windsor Castle itself. Nash, acting as the Woods and Forests architect, inspected and reported. Optimistic as usual, he stated that the 'top and lop' of the Windsor trees would meet the expense of alterations and repairs and it was decided to proceed.[9] But the work would take time and so another house had to be found to meet, for a year or two, the Prince's immediate needs – a *pied-à-terre* for brief visits. The Office of Woods suggested a cottage in the Park called Lower Lodge, once lived in by Thomas Sandby, the architect and watercolourist, and now by a Mr Frost. Again Nash inspected and reported. The cottage would need to be replanned and provided with a new staircase and the cost of this would be £2,750.[10]

Meanwhile, an estimate for the improvement of the larger house, Cumberland Lodge, was completed and the Commissioners were dismayed to learn that this far exceeded whatever could be expected from the 'top and lop'. It amounted, indeed, to a sum which the Prince 'could have no wish to ask the public to pay' (though he was probably not asked). The Treasury therefore gave orders that Mr Frost's cottage should be improved and enlarged to provide the semi-permanent accommodation which was needed.[11]

Nash's estimate for improving this little building now leapt from less than three to more than thirteen thousand pounds and this did not include the cast-iron conservatory, marble chimney-pieces and the sinking of a well. The old cottage was to be transformed – stuccoed and thatched outside, totally replanned within and enormously enlarged. The conservatory with its trellised pilasters would cost £2,737; the marble chimney-pieces, of which there would be no fewer than twenty-nine, £1,471; the water-supply another £638. Nor was that all. Further alterations and sundry additional service quarters brought the final bill to £35,243 and this was exclusive of furnishings, for which another £17,000 was required.[12]

It was certainly a pretty cottage (Plate 26A). Nash was concerned to make it look as small as possible and arranged the surrounding plantations so that not too much of the house would ever be seen at once. Innumerable chimney-stacks, however, rather spoilt the illusion. The entrance front with its two gables had the modesty of a vicarage but stretching back behind a hedge was a long front with bonneted dormers and a rustic verandah and beyond this the iron conservatory with a 'trellised temple', screening the extensive new service quarters. As Lord Brougham remarked, 'though called a cottage because it happened to be thatched, it was still a very comfortable residence for a family'.[13]

Nash's cottage did not survive for long. Renamed the Royal Lodge, it was altered and enlarged by Wyatville from 1823; the latter's Gothic dining-room was the only part to escape destruction in 1830 and to be incorporated in the early Victorian building now on the site.[14]

Nash had begun the alterations to the cottage on the instructions of the Commissioners of Woods and as their salaried architect, but as the responsibilities widened and the costs soared he considered himself to be acting as the Prince's private architect at the usual commission of 5 per cent.[15] This was not unreasonable, especially because in 1814 a radical reorganisation of public works administration had taken place, one effect of which was to abolish Nash's post at the Office of Woods altogether.

This reorganisation affected Nash's future in a number of ways and marks a distinct stage in his career. Long deliberated, it was set in motion by the sudden death in a coach accident in September 1813 of James Wyatt, Surveyor and Controller of the Works and holder of various other offices of distinction and value. Wyatt had held the surveyorship and controllership since the death of Sir William Chambers in 1796 and if his period of office was notable for one thing more than another it was for sheer administrative incompetence. He was a man for whom any sort of methodical routine was intolerable. He had a great talent for design which he exercised energetically when the fit took him. For the orderly dispatch of business and the keeping of accounts, he had no capacity whatever. He rarely answered letters unless moved to do so or attended committees if some more interesting alternative presented itself. He undertook far more than he could conscientiously carry out, could never be relied upon to keep an engagement with a client and was continuously in trouble with his official employers. His conduct had been under serious investigation since 1809 and his sudden death forestalled by a very short interval his dismissal.[16]

Action followed immediately and early in 1814 a bill was prepared 'for the better Regulation of the conduct of the Business of the Office of Works'. It became law in July. Under this act the next surveyor to be appointed would not necessarily be an architect and certainly not one in private practice. In future, three independent architects would be 'attached' to the office. They would design the buildings and supervise their execution but would be under the control of the surveyor.

In the interval between Wyatt's death and the announcement of these new arrangements there was a general scramble for the offices so dramatically vacated. The surveyorship, it was generally assumed, would go to Nash but there were scarcely less glittering prizes to be had: the controllership or the surveyorship of the Ordnance. Members of the Wyatt family were especially anxious to pick up some of the pieces. Smirke threw himself into a campaign of self-promotion. Soane was tensely expectant but probably resigned to the inevitable. The inevitable, however, did not quite happen. Nash was not appointed Surveyor-General; but he was, at the behest of the Prince Regent, made responsible for all those royal palaces which were places of his personal residence. What followed under the new Act was that a certain Benjamin Charles Stephenson, the effective head of the King's Household at Windsor, was made Surveyor-General. The three 'attached architects' were Nash, Soane and Smirke.[17]

The authority for Nash's palace responsibilities issued from the Treasury on 2 October 1813.[18] No time was wasted and by December estimates were ready for elaborate new works at Carlton House. They were the first in a long series of enterprises in which Nash tried, at fabulous cost, to create for his royal master a setting in the highest key of richness and elegance. In none of his country castles had he attempted anything of this kind. At sixty-one he was entering an altogether new field of artistic initiative.

Carlton House, a building of no original distinction, altered and extended through several generations, had been almost totally rebuilt by the Prince soon after he came of age in 1783. Henry Holland had brilliantly replanned it, built a daring and original staircase, fronted the house with rusticated masonry and prefaced this front with a *porte-cochère* which was probably the most refined specimen of the Corinthian order ever built in London. Screening all this from the public street was a raised Ionic colonnade.[19] It was on the centre of this colonnade and of the portico behind it that Nash placed the main axis of his New Street.

For a palace, Carlton House was small and Holland had made it a beautifully finished thing. He died in 1806. The Prince might well have left the house alone but the lust for building was in him and he employed next a wonderfully clever young architect, Thomas Hopper, to make alterations and to add, on the garden level (one storey lower than the street), a cast-iron conservatory in the Gothic style. This was a *tour-de-force* in casting as well as in design, with its multitudinous enrichments and pierced vault admitting daylight through coloured glass in each of the tiny cusped panels. The Prince parted company with Hopper in 1812 and in the following year brought in Nash. Nash contributed a suite of interiors on the same level as the Gothic conservatory and in line with it. They included a Corinthian dining-room (next to the conservatory), a Corinthian ante-room, with columns neatly deployed to support the octagonal vestibule above, a Gothic library, a 'Golden Drawing Room' (also Corinthian) and finally a Gothic dining-room, projecting from the main building and balancing the conservatory. Of these, the Gothic dining-room, as we see it in Pyne's illustration (Plate 26B), was the most arresting. There were five windows to the garden, each framed by a multi-foil four-centred arch. The pattern of these arches, turned upwards through ninety degrees, was repeated on the ceiling and yet again in projecting brackets, where half the pattern was swung sideways through ninety degrees into the room. The whole design was repeated on the inner side of the room and chandeliers hung from the points of the brackets.[20] It was neat and witty. But it was not, as a matter of fact, new. It was an extension of what he had done in the long hall at Corsham, sixteen years before (Plate 9).

These works at Carlton House were in progress throughout 1814 which was, for London and for Nash, an unforgettable year. The Treaty of Paris was signed on 30 May and with the Napoleonic menace apparently at an end the British government felt that the national prestige would be the better for some resonant celebrations. The first move was to invite all three allied sovereigns to London. Louis XVIII and the Tsar accepted (the Austrian Emperor did not). Landing in the early part of June, they were feted in the City and a court and grand investiture were held at Carlton House. The new rooms not being ready Nash put up some temporary buildings in the garden. The visit lasted rather more than a fortnight when, having visited Oxford and Ascot and reviewed the fleet at Portsmouth, the guests departed.

The next thing was a fête at Carlton House in honour of the Duke of Wellington, and for this Nash built a polygonal hall (it had twenty-four sides) linked to the Palace by a tent, decorated with mirrors and draperies:

> This tent led to the large new polygon room, which measures 120 feet in diameter. Each side of this spacious room was groined and supported by fasces ornamented with flowers: from these arose an elegant umbrella roof, terminating in a ventilator, decorated with large gilt cords, and painted to imitate white muslin, which produced a very light effect. The walls within the groins were decorated with muslin draperies and eight large plate glasses, round which the draperies were elegantly disposed.[21]

Supper was served in one of the rooms previously erected for the sovereigns, hung out with regimental colours. Elsewhere there were 'allegorical transparencies' and an arbour for refreshment decorated with rare plants brought from Kew. All the rooms were boarded and 'great attention was paid to their ventilation'.

But even this celebration was not enough, and 'displays of joy still more striking and appropriate to the occasion' were planned for August. They would have taken place earlier, but were so elaborate that they needed many weeks to prepare. There was some danger of anti-climax, for 'peace was now become a circumstance with which the public mind was familiarized', and one could not go on celebrating the familiar indefinitely.

Luckily the centenary of the accession of George I, founder of the reigning dynasty, was at hand, so the inscriptions were changed and the 'displays of joy' directed to this occasion. And whereas the previous celebrations had been official and more or less private, the new one was for everybody. It was staged in the Green Park, St James's Park (admission 10s 6d.), and Hyde Park.

The great day was 1 August.[22] At dusk the American fleet in miniature was defeated on the Serpentine, driven ashore and burnt, while at the same time a balloon went up from the Green Park. Then at ten artillery announced the beginning of the fireworks, and for nearly two hours the crowds watched a terrific bombardment of pyrotechnics provided by Woolwich Arsenal. When at last the storm began to abate attention was shifted to a peculiar castle in the Green Park which was gradually being metamorphosed into a Temple of Concord, with allegorical paintings relevant to the occasion. To everybody's delight the temple revolved slowly upon its axis. Nash seems to have designed the temple, though the mechanics of it were Sir William Congreve's.

In St James's Park, where there was a long strip of water, Nash had devised an astonishing Chinese bridge with pavilions at each end and a pagoda poised at the centre (Plate 27A).[23] Lamps and lanterns hung all over it and from the interior a firework display was operated with spectacular effect. The pagoda, we are told, 'appeared a blazing edifice of golden fire . . . the glass reflectors, in proper places, relieving the dazzling splendour with their silver lustre; the canopies . . . throwing up their bright wheels and stars, the pillars enriched with radiance, every rising tower of the Pagoda pouring forth its fiery showers and rockets springing from its lofty top in majestic flights, almost presuming to outrival the ancient inhabitants of the firmament'.

Not surprisingly, this dangerous exercise ended in tragedy. About midnight, the pagoda suddenly 'exhibited an appearance that excited much doubt'. Doubt resolved itself into alarmed certainty when the upper part of the structure burst into flames. A man leapt from the tower into the water, but cracked his skull on a floating stage. Another rushed out in flames and died soon afterwards. Most of the pagoda toppled over into the canal, a sizzling mass of burning carpentry and exploding squibs.

The bridge itself was unharmed, and after the display it was secured, together with the stump of the pagoda, and used by pedestrians for some years. With the hooks for the fireworks left stuck in the timbers, it soon became an eyesore. A Manchester cotton man, crossing it in 1818, expressed 'some degree of contempt for those who threw away the public money in erecting it'.[24] Canova marvelled at a nation whose government could make anything so paltry when a private company could achieve the magnificence of Waterloo Bridge.[25] It brought Nash no credit and 'Peter Pindar' made an epigram for the amusement of Soane:

> Master Nash, Master Nash,
> You merit the lash,
> For debauching the taste of our Heir to the throne:
> Then cross not the seas
> To rob the Chinese,
> But learn to be wise from VITRUVIUS and SOANE.[26]

The revolving Temple of Concord was broken up and sold in lots, but the polygonal hall in the Palace garden was presented to the garrison at Woolwich where it remains today as a museum of artillery, its somewhat frail construction reinforced by a central Doric column.

In October Nash was in France. It must have been his first visit for, with the exception of a few months in 1802–3, the continent had been closed to Englishmen since 1793. How long he was abroad we do not know and it is only by an accidental remark in a business letter-book that we know he was there at all.[27] He had always had an inclination towards French novelties and about this time, rather significantly, he developed a strong feeling for the *Grand Prix* style of the French Academy with its dramatic contrasts of plain walling and stark, frozen colonnades. We see it in a design he made, probably about this time, for an altogether new palace at Carlton House represented in an oil-painting at Buckingham Palace. It has a recessed centre, with portico and dome, and wings stretching east and west along Pall Mall: columns all the way, except where mural masses come to the eye's relief and support either attics of the

Chambers kind (as at 29 Dover Street) or rather quaint un-French turrets with pointed roofs. There is a companion design in what Repton would have called 'Queen Elizabeth's Gothic' with ogee finials instead of the turrets.[28]

It was perhaps these two visionary designs which frightened the Treasury into warning Nash not to think too seriously about this kind of thing. In December 1814 he was told that it was 'not intended that any steps whatever should be taken towards erecting a New Palace'. No preliminary expenses, even, were to be incurred.[29] Who instigated the two dangerously stimulating paintings we do not know.

Nash's comings and goings at Carlton House brought him often into the company of Lord Yarmouth. In 1812 he and Nash, together with a solicitor, a Mr Bicknell (father-in-law of John Constable, the painter), were entrusted with powers of attorney to administer the Royal farms in certain of the home counties.[30] Somewhat later the same three were made Keepers of Windsor Forest, in which capacity Lord Harcourt was added to their number.[31] The idea was that those of the old King's farms and woodlands, which he kept in his own hands as an example to landowners, should not suffer from their master's mental decline, which might in any case be only temporary. It was a worthy and innocent undertaking and nobody received a salary. But for some reason it caught the eye of a few of the more influential Whigs, including Whitbread and Tierney, who censured the appointments in the House of Commons as a malicious interference with the rights of the Crown.[32] How this could be so it was difficult to see and the attack soon crumbled, though not before Tierney, with truly sublime irrelevance, had asked the house 'what an architect had to do with parks'.

From the time that he became prominent as the architect of the Park and the Street, Nash was continuously subject to this kind of ignorant and prejudiced abuse. It was the accepted Whig strategy to abuse everything that had to do with Carlton House, with the Prince, with Lady Hertford or with any project or design which seemed to issue from or have support within that circle. The society which moved round the Prince and within his palaces, meanwhile, conducted itself with proud equanimity, fastidious extravagance and evident contempt for the Whiggish rabble and its scurrilous lackeys in the press. For Nash the Regency years were golden, filled with the excitement of command, the challenge of liberal but exacting patronage, and the realisation, in the dust and toil of London, of ideas which were nobody's but his own. To which we must add the frolic increase of battlements at East Cowes and, across the water at Brighton, an architectural adventure of dazzling peculiarity. To this we must now direct our attention.

8

The Brighton Pavilion:
the Board of Works

The Prince of Wales first saw Brighton, or Brighthelmstone as it still was, in 1783. He was just twenty-one and for the first time independent, Parliament having voted him £50,000 a year. He stayed for eleven days with his uncle and aunt, the Duke and Duchess of Cumberland, in a house which the Duke had taken on the Steyne, called Grove House. Next year he came again, living in the same house, engaged now for his sole use by his clerk of the kitchen, Louis Weltje. Adjacent to this house was a farmhouse on a small plot of ground, well screened by shrubs and roses. Of this Weltje took a three-year lease in 1786, with an option to purchase. He leased it to the Prince on the understanding that he, Weltje, would rebuild the house and that the Prince would then either pay him a rent proportionate to the outlay or purchase the property for £22,000. Henry Holland was engaged as architect for the rebuilding: the obvious choice since he was already in the Prince's service at Carlton House. The work began in 1787.[1]

Holland, however, did not rebuild the house, parts of which, impenetrably disguised, are still there. He added a circular, domed saloon to the north end of it and, to the north of this again, a duplicate of the old house, making in all a three-part composition of considerable length with a big bulge where the saloon projected in the middle. Around the bulge he set a colonnade of eight Ionic columns, with statues standing over them on the entablature. Behind the house he put a long corridor connecting all the rooms with a square entrance hall and a Doric *porte-cochère*. Two parallel service wings projected westward. To the south-west was a separate stable-court.

The house now began to be called the Pavilion, a word which went with the rather French style of the new saloon, as well as suggesting a certain agreeable lightness, as of a stately tent: an idea which Nash was to catch hold of later. In 1800 further extensions were proposed including two rooms with apsidal ends projecting obliquely north-east and south-east from the Steyne front. One was to be a dining-room, the other a conservatory. Holland was responsible for them, but he delegated the work to his 24-year-old pupil, P. F. Robinson.

While these were being built there was a sudden change of stylistic mood. Brayley, writing many years later, accounts for it by the presentation to the Prince of some fine Chinese wallpapers.[2] The date he gives for this event is 1802 but there is a design, probably by Robinson, dated July 1801, already showing the exterior of the Pavilion re-rendered in Chinese.[3] Brayley's date could, forgivably, be six months out. In any case, it seems that just about this time the Prince began to envisage the Pavilion as translated, inside and out, from end to end, into a mandarin's palace. Some Chinese interiors were, indeed, created (partly to accommodate the wallpapers) and in the great reconstructions which were to come the Chinese inspiration was never eliminated.

By 1803 Holland was in retirement and his place was taken by the 48-year-old William Porden, a pupil of Wyatt, a man of marked ability who for years had been showing good work at the Royal Academy. Porden fell in with the Chinese mood and made designs for an ambitious reconstruction and enlargement of the Pavilion in the new style, with a squat pagoda in the middle and dragons all over the roof. One of these designs he showed at the Academy in 1804.[4]

Porden's main concern, however, was with a different project altogether. The Prince, having discovered that his stables were inadequate, acquired land to the north-west of the Pavilion and ordered Porden to design a new stable, with a riding-house on one side of it and a tennis-court on the other (Plate 28). Anxious to make the most of a princely commission, Porden submitted a plan comprising a rotunda of 80 ft span and 65 ft high, inspired by the old timber-domed Halle au Blé in Paris. The design was accepted. The style of the new stable and its companion buildings was neither classical nor Chinese but *Indian*.

Porden's 'Indian', however, needs qualification. The first building in England to show the influence of monuments in the sub-continent was George Dance's London Guildhall of 1788, a very subtle blend of Islamic and Gothic forms, the Islamic element deriving from illustrations of the Taj Mahal. Porden, in his Brighton designs, followed Dance's lead. All that is 'Indian' in the stable building and its companions is the triple composition of framed multifoil pointed arches with colonettes rising into pinnacles. Nevertheless, 'Indian' it certainly is and this was important for the future of everything on the site.

It was in or about 1805, the year in which Porden showed his Indian design for the stable at the Royal Academy, that Humphry Repton was ordered to Brighton for a consultation with the Prince on the general improvement of the estate. It happened that he came with his mind full of Indian ideas. He had just been visiting Sezincote in Gloucestershire, where Sir Charles Cockerell, brother of Nash's old fellow-pupil, was building himself a house in which, with nostalgic pride, he was introducing some of the beauties and curiosities which had aroused his interest during a successful career in the East India Company. Thomas Daniell who, with his nephew William, had been the first to bring to England accurate representations of Indian monuments, was on the spot. From him Repton learnt much and was soon persuading himself that architecture and gardening were 'on the eve of some great future change . . . in consequence of our having lately become acquainted with the scenery and buildings of India'.[5]

When Repton came to Brighton he was delighted to see that the 'great future change' was already on the way. In Porden's Indian stable he recognised 'a stupendous and magnificent building which, by its lightness, its elegance, its boldness of construction, and the symmetry of its proportions, does credit both to the genius of the artist and the good taste of his royal employer'. His only criticism was that the dome resembled 'rather a Turkish mosque than the buildings of Hindustan'. Repton had a different kind of dome in mind – the bulbous onion which Cockerell had constructed at Sezincote. When the Prince required him to deliver an opinion on the style of architecture best suited to the Pavilion, Repton's answer was unambiguous. Indian it must be; and without delay he produced and submitted a scheme of improvement which included not only a reorganisation of the gardens but a dramatically enlarged and extended Pavilion with three gloriously bulbous domes and a whole forest of pinnacles and minarets.[6]

It caught the Prince's fancy, or so Repton understood. 'Mr. Repton,' he had said, 'I consider the whole of this work as perfect, and will have every part of it carried into immediate execution; not a tittle shall be altered, – even you yourself shall not attempt any improvement.' That the Prince was merely trying to terminate with a pleasantry an interview of more than ordinary tedium seems probable. In 1808 Repton published his designs, dedicated to the Prince.[7] But they were already forgotten. The style, however, was not.

The next few years were unpropitious for building at Brighton. The stable group had cost £80,000 and the purchase of the original Pavilion estate from Weltje's executors another £17,000. Money was short. A new era of expenditure opened, however, in 1812. The Prince was now Regent and the Pavilion therefore a palace of the sovereign. Marlborough House (the former Grove House), standing to the north of the Pavilion, was acquired and the chief royal architect, James Wyatt, Surveyor-General of Works, instructed to consider its improvement. He must have been required to consider a good deal else as well, for he delivered an estimate in the enormous sum of £200,000.[8] But in September 1813 he died. Nash stepped into his place, not indeed as Surveyor but as Deputy, charged with all royal building works.

No more was heard of the schemes for which Wyatt had estimated and through 1814 Nash's attention was concentrated on the work at Carlton House, the celebrations in Hyde Park, the Windsor cottage and the uphill work of setting the machinery of the New Street Act in motion. Then, on 24 January 1815, he went down to Brighton and met Sir Benjamin Bloomfield, the Regent's private secretary, to consider the next move.

The Prince, at this stage, was concerned about two things which seriously detracted from his enjoyment of the Pavilion. He disliked the oblique wings of 1801–4 containing the dining-room and an almost useless conservatory. What worried him even more was the ludicrous contrast between the grandiloquent stable with its Indian arches and rotund covering and the frail saucer-domed Pavilion. One solution might have been to 'plant out' the stables with trees so that the two buildings would never be seen together. But trees take time to grow and the stables are very high.[9] An alternative was to enlarge the Pavilion to meet the challenge of the stable, but this would have meant total rebuilding on a much increased scale. The solution adopted was, it must be admitted, brilliant (it must also be admitted that Repton had thought of it first). It was to raise on the old Pavilion a set of domes of so provocative a shape that they would assert complete dominion and whip the stable into submission. The Indian profile, aerial, exotic and improbable, was the answer. It worked and still does.

The domes of the Pavilion did not, however, immediately appear. First, Nash increased the extent of the building westwards by widening the north-south corridor into a gallery and filling up half Holland's courtyard with new rooms. The gallery, low and rather dark, is a recognisable derivative from his country-house plans, all the way from Kentchurch, through Ravensworth, Aqualate and Caerhays; as at Corsham, there is a grand staircase at each end. The Brighton stairs, however, are made wholly of cast and wrought iron, with inset brass ornaments.[10]

This part of the Pavilion was finished by the end of 1815. The following year was taken up with the building and rebuilding of 'offices', followed by the new kitchen with its highly original iron columns, decorated with copper palm-leaves. Then came two great new apartments, replacing the despised oblique wings and continuing the main volume of building at its north and south ends. These were the Music Room on the north and the Banqueting Room on the south. Externally they appeared as plain square boxes with windows of a faintly Indian type and on their roofs concave cones suggesting the idea of a tent.[11] This was the theme which Nash had exploited in his polygon room in St James's Park in 1814 and which, here at the Pavilion, seemed strikingly appropriate to a building so named.

The design of these two rooms is very remarkable. In considering them it is as well to put aside the question whether they are 'Chinese' or 'Indian' or anything else. They are, in fact, domed square spaces with two lateral extensions, classical in spirit and, in principle, not all that remote from Soane's halls at the Bank of England. Soane's halls, however, were built of brick, stone and hollow tile, with real arches carrying real domes. The Pavilion rooms are of brick, timber and iron and it is obvious at a glance that there is not a single 'working' arch in either. The flat ellipses which appear to support the dome of the Banqueting Room are mere wall ornaments in relief. The arrangement in the Music Room is rather different, with eight arches seeming to carry the dome across the curious vesica-shaped openings above the cornice. The domes themselves, with their moulded plaster surfaces, are fixed to trusses which are part of the carpentry work supporting the externally visible cones (Plate 29B).

The extensions to both these rooms are charmingly handled, with curved ceilings sweeping down from the cornice in imitation of the sagging lines of a tent. Both rooms have a romantically improbable look as if something rather daring was being done. But they are really very simple. They were probably designed in a flash and certainly finished at top speed for both were structually complete by the end of 1817.

In 1818 came the total transformation of the exterior (Plate 27B). Holland's low saucer-dome over the saloon was removed in May. In August the Prince came down with Nash and 'several eminent architects' to enjoy the spectacle of the iron frame of the new dome being erected.[12] This was designed by Nash as an armature round which the 'Hindu' silhouette could be shaped. Its construction is difficult to ascertain but the section given in Nash's own book on the Pavilion seems to show that it rests on girders, the ends of which bear on the brickwork (presumably rebuilt or thickened) of Holland's walls. The outer skin of the dome is of sheet iron, covered with Hamlin's mastic, in which material the ornaments are moulded. Inside the dome are three perfectly usable rooms and various smaller spaces.

The lesser domes over the drawing-rooms and the many minarets of Bath stone followed soon after. For Holland's Ionic columns were substituted columns of an 'Indian' order which seems to be based on Daniell's illustration of a hall at Allahabad. The same order was applied to the box-like exteriors of the Banqueting Hall and Music Room, a variant secondary order being made to screen the bays of the intervening blocks. The disposition of these 'orders' brought the whole range of the Steyne front into a fairly convincing unity. A final touch, of a most persuasive kind, was the construction of *jalis*, or stone trellis, between the columns of the greater of the two orders.

On the entrance side (Plate 29A) Nash provided a *porte-cochère*, planned like the Gothic porches of his country houses, but here Indianised, it seems, on the basis of a temple on the Ganges illustrated in Colonel Forrest's *Picturesque tour along the Rivers Ganges and Jumna*.[13] As Forrest's book only appeared in 1824 it is obvious that Nash did not work from published sources alone. This front was followed in 1819 by an extension on the north, containing what were to be the King's private rooms, contributing to the intended (but never completed) symmetry of the west front, but recessed a little from the east front whose balance was thus unmolested. Then in 1820 to 1822 came the decorations of the great rooms. These, like all the interior ornaments since 1802, were in a Chinese style. They were the work of John Crace and Sons, with Frederick Crace as the chief designer and, in the last phase, of Robert Jones collaborating with him.[14] There is nothing to tell us how much, if at all, Nash influenced these effusions of lyrical orientalism, or whether he had something of the sort in mind when he designed the music-room and banqueting-room. His own hand is easily detected in the modelled detail of ceilings, coves and cornices; his idiom is neither Indian nor Chinese nor anything else – unless it be insisted that the presence of cusps and quatrefoils points towards the Gothic. Without the Crace decorations Nash's interiors would be interesting enough compositions, though perhaps a little meagre. The decorations, artistically so much stronger than the architecture, provide generously for its weakness and exploit its originality.

The cost of all this was, of course, prodigious. The estimates up to 4 May 1820 totalled £134,609 16s. 5d., but Nash exceeded these by £11,109.[15] He offered various excuses. One was that the work was 'difficult and unusual', and another that the estimates did not allow either for carriage of materials or for ordinary annual repairs to the existing work.

On the whole, £11,000 was not an outrageous excess considering the peculiar nature of the work and the unpredictability of the client. But unhappily the matter came under review just at the moment when the economy campaign of 1820–1 was in full swing, and, for some reason which is not clear but which obviously has to do with the Pavilion expenditure, Nash suddenly found himself in the shadows of royal disfavour. In a letter, perhaps of 1821, he expresses a somewhat mystified ignorance of the cause:

> How then and in what can I be blamed and how have I lost the countenance of the King? I am conscious that the work has been done at the least possible expense, indeed infinitely less than if it had been done in the usual way under tradesmen – but Nixon more than me is entitled to this praise – he is the most diligent attentive and the most honest Clerk of the works I have ever met with – and when His Majesty recollects that in two instances which did not concern me that I procured carving to be done for 500£ for which 1100£ was about to be given & ormoulu for 800£ when 1500£ was about to be given His Majesty may infer what the buildings would have amounted to had they been in similar hands.[16]

The tribute to Nixon was a graceful way of emphasising his own innocence of improvident spending; but the tribute was genuine enough, for Nixon was subsequently selected to rule the works at Buckingham Palace.

Much of the anxiety which the Pavilion expenses entailed fell upon Sir Benjamin Bloomfield, the King's private secretary, who seems to have been a good friend of Nash. Writing to Gray, the Keeper of the Privy Purse, he was inclined to be lenient about the excesses.

> That he [Nash] has labored under peculiar disadvantages in the conduct of these concerns, I am free to allow and that much excess must be ascribed to the alterations that have taken place after the works have been nearly completed. He seems prepared to close the accounts which, after all, is the main object & I know their investigation will not be delayed.[17]

But to Nash Bloomfield had evidently sent a less complacent letter, for on the very day that the last extract was penned Nash was writing back in a tone of chastened anxiety:

(*private*)

My Dear Bloomfield

   I am grieved beyond everything because I feel that I have inflicted (though unintentionally) pain on you – I will not agravate your feelings by arguments in justific[n] of myself – though much very much should be taken into consideration – that passage in your Letter when you said you had a 'pride in saying to thousands that so gigantic a work had been done within my estimates' – there is so much friendship in the sentiment that I shall never forget it – I have but one thing in my power in regard to the Accounts. I have not, nor will I charge the King anything for myself. On 156,000£ my Commission would be 7800£ – this charge most likely is expected and let it go to pay part of the balances – I have saved 4 or 5000£ in the Carpenters & Brick layers work, that too will lessen a little the balances – I do not my dear friend do this out of any personal motive to myself but to alleviate your distress – and as I will send you an exact statement of the Estimates as delivered to you seriatim, I believe you will find that the Estimated works have [been] very little exceeded – the accounts are now all perfect as I have compared the payments with the several tradesmen that there may be no differences with them – I will write to you on other subjects tomorrow it being now postime.

   I am my D Bloomfield ever gratefully yrs

J. Nash[18]

By August the clouds were dispersing, and Nash does not appear to have foregone his commission.[19] Nevertheless, in 1822 he was again in serious trouble, this time because the Pavilion roofs were letting in rain. The King refused to have any communication with him except through official channels, and in a letter to Gray Sir William Knighton intimated His Majesty's stern disapproval:

It has been represented to His Majesty that the Dehl Mastic employed on the Roofs, has *completely failed,* that the covering of the Magnificent dining Room, the interior of which, has cost so large a Sum, is now in that state, that to secure it from Injury Pans are obliged to be placed over the Surface, to guard the Interior from the Influence of the Rain. . . .[20]

The flat roofs, he continued, were in even worse condition, and he went so far as to suggest that the use of the mastic was a mere experiment, 'which his Majesty feels most inconsiderate conduct'. Gray was instructed to take up the matter with the architect.
   There is some confusion about Nash's roof-coverings at Brighton. The 'Dehl Mastic' mentioned by Knighton seems to have been the same as 'Hamlin's Mastic' with which, as we have seen, Nash covered the iron-sheeted domes and in which many of the ornaments were modelled. This material had lately been introduced into England by a

certain P. Hamlin (or Hamelin) who supplied it to the Brighton works.[21] It was a mixture of litharge, pulverised stone, sand and linseed oil.[22] For most, if not all, of the *flat* roofs at the Pavilion, Nash used a totally different material – 'Lord Stanhope's composition'.[23] This consisted of powdered chalk, tar and sand, laid on hot and covered with slates. This was recorded, more than twenty years later, as having been completely successful at Brighton as elsewhere in Nash's practice and Knighton's remark about the flat roofs is puzzling.[24] The 'Dehl Mastic' was obviously not a success and was, as the King indignantly suggested, something of an experiment. Nash had in fact tried it out only twice, at the Haymarket Theatre and his own house in Regent Street.

The King's complaint threw Nash into a fever of anxiety. He was diffident about going to the Pavilion, where his presence, in the circumstances, might be resented.

> It would seem a matter of course [he wrote to Gray] that I should go to the Pavilion in the first instance, but reflecting on the terms on which I have been received there and ignorant of H: M: present disposition towards me I am fearful of giving offence by appearing there without H: M: permission. In the mean time I beg to state that *I know* the Mastic in a *perfect state* to be *impervious to wet*, and can show it to be in a hundred instances & *therefore* I have not the slightest doubt of being able to remove the defects and secure the Eating room and drawing room ceilings from damage.[25]

Nash could only have been referring here to Lord Stanhope's composition. Anyway, he was ordered to the Pavilion and evidently succeeded in putting everything right, for nine years later he boasted of the success of the roofing, saying that the water had *never* penetrated.[26]

In May 1821 the conversion of the Castle Hotel Assembly Rooms into a royal chapel was begun. It was completed in January, by which time the Pavilion had acquired most of the features which it possesses today. In 1823 it was positively finished, and perhaps as a result the King began to lose interest. He was there for Christmas 1824, but three years elapsed before his next visit and on 7 March 1827 he left the building for the last time.[27]

In the building of the Pavilion over £160,000 had passed through Nash's hands. The settlement of the accounts was an anxious business for Knighton and Gray, as well as for Nash and when they were finally closed, on 8 February 1823, Knighton expressed himself 'very happy and *much satisfied* with the event'.[28]

For George IV the pleasures of architecture were always more in anticipation than in achievement and it was while his excited admiration was at its height that he planned a picture-book to give away to his guests. He commissioned Nash to prepare it and the first plates were begun in 1820. Nash put the illustrations in the hands of Pugin, who made many of the drawings himself and organised a team of engravers, aquatinters and colourists to work under him.[29] The book was ready by the spring of 1827, when eighty-six copies were embossed with the Royal arms. The cost of production was £3,628 18s. 6d., which included Pugin's commission of 7½ per cent. Each view was engraved in line and also in aquatint, the aquatints being coloured from diagrammatic sketches made by Pugin. These marvellous illustrations preserve for us the bloom and freshness of the Pavilion as the King knew it and two of the plates show George IV himself among his guests. In the plate of the Banqueting Room, the guest sitting at the end of the table nearest to the observer, is very easily recognisable as John Nash.

It was, perhaps, inevitable that so curious and outlandish a building as the Pavilion should become the target of every kind of abuse and sarcasm. All the wits and wags had their fun with it and serious contemplation of its architecture, if there was any, has left no printed trace. Today it is easier to see it for what it is, or rather, what it has become: one of the curiosities of European architecture. It is a fragment of the visible history of the British raj, just as are the grim brown warehouses of the East India Company still standing in the City of London or, a whole world away, the colonnaded vistas of New Delhi. Unlike the warehouses but like New Delhi it seeks to derive aesthetic as well as material gain from the tributary civilisations, while preserving the rationality of western tradition. As architecture, we must admit, it is flawed; partly because it is an improvisation done over another improvisation and hustled into dubious pictorial harmony by the imposition of a spectacular skyline; and partly because, in the matter of style, associational factors are introduced with a crudity which offends. Yet there are some fine strokes of design: the swinging lines of the two great rooms, the exploitation of the 'stately tent' idea; and the happy marriage of the verandah with the classical portico. Moreover, by virtue of the sheer amount of novelties it contains – novelties of style, of construction and of decoration – it is unmatched as a palace of varieties. All in all it is a felicitous materialisation of the careless, humorous, audacious genius of its architect.

The Royal Pavilion was the Prince Regent's private architectural adventure. He paid for it out of his Privy Purse, both as Regent and King, and Nash was his personal architect, employed in the regular professional way and not as the holder of any kind of office.[30] But Nash did simultaneously hold an office under the Crown as one of the three 'attached' architects at the Board of Works. This triumvirate had come into being as part of the new establishment set up under the Act of 1814 which, as we have seen, followed the sudden death of James Wyatt in that year. Nash and his two colleagues, Soane and Smirke, entered office on 6 April 1815. Their duties and rewards may be briefly stated. To each of the three was allocated a certain area of the Board's responsibilities, consisting of palaces or other public buildings or Royal parks. They were not responsible for ordinary maintenance at these places – that was carried out under resident clerks of works – but they could at any time be called in for advice and in the event of rebuildings or extensions they would be expected to design and supervise the work. In general, they were obliged to make themselves available 'on all occasions when their professional abilities are required'. They took their orders from the Surveyor-General, Colonel Stephenson, who, though Wyatt's nominal successor, was not an architect but a man with a military background, a legalistic mind and a somewhat unsympathetic personality. He in turn took his orders directly from the Treasury and saw to it that the chain of command down to the humblest clerk was never in the minutest degree impaired.[31]

The Surveyor-General was a permanent official, with a deputy surveyor under him and a staff of half-a-dozen clerks in the office, which was situated, as it had been for nearly three centuries, in Scotland Yard. The attached architects conducted their private practices, though giving priority to instructions issuing from the Surveyor-General. They received an annual salary of £500 a year with, in addition, a commission of $2\frac{1}{2}$ per cent (instead of the usual 5 per cent) on any new work which they designed and supervised.

In the division of the Board's responsibilities, Nash's 'district' (as the allocations were rather oddly called) consisted of St James's Palace, Carlton House, the King's Mews, Kensington Palace and Gardens, St James's Park, the Green Park, Hyde Park and Windsor Great Park. Soane was given the Queen's Palace (Buckingham House), everything in Whitehall and Westminster, Hampton Court and Bushy Park; while to Smirke went Windsor Castle, Greenwich Park, Somerset House, Rolls House, three prisons and the British Museum.[32] As things turned out the only major buildings built by any of the three architects in their own 'districts' were Soane's Law Courts at Westminster and parts of the House of Lords and Smirke's British Museum. The great rebuildings at Windsor and Buckingham House were conducted, as we shall see, on a different footing.

Apart from work proceeding out of these ordinances, the architects had one very tedious and difficult duty – to maintain an up-to-date schedule of prices to be applied throughout the works undertaken by the Board. The prices were based on the prime cost of materials and this could only be obtained from merchants and dealers, with the help of the clerks-of-works and sometimes of the architects themselves. To the prime cost was added $12\frac{1}{2}$ per cent for profit and tradesmen working for the Board were obliged to accept the resulting figure. Naturally, it fluctuated from time to time. In 1815 the architects met every quarter to settle the prices but by 1818 they found it necessary to meet every month.[33]

Nash knew all about prices, took the work seriously and regularly attended the meetings. When in 1824 the Board was studying a more efficient method of getting at the prime cost figures, he wrote to Stephenson: 'I have bestowed three whole days on it and fragments of others and have scribbled many sheets of paper with remarks and figures but I am very far from the end'.[34]

Nash's relations with Stephenson were not always as co-operative or agreeable as this extract implies. As the King's private architect he was inclined to take a rather cavalier attitude to the meticulous procedures laid down by the Treasury. This irritated Stephenson whose own relations with the King were far from cordial; there was an occasion when the King, finding his wishes frustrated by some pettifogging restrictions of the Surveyor-General, ordered his dismissal and the poor man was only saved by the energetic interposition of Lord Liverpool.[35] Nash took what Stephenson regarded as gross liberties. In 1816, on the Prince Regent's instructions, he made a new doorway at Cumberland Lodge in Windsor Park. To Stephenson's inquiry as to his authority for this he replied loftily that 'he conceived the Prince Regent's commands were sufficient'. A few weeks later Stephenson was after him again for allowing one of his 'private clerks' to 'make enquiries' on the works at Carlton House. The 'private clerk' turned out to be George Repton. 'I beg to state', wrote Nash, 'that it was Mr. Repton (united to me in business) and not a "private clerk" who I desired in my absence to "enquire" for my *information* what his workmen were doing.'[36]

Any matter concerning architecture or building which appeared to be of public importance could be referred to the Board by Parliament or the Treasury. The matter might be as relatively trivial as the feasibility of using mechanical appliances instead of chimney-boys to sweep chimneys, a problem put to the architects at the humanitarian instance of Lord Sidmouth in 1818.[37] Or it might be of high architectural significance, as it certainly was in relation to the Act for Building New Churches, passed in 1818.

Under this Act, Parliament had voted one million pounds for building an unspecified number of churches, mostly in impoverished areas or where lack of church accommodation was conspicuous.[38] The architects to the Board were immediately asked 'to consider of the most economical mode of building churches with a view to accommodating the greatest number of persons at the smallest expense'. No church was to cost more than £20,000.[39] This was hardly an inspiring invitation (the most recent London church, St Marylebone, had cost £60,000). Nevertheless, here was an opportunity to design something original and appropriate to the times after the lapse of a century during which very few churches indeed had been built. The great prototypes were still Wren's churches and those built by Gibbs, Hawksmoor and Archer under Queen Anne's Act of 1711. Each of the Board's three architects submitted a report with alternative plans and estimates. As none of the three had ever built a completely new church in his life he had to form his own idea of what an English church of the Regency should look like. This was not easy and the designs which survive in the archive of the Church Commissioners are a very curious assortment.

Nash submitted ten designs, Soane two and Smirke four. Soane's were the most thoughtful and one of them is a highly original expression of the Gothic type of church in his own precious and peculiar idiom. Smirke's are massive halls, modulated on the severest Greek precedents with no felicities of lighting or silhouette. Nash's ten designs are altogether less restrained, running through Palladian, Gothic, Greek and modern French in such diverse terms that it is really impossible to believe that he designed them all and perfectly credible that he designed none. The impression they give is that anybody in the office was allowed to have a go.

Among the four classical designs, one borrows Mr Ward's thin tower at Cowes and makes it ride agonisingly on a Greek pediment; another takes the choragic monument of Lysicrates from Stuart and Revett, stands it on a square podium with a clock and loads the podium on to a Roman Doric portico; a third, on a cruciform plan, has four corner towers with pointed hats and, over the crossing, a Gothic spire with a circular colonnade round its base. The fourth, very clearly inspired by Pliny's description of the prototypal Mausoleum, consists of a perfectly square hall of a somewhat methodistical appearance with a pyramidal covering made up of forty steps leading to a miniature Greek temple, above which another twenty steps run up to a cross at the apex.[40]

Of the six Gothic designs, two show such a respectable command of medieval ornament that we may suppose A. C. Pugin to have had a hand in them; he was certainly paid for making drawings of at least one of the designs. The other four are indifferent specimens of the thin pointed manner which every architect of the time could supply on request.

One outcome of the commissioners' consultations with the Board of Works was that each of the three architects was invited to build some of the churches. Soane built three in London, Smirke three in London and four elsewhere. Nash built two, both in London: All Souls', Langham Place and St Mary's, Haggerston, begun in 1822 and 1825 respectively.

All Souls' is one of Nash's major works, partly because of the intrinsic originality of the design but mostly because of the brilliant way in which he clinched the problem of orientation with that of creating a terminal feature for Regent Street.[41] To that aspect we shall come later. Meanwhile the church commands respect for the dignity of its interior: somewhat Wren-like but with a flat coffered ceiling instead of a vault. But the most challenging parts of it are the tower and spire (Plate 30A). The spire is lifted straight out of one of the designs submitted to the commissioners in 1818. In that design, where it stood over a central space, it looked merely quaint. Placed over a cylindrical vestibule with a circular portico it comes into its own. It is nevertheless a curiously ambiguous design. A spire is, by association, Gothic. But a fluted cone is not necessarily Gothic or anything other than a geometrical figure; and a fluted cone rising out of a Corinthian peristyle suggests the thought of some of the more experimental French designers of the late eighteenth century, like Lequeu or Delafosse. So the spire of All Souls' has a double association. As Nash put it in his covering letter to the commissioners, 'the spire (I submit) is the most beautiful of forms . . . and particularly appropriate to a church'. It is, he might have said, both 'Modern French' and 'Old English'.[42]

This pleasant ambiguity was not to everybody's liking and in March 1824 Henry Grey Bennet asked in the House of Commons 'who was the architect building the church in Langham Place? There was certainly,' he said, 'something very extraordinary in that work – something so sublime as to be beyond comprehension. Persons shrugged up their shoulders and exclaimed, "Who is doing this work?" He wished to know who was the architect, what it was to cost, and who was to pay for it? Indeed, he must say he would give a trifle to have this church pulled down.'[43]

Arbuthnot of the Woods and Forests, stood up to reply, but asked to be allowed to withhold the architect's name, hinting, however, that it was 'not unknown to him, nor indeed to fame'. Cries of 'Name, name' forced him to reveal that the author of the design was 'an obscure individual of the name of Nash'. A week later, a print by 'Q in the corner' came out showing the architect perched like a weathercock on top of his steeple (Plate 31).

Even C. R. Cockerell, whose criticisms of Nash were always just, could not reconcile himself to the steeple of All Souls'. He felt that it 'had an inapposite association, reminding one of a village church and not such as fits a metropolis'. He found it 'too homely'.[44] Perhaps it is the homely aspect of the silhouette which, since Cockerell's time, has endeared it to so many people to whom the more austere associations of revolutionary classicism would have little appeal.

All Souls' cost £19,612. Rather cheaper, at £15,153, was the church at Haggerston, in a fast growing area off the Kingsland Road. This church was awarded an ample site and Nash persuaded the owner of the adjoining land to build handsomely round it. He wanted the church to be classical, out of respect for the mother church of St Leonard, Shoreditch, but he was diverted to Gothic. St Mary's (Plate 30B) had a plain brick body with nave and aisles, but the west front was in Bath stone and its main feature was a tower of arrestingly slender proportions. It shot up to a considerable height and exploded with a diminutive parody of Boston stump. Bumpus, in 1909, called it 'the bathos of Gothic burlesque'.[45] It was Nash at his most naive. It vanished abruptly when a bomb struck it in 1941.

9

Building the Park

The steeple of All Souls, rising in Langham Place in 1824, marked the end of a decade in which more of the architecture of John Nash was put on the ground than in any other. During these ten years the whole of Regent Street had been built. The Park, too, had moved forward, though with less expedition. Inhibited at first by its dependence on the Street and its future overcast by the failure of the builder who had undertaken the great circus on the New Road, difficult and despondent years followed. The recovery and the great drive to completion in the eighteen-twenties has now to be narrated.

In 1813, Charles Mayor's half-built and abandoned houses stood at the very gateway of the park, a ghastly warning to other builders and a profound embarrassment to the commissioners. In November of that year a long letter was addressed to Nash over the signature of one of their secretaries, James Pillar. It is a curious letter – lame, querulous, badly expressed and ranging over a variety of topics, some vaguely large, others largely trivial. It reflects the state of mind of people who had committed themselves to a leader who was nevertheless also their paid servant and must on no account be allowed to get above himself. There were eleven paragraphs. Nash, in his reply, copied each paragraph in turn, appending a clear and courteous reply.[1]

One particularly wordy paragraph seemed to accuse Nash of negligence. 'The Board believe that your various avocations in the service of Government or other sufficient reasons must have prevented you from making any report on villas.' The early erection of villas, the letter continued, 'would contribute more than anything else to the accomplishment of the whole of the splendid Improvement chalked out by you which otherwise may add one more to the many which exist in almost all the Countries of Europe of great and magnificent national undertakings which have remained, in some cases, for centuries incomplete and thereby have become objects of deformity and inconvenience instead of ornament and advantage'. In this dreadful sentence, the thought is not uncharacteristic of Glenbervie; the language is no doubt Pillar's.

Nash replied that he would immediately submit a plan showing the villas and their grounds but that every villa site which it was possible to mark out had been dug and planted two years ago.

Few of the questions deserve our attention but some of Nash's answers do. Asked whether the planting of the villa sites before the building of the villas might not be prejudicial to the tastes of the individual lessees in this matter, he replied:

> The planting of sites of villas is only for the scenery of the Park and to screen the villas from each other, the leading object being that of presenting from without one entire Park compleat in unity of character and not an assemblage of Villas and Shrubberies like Hampstead, Highgate, Clapham-Common and other purlieus of the Town.

The theme of 'one entire park compleat in unity of character' comes again in the answer to a question about the great double circus proposed as the central feature of the Park. This time, however, continuous *urbanity* is the theme:

> I have always been of opinion that in forming the Regents Park the buildings and even the Villas should be considered as Town residences not Country Houses. It is in the former character only we can expect the Houses will be occupied by the higher classes; to effect this the security of a contained and unbroken metropolis of Streets and Houses must be preserved.

The recommendations of Spencer Perceval had much reduced the urban consistency at which Nash initially aimed and there would be, inevitably, some rather un-neighbourly tracts:

> I still adhere to the ultimate appropriation of the apex of the Park to the double circus as laid down in the last plan approved by that minister. If a unity in the character of the houses can be preserved so as to exhibit the entirety of a single building, its commanding situation will produce an effect of grandeur in the greatest degree striking. It will be the rallying point of the surrounding houses, embodying them as one connected Town and obtain the comfort of security by apparent neighbourhood.

Nash was in no hurry, however, to build the double circus which would in any case have attracted no speculators at this early stage. He believed it should be the last thing to be built when, with all the rest of the Park in perfect array, it would be an irresistible object of investment. But that time never came.

No buildings appeared in the Park for three years. It had been hoped that as soon as the Act for the New Street had been announced there would be a rush of wealthy people and ambitious builders to take leases. But nothing of the sort happened. Nobody, it seems, not even architects, believed that the new street would ever be built. Things like that did not happen in London. The buildings on the ground were there for ever or until they fell down. As for making Portland Place a thoroughfare, Foley House blocked it at one end, the Duke of Portland's iron gates at the other. To the ordinary citizen the whole thing was moonshine.

By 1816 the roads, fences and plantations had been completed and the bed of the ornamental water excavated. To the plantations Nash attached immense importance: they were to make the Park scene handsome and harmonious before ever a house or a terrace was built. He had learnt about planting from Repton: now, exercising the art in his own way delighted him. The planting was of two kinds: the regimented kind on future building ground; and the more random kind round villa sites and on the canal banks. The planting on building ground consisted of young forest trees set anything from 12 ft 6 in. to 17 ft apart in ranks of two alternating varieties. On one site it would be birch and plane, on another sycamore and oak, on another larch and Spanish chestnut, on another ash and beech, and so on. Some 14,500 trees were planted in this way by two competing firms of nurserymen, one, William Malcolm, starting at the south-west and moving east and the other, Jenkins and Gwyther, starting at the centre and moving east, then north and west. Another firm, the old-established Lee and Kennedy, who had supplied trees at Corsham for Capability Brown, undertook the random, picturesque planting on the canal banks.[2]

This was all very fine but it cost a great deal of money. Over £53,000 had been spent and the returns on the development were nugatory. The sale of old materials, grass rents, nursery grounds, potato fields in the plantation and six acres of mangel-wurzel were almost the only sources of revenue and the letting of sites made no headway.[3]

The commissioners turned to their architect for an explanation, and Nash had to confess he was disappointed.

> The numerous applications I had from men of rank and fortune, when the design was in agitation, to set down their names for Sites for Villas within the Pale of the Park, justified the expectation of that part of the Improvement immediately commencing; but before the roads were completed and the Park inclosed, the disposition to building suddenly became paralysed.

He points out (what was certainly not apparent in his report) that he 'always looked to a remote period for a full consummation of the hopes . . . held out as to Revenue', and pleads his tree-planting proposals as evidence of this forethought. The low price of government stock has, he says, diverted capital from building; as the stock rises capital will tend to flow back again:

> So fully am I persuaded of this result, that I recommend to restrain the anxiety

for *immediate* Revenue, to give opportunity of selecting a higher class of tenants, remembering, that as the Park increases in beauty it will increase in value, and that the first occupiers will stamp the character of the neighbourhood.[4]

No less alarming than the delay in the consummation of the Marylebone plans was the state of the Regents Canal project. Trouble had been in sight for some time, but in 1814 Mr Agar, a considerable landowner in St Pancras, actually obtained an injunction against the company, and shortly afterwards took proceedings on account of his land having been forcibly entered in 1813 by Morgan and a number of workmen, who (he said) first assaulted his employees and then began to dig. The mediation of one of the proprietors temporarily averted Agar's mischief.[5]

Another calamity of 1814 was Morgan's blunder in recommending a patent 'hydro-pneumatic' lock invented by Sir William Congreve, whose pyrotechnical devices contributed so much to the spectacles in St James's Park in that year. A prize of £50, offered in 1812, had failed to elicit anything better than Morgan himself could devise; then Congreve produced his design, which was adopted at once for the lock near the Hampstead Road. The invention was certainly too good to be true; it was supposed to save the whole of the lockage water, thus making the canal independent of a regular supply and solving one of the great difficulties of the enterprise. It was not till 1817 that the invention was found to be incompetent and the whole of Congreve's costly machinery was sold for little more than £400.[6]

But even before this blunder of Morgan's came to light the sub-committee in charge of the works began to suspect that 'their engineer had not such experience in canal works, or even knowledge of the various transactions left to his superintendence as they had conceived him to possess'.[7] Moreover, funds began to run short and a select committee inquiring into the condition of the concern at the beginning of 1815 was obliged to report that an additional sum of £168,935 was needed. Soon afterwards it was found that the worthy Homer, originator of the whole scheme, had been quietly embezzling funds for years.

At this crisis all work was suspended and the undertaking seemed to be on the brink of disaster. However, in 1816 a new Bill was obtained authorising the raising of more money and defining the canal's course through Agar's land. On 12 August, the Prince Regent's birthday, the canal was opened as far as the Hampstead Road. An appeal to the shareholders for a further subscription having failed dismally, a suggestion of Nash's was taken up and a number of bankers were approached with personal introductions.[8] But the bankers' terms proved unacceptable. A tontine was then tried, but this also failed, and for the second time things looked desperate. Finally the Government appointed commissioners to issue exchequer bills on proper security. The work pressed forward and in 1817 the collateral cut to the markets in the Park was begun. It was now discovered, however, that the company could not, without a further act of Parliament, lease from the commissioners the land required for the wharves round the basin. This should have been foreseen but had not, and Nash coolly took the whole of the land in his own name, at the same time promising not to let the wharves to any persons who would not agree to pay their share of the masonry lining of the basin.[9]

At last, early in 1820, the whole length of the main canal was finished and a grand ceremony was announced for 1 August. The King sent an encouraging message. It was a fine day and at ten o'clock a procession started. First came a little boat with Morgan and his assistants, then a barge full of 'beer, workmen and musick', then two barges for the proprietors, then the immense gilded Grand Junction barge containing the general committee; then more barges, more musick, more beer. As the procession emerged from the Islington tunnel salutes were fired from each bank. Emerging into the Thames, they landed at London Bridge, and between six and seven the party dined at the City of London Tavern; Nash had a place of honour at the chairman's table.[10]

By this time the deplorable Homer had been forgotten, and Nash was credited with that gentleman's part in the undertaking as well as his own. *The Times* described the canal as 'one of the works for which the public are indebted to Mr. Nash, by whom it was originally projected and under whose direction it has been carried on'.[11] Nash certainly deserved all the praise he got, for he could have ruined himself in seeing the thing through. As lessee of Crown land in addition to being a large shareholder, his position was unenviable, especially as he had leased the land for the basin on his own official valuation, which was a high one and much more than his valuation of the same land before the collateral cut was contemplated.[12] As a speculation the canal certainly turned out disastrously; the first dividend was only paid in 1829, and then it amounted to 12s 6d. on each £100 share. Nash, however, seems to have got rid of most of his shares and in 1827 was possessed of only forty-six, having at one time, when the canal was in a really bad way, amassed as many as 1,280.[13]

In their Third Report (1819) the commissioners were at last able to state that three of the villa sites had been let. Two of the villas were already built and in occupation. One of these, on a charming site on the east side of the ornamental water, was 'The Holme', built by James Burton for himself in 1818 with his 18-year-old son Decimus as architect.[14] Neat, symmetrical, with its domed Ionic bay jutting towards the water, one would suppose it to have struck exactly the right note for a show-house in the still somewhat raw parkland. The commissioners, however, took strongly against it and complained to Nash. Nash agreed that it was unsatisfactory and blamed the commissioners for allowing it, to which Milne, for the commissioners, replied rather sharply that it was Nash's business to prevent bad designs from being executed in the Park.[15]

Just what was wrong with The Holme it is difficult to see. It is still standing, but so much altered (with Corinthian instead of Ionic columns) that it is hard to visualise it as first built or to detect any feature which might have given offence. It looks pleasant enough in old drawings and engravings.

The other pioneering villa-builder was a very different character. Charles Augustus Tulk, MP, was a radical in politics, a friend of Joseph Hume and, at the same time, a student of the occult and an enthusiastic follower of Swedenborg. His villa, called St John's Lodge, situated on the inner circle, was designed by an obscure architect, John Raffield, who had once been in the service of Robert Adam. As originally built in 1817 it had more the appearance of a masonic temple than of a private dwelling. The exterior is now unrecognisable but Raffield's lofty church-like hall is still intact. It is all slightly eccentric but was accepted, it seems, without murmur by Nash and the commissioners.[16]

These two outposts of the new Marylebone – the house of the thrusting builder and the house of the radical mystic – stood alone in their groves of saplings for three or four years. In 1821, however, with the new street an actuality and driving every day further ahead towards the park, the terraces began to arrive. Before we describe them it may be as well to look at the building procedure. The sites were not exactly pre-determined nor advertised in the press and it was left to the enterprise of builders to approach the commissioners and negotiate. An application for a building site would be referred to Nash. He would bargain with the builder, discuss the design and, if a satisfactory arrangement was reached, make a recommendation to the commissioners. The commissioners would then submit the proposal to the Treasury and obtain a warrant to lease the land. A building agreement was then signed, conveying the land at a peppercorn rent for three years and a full ground-rent thereafter, the rent being assessed either on the acreage of the site or on a price per foot frontage. The outline plan and the main elevation only had to be designed or approved by Nash. In most cases he made the design and, in one case certainly and possibly in others, charged the builder a fee.[17] Nash was responsible for checking that the materials and construction were satisfactory. When the houses were roofed, Crown leases of 99 years were granted to the builder or, if the builder had disposed of the houses, to the purchasers as his nominees.

The leases contained important conditions respecting the interior and exterior maintenance of the houses. The lessee covenanted to 'clean, recolour and rejoint in imitation of Bath stone the outside stucco or mastic work . . . in the month of August', to paint the outside sashes fronting the Park 'in imitation of oak' and the iron railings of the areas and balconies 'of the colour of Bronze', once every four years.

The first terrace to be built was Cornwall Terrace, in the south-west corner of the estate.[18] The builder was James Burton. The designer, rather surprisingly, was young Decimus, in spite of the trouble over The Holme. One would have expected Nash to keep this, the first of the terraces, in his own hands and make a precedent of it. But not so. He dismissed Burton's first submission as being too plain, looking like 'an hospital, alms-house, work-house or some such building', and then suggesting that it should be divided into three, four or five distinct buildings, 'each assuming the character of a nobleman's villa'.[19] A scenic *trompe-l'oeil* of this kind was probably too revolutionary for the Burtons and Nash eventually accepted a design based on the traditional five-part terrace formula, with strongly projecting porticos. The terrace was entirely acceptable to the commissioners and, in fact, was the cause of Charles Arbuthnot, as first commissioner, awarding its architect some handsome public commissions later on.

In 1822 a builder, William Smith, applied for a large piece of ground north-west of Cornwall Terrace.[20] This time Nash turned his attention, full strength, upon the project, and produced in Sussex Place something in the palace-building spirit which had just then begun to take hold of him, for reasons we shall shortly understand. Sussex Place (Plate 34B) consists of twenty-six houses, the biggest in the Park. It has a colonnade of fifty-six Corinthian columns – sixteen more than Gabriel used for his two palaces in the Place de la Concorde. The march of these columns is interrupted only where ten bay-windows rise into pointed domes. At each end the colonnade comes wheeling round towards the road, to be halted dramatically by two of these tower-like bays. 'Too much the air of an experiment in brick and mortar,' observed an anonymous critic of this regally enter-taining but somewhat reckless composition.[21]

Hanover Terrace, to the north of Sussex, was built by J. M. Aitkens in 1822–3 to a design by Nash.[22] If Sussex is more than a little wild, Hanover is provocatively conventional: a five-part composition with full-dress Doric porticos at centre and ends, a continuous entablature, sculpture in the tympana and acroterial figures on the pediments – a model composition which would have been acceptable at any time in the preceding century. The continuous balcony supported on an open arcade of segmental arches, approached by flights of steps, is the only feature out of the common. The sculpture fully deserves Elmes's observation that it was something which 'the architect would do well to remove'.[23]

James Burton now (1822) took a site between Cornwall and Sussex terraces. He wrote to Milne saying that he was 'desirous of having a sonorous and commanding name for this pile of buildings'.[24] The choice being limited to the titles of the Royal family, Milne assigned him the venerable and romantic 'Clarence'. Decimus again provided the design which Nash was happy to accept as 'very respectable'. It looked rather more than that in the Academy perspective,[25] but rather less after two extra houses had been squeezed into the spaces behind Decimus's open Ionic screens.

Also to 1822 and the following year belong the two long blocks of York Terrace (Plate 35A) with the opening to York Gate (Plate 35B) between them, where the portico and steeple of Marylebone parish church stand impressively framed. The church's presence prompted this part of the plan. Its siting had been a problem for years. In 1811 the vestry had considered a site in the south garden of Foley House, but Parliament would not sanction the raising of the necessary funds. In 1812 the King authorised the presentation to the vestry of the site in the New Road circus but the Duke of Portland protested that the parish church must be on his land, he being Lord of the Manor.[26] The vestry then contented themselves with building chapels-of-ease, one at St John's Wood and another on ground given by the Duke adjoining the old parish church in the High Street. No sooner was this begun, however, than a new decision was taken: the High

Building the Park

Street chapel was to become the parish church. The architect, Thomas Hardwick, enlarged his plan, added two columns to his Ionic portico, made it Corinthian and designed a steeple.[27] It was at this point that Nash made his gesture of the formal opening to the Park on the axis of the new church.

York Gate and the two York Terraces make a single grandly-extended composition. Burton took the west part of it and William Mountford Nurse the east, both agreeing to conform with Nash's design.[28] The scheme of the terraces is very simple – the usual five-part treatment with an Ionic portico in the centre, Ionic colonnades at the ends of each block and Greek Doric columns running between at ground level. The Ionic comes into its own in the two facing blocks of York Gate where, contained between plain slabs of wall, it becomes really striking. Nash saw York Gate as 'the great central entrance to the Park' and was anxious to suppress all signs of individual ownership in the two facing blocks, urging that no garden fences should be allowed. He also had in mind a continuation of the Doric colonnades across the road as a screen with gates.[29]

To east and west of the two York Terraces are houses which, though numbered in the same series, have every appearance of being large detached mansions, which they are not. Doric Villa, to the east, with four giant Greek columns under a pediment, is two houses (Nos 19 and 20) and so is the much larger Corinthian block (Nos 21 and 22) next door. On the west are several more of these 'noblemen's villas' (as Nash wants us to imagine them) ingeniously obscuring the monotonous truth which only the party walls and chimney-stacks emerging above their roofs betray.

Eastwards of the whole York Terrace series, there had been by 1823 an important change of plan. The southern half of the circus on the New Road having been completed, it was decided to abandon the northern half and form instead a square with its north side open to the park. Thus the southern half of the circus became Park Crescent (Plate 34A) which, instead of facing a duplicate of itself across the New Road, now faced a planted garden with terraces to east and west of it and the open Park beyond. Park Square came into existence in 1823–4.

The two sides of this square continue the Ionic theme of the Park Crescent porches, though here the columns are attached to the walls. Above, an arcade in relief frames the first-floor windows and the second-floor windows are dressed to match; all of which is a rather doubtful improvement on the simpler terms of Park Crescent. At the north end of the square the buildings turn towards the Park giving us Ulster Terrace on the west and St Andrew's Terrace (now Place) on the east. The Ionic order still runs on. The upper parts are plainer, but robustly bulging bay-windows attempt to offset the bleakness of a northern aspect.

W. M. Nurse was the builder of Park Square West and Ulster Terrace. The equivalent blocks on the east were built by Jacob Smith whose interest in the development went somewhat beyond the building and selling of dwelling-houses, for behind the three central houses in Park Square East he erected his 'Diorama'. This was one of those

121

installations which fed the appetite for illusion which the cinematograph theatre was later so amply to assuage. Built on a Paris model, the Diorama consisted of a circular auditorium and two 'picture-rooms'. On the back walls of these were exhibited realistic paintings of exotic architecture and scenery, rendered more intensely convincing by manipulated lighting. Before the audience could weary of one of these manifestations twenty tons of machinery, mounted on a massive stone base, went into action in the basement and rotated the entire auditorium to bring into view the scene which had been prepared in the second picture-room. Morgan was the engineer. The carcase of the building, which Pugin designed behind the Nash facade, still stands in 1979.[30]

St Andrew's Place terminates eastward in a curiously planned house, entered both from the Park side and from Albany Street, designed by Nash in 1826 and built by George Thompson. On the north was built, in 1824, on the site now occupied by the Royal College of Physicians, the Adult Orphan Asylum. This was an institution for the education and maintenance of the orphaned daughters of clergymen and officers of the armed forces, the girls being accepted at fourteen and turned out as potential governesses before they were nineteen. The committee had begged a site at a nominal rent. Unable to comply, the Treasury directed the commissioners to make an annual donation of £50, and Nash made the design of this very genteel barracks for nothing.[31]

The next arrival was another palace of illusion, but on a bolder scale than Jacob Smith's Diorama. This was Thomas Hornor's so-called 'Colosseum'. Hornor had made some two thousand drawings from a cabin on the dome of St Paul's when the ball and cross were being dismantled and replaced in 1822. He persuaded a young painter, E. T. Parris, to make a panorama of London out of them. To turn this idea into a profitable investment he found a backer, took this site in the Park and employed Decimus Burton to build something like the Roman Pantheon but with a Greek portico, to house not only the panorama but the original ball and cross. It seems strange that the commissioners should have accepted such dubious clients. The project ended, as anyone might have guessed, in Hornor and his backer absconding in a cloud of debt. Burton's first design had not pleased Nash who made him reduce it in size and add some pilasters. The building served a variety of purposes but fell on evil days and was replaced by the francophile Cambridge Gate in 1875.[32]

With two successive sites being let to individual buildings Nash was anxious that the next should restore the sense of horizontal continuity and he welcomed the application of Richard Mott to build another terrace.[33] This was Cambridge Terrace, for which Nash provided one of his more reserved designs, with no columns except in the porches, which display that peculiarly mannered device which consists of interrupting the shaft of a cylindrical column with square blocks: a somewhat freakish revival for 1824, the year this terrace was begun.

It was in December of this year also that James Burton made approaches for the next site northwards, the site of Chester Terrace. This would be the longest terrace in the Park, 'nearly as long as the Tuileries', as Nash observed with satisfaction.[34] Such continuity was a rare thing in London building and Nash relished the opportunity to show how sublime the sheer horizontal can be. In 925 feet the skyline would be unbroken.

Of Nash's first design for this terrace we have a sketch-plan. It shows the five attached colonnades which he introduced to give animation and relief to the composition; it also shows the ends of the terrace brought forward towards the Park, with more colonnades. There were, it seems, to be fifty-two columns in all and over each column was to be a statue. This combination of columns and statues, imposed for purely scenic effect, would cost Burton at least £4,000 and Nash considerately suggested that, in compensation, he should be relieved of the ground-rent for two small planted areas at the ends of the terrace.[35] This consideration for Burton, however, did not last long.

In 1825 the terrace was built. Unfortunately it came up to nobody's expectations. In building the two forward blocks, Burton had left gaps between them and the main block, presumably in order to gain entry to houses built *behind* the forward blocks. Whether he had done this with or without Nash's sanction is not absolutely clear but in any case severe criticism reached the commissioners. Nash agreed that the gaps made the forward blocks look ridiculous. They gave the impression 'that some ill-natur'd fellow, having the right, has built Houses before his neighbours windows'.[36] The forward blocks themselves he defended as being in a highly respectable tradition of design. Nevertheless, the commissioners were for removing them. Burton very naturally demanded compensation and William Wilkins, the architect, was brought in to estimate a just figure.[37] The matter was complicated by the fact that Burton had already parted with his interest in the terrace to a Mr James Lansdown and compensation had to be assessed in relation to both builders.

At this point Nash attacked Burton and Lansdown for all sorts of deviations from his designs – the omission of balusters or their excessive enlargement, badly-executed cornices and so on. He also ridiculed the figures which had begun to make an appearance over the columns. These were the work of J. G. Bubb, who had devised a programme of 'British Worthies', which he claimed Nash had seen and approved. James Watt, lately deceased, and John Smeaton, had been nominated 'worthies' and were already on view. Nash made fun of them and begged that they should be taken down.[38]

Wilkins, reporting on the whole affair, found himself unable to support Nash's allegations of culpable deviation but he did agree that the statues should go. As to compensation due to the builders if the forward blocks were demolished, he arrived at a figure of £8,132. The Treasury declined to see why they should pay this sort of money to correct an architectural blunder and the forward blocks remained.[39] Nash was content; he already had a solution to the architectural problem in his head. Burton apparently had attempted to link the blocks to the terrace by some kind of screen – 'mop-stick posts which Mr. Burton calls columns'.[40] For these Nash now proposed to substitute two fairly massive 'triumphal' arches and these are what we see today (Plate 36A). If they deprive the houses behind of even more light than the previous arrangement, they certainly bring coherence, as well as a welcome touch of theatre, to Nash's severe essay in the horizontal.

Chester Terrace was the last of Burton's undertakings in the Park. It was now the turn of William Mountford Nurse, who had built so much of the York Terrace and Park Square areas, to increase his holding. He had tried for the site of Chester Terrace in 1824 but was disappointed. In the following year he agreed terms for a terrace of about 850 ft, northwards of Chester Terrace, and built in 1826 the mass of houses which was to receive the title enjoyed by the King's youngest brother, the Duke of Cumberland.[41]

Cumberland Terrace (Plate 36B) is the most elaborate, the most ornamented, the most ostentatious and spectacular building in the Park. The reason for this is nowhere stated but can be guessed. When it first appears on plans of the Park it is seen to be sited opposite the place where the King's *guinguette* was to be built. Thus, Cumberland Terrace was designed as a 'royal salute' and that is exactly the appearance it has. It is a palace, not indeed for the sovereign's residence but for his visual entertainment.

Cumberland Terrace is the antithesis of Chester. Chester lies low and stands still; Cumberland springs into movement. Twenty-seven houses are disposed in three blocks, linked by the arched entries to three little courts whence drives lead down to the mews behind. An Ionic order ranges through the entire composition advancing in the end pavilions of all three blocks and, in the centre block, marrying with a colonnade of ten columns which advances yet again and takes command. None of these groups of columns carries a pediment. The only pediment is the one standing on the attic over the central colonnade: a huge triangle, palpably unfunctional, designed only to display sculpture in a frame.

The terrace is a composition of great energy and brilliance. To complain of the poverty of the detail, insensitive profiles and ill-considered junctions would be to say again what has often enough been said: the thing is the work of men in a hurry and looks it. But the invention and spirit of a great design are there. How did the composition form itself in Nash's mind? It may be seen, perhaps, as a fantasia on the theme of Chambers' river front of Somerset House. In that building three blocks are linked by Palladian bridges, while above and behind the central portico a pediment stands on an attic storey, as it does in the terrace. For the Palladian bridges Nash substituted archways. The form of these may have been suggested by the archways similarly used by Chambers' pupil, Gandon, at his Four Courts building in Dublin which Nash would have seen on his Irish travels. From Versailles certainly come the six quartets of columns, spaced in pairs with figures over columns standing against the attic.

Of figure sculpture there is any amount. It is all by J. G. Bubb and pretty poor stuff. Distantly seen it creates a fine aura of Roman prodigality. There is no need to scrutinise it, but the curious student will find in the pediment Britannia presiding over 'the arts, sciences, trades etc. which mark her empire'.[42] Thirty-five standing figures at various other points are less usefully employed and of them no interpretation seems ever to have been offered.

As executive architect for Cumberland Terrace, Nurse employed a young architect of considerable taste, James Thomson, the author of *Retreats* (1827), a book of villa and cottage designs which ran to several editions.[43] His hand may perhaps be seen in the nice detailing of the pairs of houses in the two courtyards. Thomson is also supposed to have worked on Cumberland Place, the separate block of four houses for which Nurse found room on his land but whose general design is presumably Nash's.[44]

Proceeding north, the scene changes abruptly from festive Roman to sober collegiate Gothic. St Katherine's Hospital was a royal foundation of the thirteenth century, standing eastward of the Tower of London. In 1825, the site being coveted by the St Katherine's Dock Company, it was sold to them for the enormous sum of £125,000, with another £36,000 for a new building and £2,000 for a site. What became of all this money is a matter of some obscurity. The Treasury told the Woods and Forests to provide a site in the Park for nothing and a sum of £41,521 was set aside for building. The master of the hospital was a soldier–courtier of great distinction, Sir Herbert Taylor, and it was within his competence to appoint the architect for the new college. It might have been assumed that the only possible architect was Nash and that, indeed, was Nash's view. Taylor, however, chose to award the commission to a young architect who had come to him with an introduction and a plan in his hand which happened to take Taylor's fancy. The architect was Ambrose Poynter.[45] He had been a pupil of Nash in 1814–18 and taken as great a dislike to his master as his master had to him. Learning of the appointment Nash exploded. But there was nothing he could do and Poynter proceeded in 1826–8 to build a tasteful enough Gothic group in white brick (Taylor would not have stucco) with a chapel fronted in Bath stone. Opposite, in the Park, he built a Tudor residence for the master. This was destroyed by a 1941 bomb.

Beyond St Katherine's stands the last of Nash's terraces within the Park: Gloucester Terrace (now Gloucester Gate), built by Richard Mott in 1827. It is nearly as conventional as its opposite number on the west of the Park, Hanover Terrace and, in fact, very much the same thing, only Greek Ionic instead of Roman Doric and with pediments set back on attics instead of standing over columns. The entablature has a bolder profile than Nash usually gives us and for this there is a reason. Mott, the builder, employed as executive architect a man of some future celebrity as a Catholic church architect, called J. J. Scoles. Scoles, no doubt, thought Nash's profiles old-fashioned and niggling and, on his own initiative, omitted some members and enlarged – doubled, so the story goes – others. Nash, inspecting the finished building, merely observed that 'the parts looked larger than he expected'.[46] The story is meant to underline Nash's notorious neglect of detail. But one wonders if James Burton would have got off so lightly.

Gloucester Gate dates from 1827. To the north of it Nash built an architectural entry to the Park, or, to put it another way, an exit to Camden Town: two lodges joined by a Doric entablature with two columns to carry it. The columns and entablature soon disappeared and one of the lodges was moved across the road and attached to the other.

If we now cross back to the west boundary of the estate we find a Nash terrace which

125

is not part of the Park series but has its back to Hanover Terrace and looks on to Park Road. This is Kent Terrace, built by William Smith in 1826–7.[47] Smith had built Sussex Place and apparently survived the crippling load of fifty-six ornamental columns. But Kent Terrace broke him; he went bankrupt.[48] It is a fine block, with a recessed Ionic colonnade recalling York Gate in its middle section, the Ionic briefly re-emerging in four pavilions. A little way up Park Road is the lodge of Hanover Gate which must be noticed as a spirited departure from Nash's routine classicism; its angle-piers, carrying baroque consoles, linked by swags, suggest a French model.

In their Fifth Report, published in 1826, the commissioners announced, complacently and without apology, that they had decided to bring the building programme in the Park to a close. They merely stated their belief that 'the carrying into execution, to their full extent, the original Plans for occupying so much of the Ground, and particularly in the interior of the Park, by Building, would so far destroy the Scenery, and shut out the many beautiful Views towards the Villages of Highgate and Hampstead, as to render it very advisable to reduce the number of Sites to be appropriated for Villas, and also to leave open the Northern Boundary of the Estate, formerly intended to be built upon'.[49] With this opinion the Treasury, content with a (not very spectacular) revenue from ground-rents of £13,024, concurred. The number of villas was to be reduced from twenty-six to eight. Five being already built or in progress, three other sites were let on lease but only one of these was used ultimately and two villas were built in the marginal area on the west of the estate. Hanover Lodge appears to have been designed by Nash about 1821 and built by Burton.[50] All, or nearly all, the others were designed by Burton.

So the built environment of Regents Park was cut off in its stride and brought to a premature though by no means inglorious conclusion (Plates 32B and 33A). Of Nash's feelings about the decision we have no precise evidence. Nothing he wrote to the commissioners or to anybody else that we know of evinces any disappointment or bitterness. He was so very much the empiricist that he probably saw that what he had achieved was, if not precisely the image of his early visions, something absolutely real and effective. Thwarted in the pursuit of one objective he had attained another which was perhaps, after all, the right one: the open Park, with water and trees, an architectural circumference of spectacular beauty so far as it went, and to the north, a vista which the future would fill in its own inscrutable way.

There is, nevertheless, a plan by Nash, dated 1828 (Plate 33B), which does seem to cling rather nostalgically to the original vision.[51] It shows terraces on either bank of the canal, along the north, with planted sites for twenty-six villas, the formal 'basin' and even the *guinguette* which is now clearly marked 'Royal Guinguette' and is described in the key as 'planted and formed by the King's direction', as if it were actually on the ground. It does not, indeed, show the double circus, though this, curiously enough, had not been specifically excluded by the decision announced in 1826. But it does, of course, show the inner circle as a road with two alternatives for the treatment of the ground it encloses. One of these is a planted garden. The other, drawn on an overlay, has a square building enclosing a courtyard and, within the courtyard, a circular building marked 'chapel'.

No clue to the purpose of these buildings is supplied but what they represent is, without doubt, a proposal for accommodating King's College. This institution was the establishment's answer to University College – that 'stye of infidelity' founded in Gower Street in the previous year. In 1828 the King's College committee, having turned down a variety of sites, received encouragement from the Prime Minister, Wellington, and then from the Commissioners of Woods to apply for the ground within the Inner Circle, which they would certainly have taken had not the residents in the Park created an uproar. With students in the Park, they declared, their more timorous women-folk would never feel safe, their maid-servants would be insulted. It would be worse than the Zoological Society's Gardens, which had been opened in the previous April. There, at any rate, the animals were behind bars.[52]

So King's College went to the Strand and built itself into the eastern limb of Somerset House. Of Nash's design we have nothing but the block plan; but if the circular chapel was to carry a dome (a pretty certain assumption) we may see in it the last refulgence of the Valhalla idea – now finally to be extinguished.

In 1832 Nash made what was probably his last contribution to the plan of Regents Park.[53] It seems that the commissioners had asked him what further improvements he had in mind. He was now eighty and in poor health and his suggestions were neither striking nor altogether realistic. A formal seven-fold avenue had already been planted on the line of what we now call the Broad Walk, stopping at the road leading to the Inner Circle. Nash now wanted to continue this avenue northward to the zoo, terminating it with an obelisk, while on the south he proposed clearing some of the shrubberies in Park Square so that Gahagan's statue of the Duke of Kent would close the vista on the south. This would never have worked. The statue is far too small and, anyway, has its back to the Park. The obelisk, unless of gigantic size, would have seemed a mere bauble. He also laid before the commissioners the curious idea, which he had never expressed before, of arranging new plantations in such a way that the terraces on the east side of the Park would never be seen together but would be enjoyed separately, 'as so many distant pictures' (rather like the presentations in the Diorama!).

The *guinguette*, now that George IV was dead, was a faded dream but Nash was not inclined to let it disperse altogether. 'The Plantation made for the express purpose,' he wrote, 'of forming a site for a guinguette which his late Majesty meant to build I have proposed to preserve.' To this day, two plantations mark the site of this Trianon which never was.

On the eastern part of the Crown's Marylebone estate is a long thin piece of land which Nash had, from the first, designated as the site for the 'collateral cut' from the Regents Canal and for a marketing area which the cut would serve. This land is divided from the Park by Albany Street, the northward continuation of Great Portland Street to Gloucester Gate. Part of the land had been sold to the Canal Company in 1817 for the construction of the collateral cut. In this Nash was, as we have seen, heavily involved, having taken on building lease from the company sixty-seven plots on the ground surrounding the Regents Park Basin, the pool where the barges loaded and unloaded. Fifty-three of these plots constituted a little street called Augustus Street.[54] The portentous name is still on the map but the diminutive houses, which had an air of having a somewhat more sophisticated source than most of their kind, have gone.

South of the Basin, Nash laid out three squares, connected by short streets and intended for the marketing, respectively, of hay, vegetables and meat, the supplies coming mainly by water. But the canal seems never to have attracted this kind of traffic, even before the arrival of the railways. The northernmost square, Cumberland Market, did indeed become a hay-market in 1830 and continued as such for as long as London remained a horse-drawn city. The two other squares became residential at an 'artisan' level. The southernmost began as York Market but was changed to York Square, then to Munster Square. It was built from 1823 onwards and lined with houses whose tiny dimensions and single-window fronts made the square seem magically large and serene. Clarence Market came next, was cultivated as a nursery garden and became Clarence Gardens. Cumberland was the only one to adhere to its original name and purpose.[55] The houses in Clarence and Cumberland were the work of ordinary builders who took ground on Nash's valuation and put up their run-of-the-mill products without the slightest obligation to make architecture.

In the northern part of this same stretch of land, bounded on the west by Albany Street and skirting on the east the Southampton estate, something very different happened. Here was a piece of ground, narrowing rapidly to the north, with the cut bisecting it lengthways and no sites on either bank likely to tempt a Burton or a Nurse. But they attracted Nash. He took all this ground in 1823 and tells us that he did so more for amusement than for profit, having in mind the building there of a settlement of houses of a kind he had built, years before, 'in another part of the Kingdom'. That this is an allusion to the 'hamlet' at Blaise which he built for J. S. Harford in 1810–11 is proved by a copy of Nash's original plan (Plate 37A) in the Crown estate records.[56] This shows not only the street layout but, in eight little vignettes, the kind of cottages he proposed. Five of these are very close indeed to cottages in the Blaise series. Another is a cottage-terrace of three houses. Another is a miniature Cronkhill with a round tower. This was the beginning of the Park Villages.

Nash leased the plots at a comfortably low ground-rent and the houses went up from 1824 to 1828.[57] As built, none resembles the cottages at Blaise or, indeed, the sketches on Nash's plan. Not unnaturally, they aim at a rather higher class of occupier and were, in fact, respectably inhabited from the first.[58] In Park Village West, with its picturesque loop road, No. 12, with an eight-sided, Italian-roofed tower, is in the Cronkhill spirit; while the Tudor-style pair, Nos 18 and 19, is a distant relation of Longner. Of Park

Village East not much remains, all the houses on the east side of the road having been removed when the London and North Western Railway multiplied its tracks under an Act of 1883. There seems to be no record of what the houses on that side of the road were like. Those opposite (Plate 37B) are a quaint set of variations on the styles, starting at the north end with Nos 2 and 4, castellated Tudor (with a touch of Aqualate), going on to broad-eaved Italian (Nos 6 and 8), then something with eaves of the sort usually considered Swiss (Nos 10 and 12), then various versions of the classical vernacular and so rapidly descending to the nondescript.[59]

The Park Villages are among the most amiable curiosities of the Picturesque. Here, in these last marginal acres of the Crown estate, Nash the cottage architect came back to his favourite employment and left behind him a model – slight, hasty as ever and gently humorous – for a suburbia of the future. It did not pass unnoticed by estate developers of the next generation.

One other building by Nash on the Marylebone Park estate requires notice. This was the Ophthalmia Hospital, built on the east side of Albany Street in 1818 at the instance of Sir William Adams, George IV's oculist. It was for soldiers whose eyesight had been affected in the Egyptian campaigns and for several years Adams gave his services free. Nash took the site on a ninety-nine year lease, built the hospital, a very plain brick structure, and rented it to the government. In 1822 the government closed the hospital and the building remained on Nash's hands. It was not easily disposed of. Used for a time as a manufactory for Bacon's and Perkins' 'steam guns' and later by Sir Goldsworthy Gurney for the construction of his famous 'steam carriage', the building eventually found a purchaser in Sir Felix Booth, the gin distiller who earned a baronetcy for promoting arctic exploration. It must surely have been Booth who gave the building the pretentious stucco frontispiece which formed a conspicuous feature of Albany Street till its demolition soon after 1960.[60]

10

Regent Street,
Charing Cross, the Strand

Few people born after the death of Queen Victoria remember much of old Regent Street and for those who do there is little joy in remembering. By the 1920s Nash's fronts had long ceased to stand on the ground or anywhere near it. The shopfitters had seen to that. The surviving upper parts were patched and particoloured, disfigured by the inscriptions and devices of trade and discomposed by irresponsible repainting. Against the sky was a jangling mass of dormers and mansards, antique chimney-pots and patent cowls. If there was one aspect of the street which did memorably survive the decline it was its amplitude. Its width was nearly twice the height of the buildings enclosing it – a ratio of approximately 90 ft to 50 ft. Therein was a title of nobility which it retained to the end.

To imagine Regent Street in its prime we must go to the topographical artists, to Thomas Hosmer Shepherd, Thomas Shotter Boys and a few other worthies, who drew the street before it had begun to be forgotten as architecture, which was very soon. With their help it is not difficult to visualise Regent Street as it stood, bright and new, at the close of George IV's reign. But it is easy to misunderstand the old street. It is often spoken of as 'elegant' which is not the right word for it. It was never a refined and harmonious architectural symposium. It took its character from the way it was built and that, as we have seen, was opportunist, improvisatory and rapid. It was sometimes strictly formal, sometimes deliberately picturesque but also sometimes accidental. As Nash knew and wryly confessed, it was poorly executed.[1] Nevertheless, through the whole long stretch of it ran a spirit of artistic intention reflecting the personality and contriving genius of its architect.

The street was built from south to north and was evidently so designed. This was apparent in its architectural composition. All the formal vistas except one, all the picturesque surprises and architectural groupings, favoured the passenger proceeding northwards. Its progress was episodic. From the absolute and strictly residential formality of Waterloo Place it proceeded to semi-formal and semi-residential improvisation in Lower Regent Street. After Piccadilly, the Quadrant imposed formality of another, more dramatic, kind and led in stately fashion to the main shopkeeping stretch where the architecture became an almost random sequence of architectural events with little correspondence from side to side till the approach to Oxford Circus. After that, residential formality again prevailed.

The street began at Carlton House Palace, before whose famous screen (in line with the south side of Pall Mall) was Waterloo Place, built by James Burton in 1815–16.[2] While the Palace stood, Waterloo Place (Plate 38A) was an enclosed square of private houses, perfectly uniform and more grandly pillared and pilastered than the Place Vendôme. An Ionic order, standing at first-floor level, marched round all three sides, coming into relief as porticos, left and right, where the north side opened into Regent Street. The order returned northwards as far as Charles (now Charles II) Street. Regent Street then began. The first vista, up a steep incline, was closed, beyond Piccadilly Circus, by the County Fire Office, with Britannia enthroned on the skyline.

But before we come to the Circus it is worth investigating how this lower part of the street ('Lower Regent Street' as we call it) was put together (Plate 38B). The inclusive dates are 1817–20. Here the strict discipline of Waterloo Place was abandoned. Buildings other than private residences were admitted and plots were let singly or in twos and threes to different builders and different sorts of user.

To start with, there was a hotel on the left (No. 1, Regent Street) and a club on the right (No. 2, Regent Street), two functions which seemed to match tolerably well. But Warren's Hotel was designed by Nash,[3] while the newly-formed United Service Club had Robert Smirke for its architect. Nash's design was strikingly vulgar, Smirke's austere and refined, so the street commenced its course with a flat contradiction in style by two architects of the highest eminence. Such disagreements were, as we shall see, in the nature of the street. Next to the club, on the right, came a massive five-house block (Nos 4–12) called Carlton Chambers, a project of Burton's with a ground-floor portico.[4] This was a new sort of enterprise, designed either for residence or business; it could claim to be Regent Street's first office block. Opposite, on the left, was the narrow three-window front of Hopkinson's Bank, designed by G. S. Repton, with the traditional banker's device of a Doric ground floor.[5] This was followed, first by a trio of houses, the middle one pilastered, then by a narrow house-front, probably by Repton. Then came St Philip's church.

The church, one of the three in the street whose sites were provided by the Crown under the terms of the church-building Act of 1818, was designed by Repton, whose brother, Edward, was the first incumbent. Nash had awarded it a site directly opposite the opening from Carlton Street, so that its Roman Doric portico and Lysicratean steeple closed the vista from the Haymarket. The portico was of Bath stone, the steeple of sheet iron covered with Hamelin's mastic. It cost about £15,000 and was consecrated in July 1820.[6]

The stretch of street from here to Jermyn Street was interrupted on each side by a recess protected by iron railings and gates and seeming to be the courtyards of large mansions, with projecting wings. The recess on the left was filled by the residence designed by Nash for Charles Tufton Blicke,[7] while the 'wings' were separate houses of identical design. The recess on the right belonged to two houses, each occupying one wing and part of the centre block. This was the pair of residences which Nash designed and built for himself and his cousin Edwards. Of this more later.

On Blicke's side of the street, the house pretending to be the north wing of his mansion was duplicated on the corner of Jermyn Street, the houses between the two being designed to unite them into a continuous whole which, in the economic sense of being a single undertaking by James Burton, is what they were. On the Nash–Edwards side, the house at the corner of Jermyn Street again duplicated the design of Blicke's 'wings', so this particular frontage (characterised, incidentally, by 'Ammonite' Ionic capitals) appeared four times in the street.

From Jermyn Street to Piccadilly Circus the right-hand side of the street was a mirror-image of the left-hand side. The elevations showed two very big three-window houses, one with a pediment, one without. Both sides were undertaken by Frisby Howis. But Howis in fact built three houses behind the elevation on the left and four behind that on the right.[8]

This curious mixture of *laissez-faire* and spasmodic control reflects Nash's philosophy of street design as it evolved in the unique circumstances with which he was faced. It was nothing if not realistic. It allowed individual expression by different users but at the same time aimed at shuffling the accidental into picturesque coherence. It was a landscape philosophy brought to bear on townscape. It was business but also a sort of art.

Here we must pause to look at what was certainly the most interesting building in Lower Regent Street, the pair of houses (Nos 14 and 16; Plates 39A and 39B) which Nash built for himself and his cousin in 1819–23.[9] There was no party-wall separating these two residences; they interlocked. Nash had the south wing and the ground floor of the main block. Edwards had the north wing and the first floor of the main block. Towards the street, the houses looked like one very big house, of the social rank of great dynastic residences like Devonshire, Chesterfield or Burlington. The relationship to the street, however, was very different, the wings coming forward to the pavement and occupied, on the ground floor, Paris-fashion, by shops. Nor was the architecture in the tradition of the Palladian town-house, but decidedly French in proportion if not in ornament. For London it was something new.

Identical front doors faced each other across the court. Nash had the grander entrance hall of the two and a stair which, rising in two flights, led to the principal floor. Here a square drawing-room faced the street; behind it was a gallery 70 feet long, leading to the dining-room at the back, while the private bedroom, dressing-room and bathroom were alongside on the south. The Nashs lived on one level. John Nash's professional office, however, occupied the ground floor of the main block. The great showpiece was the gallery, of which there is a good engraving done under Pugin's eye (Plate 39C). Elmes's impression of the interior is as follows:

> The principal story is . . . a most gorgeous affair of gilding, ultra marine, and the newly invented Musaic gold [a patented alloy resembling brass] in the richest Parisian style imaginable. The Café de mille colonnes, or Napoleon's Salle des Marechalles, are nothing to it, for flutter, multiplicity of mouldings, filagrain, and leaf gold. Mr Nash seems to have emulated in these apartments the laboured elaborateness of finish that characterizes the works of M. Percier.[10]

Elmes exaggerated. He may be right about the Parisian influence but there was nothing in the gallery at all like Percier and the detail was from Nash's own rather limited repertory of ornament. Thomas Hope's famous gallery at his house in Duchess Street may have been an influence.[11] The charm of the room was in its shape: a series of seven recessed bays, connected by round arches on each side, with a segmental ceiling over the middle part. Each bay had its own skylight and there were round openings in the ceiling, so the floor above must have been nothing but a light-well.

The main adornment of the gallery was a set of copies of Raphael's *grottesche* in the Vatican loggias. Nash had sent an assistant of Sir Thomas Lawrence's, Richard Evans, to Rome to make or procure these, as well as various other works of art, including copies from Titian, Caravaggio, Guido and Guercino.[12] To these were added casts of famous statues – Apollo Belvedere, Diane à la Biche, the Petworth Amazon, the Capitoline, Antinous – and a collection of architectural models (probably by Fouquet) which Nash told Farington had cost him £1,000. Apart from these, the gallery outfit cost Nash nearly £3,000. We have the impression of a somewhat conventional collection brought together *ad hoc* to make a brilliant impression. It impressed Prince Pückler-Muskau, who saw it in 1828.[13] He, like Elmes, was struck by the polished brass; but, unlike Elmes, remembered the walls as 'pale red'.

Returning now to our inspection of the street, we have before us Piccadilly Circus. The four segments of this were shared between several builders, but Nash imposed an overall design: Ionic on the ground floor and, above, a system of vertical and horizontal panelled strips of the kind most commonly seen in chimney-pieces of the period. Here, shopkeeping took over, and in 1820 the shopkeepers were asking to be allowed bowed windows between the columns.[14]

North of Piccadilly Circus was a peculiar piece of planning which was half blotted out when Shaftesbury Avenue was formed in 1885 and is not easy to visualise. Lower Regent Street, entering the Circus from the south, made its exit on the north and continued north for some twenty yards before the Quadrant swooped into it on the left. This junction between the Circus and the Quadrant was not particularly well managed. Each of the Circus fronts returned upon a commonplace little house-front whose cornice and floor levels were, because of the sloping ground, a few feet higher than those of the Circus. On the left, the house-front butted against a tower which was the end feature of the Quadrant. Here the sills and heads of windows were juggled to look more or less right. The same thing, with variations, happened on the other side where an insignificant bit of a street with no name crept in from Tichborne Street. Here again there was a tower, though not precisely opposite its fellow on the left and not far enough north to make a terminal feature to the entering Quadrant.

But if improvisation stumbled at this juncture the eye was convincingly held by the building which closed the composition on the north: the County Fire Office (Plate 40A). Here was a site of no great depth on the west and sliced off to nothing on the east, but offering the most spectacular opportunity for architectural effect of any site in the street. It was taken by J. T. Barber Beaumont, history painter, crack rifleman and founder, in 1807, of the County Fire and Provident Life Office.[15] Beaumont approached the commissioners in 1817. He said he wanted to build a house 'with a stone or stuccoed front somewhat similar to the elevation of the Bank of England [i.e. Sampson's Palladian front, not Soane's] or of Somerset House, and an open ground floor like the "piazza" at Covent Garden'. Nash met this proposal half-way by insisting on a literal copy of Henrietta Maria's gallery at *old* Somerset House, supposed to be a work of Inigo Jones and easily adaptable to the Covent Garden idea.[16] Beaumont's architect, Robert Abraham, made a drawing. Nash disliked it, complained that it was not literal and began revising it himself, taking his time. Beaumont was in a furious hurry to build, but six months elapsed before the design was approved. Abraham, snatching occasional interviews with Nash, argued for some variations; he wanted columns in the round, rather than the flat Jonesian pilasters and this point, as well as the addition of a balustrade, Nash did eventually concede. Fortunately, perhaps, when we consider that the facade was expected to make an impact all the way from Carlton House.

Now, as we face the County Fire Office and move towards it, the perspective of the Quadrant unfolds. An effort of imagination is required to recapture the long-lost effect. We see two parallel colonnades proceeding away from us to the left, then curving out of sight to the right and, for all we know, going on for ever. The colonnades are unbroken and magnificently severe: simple Roman Doric, the columns twenty feet high from the ground, carrying nothing but their own ponderous entablatures, a balustrade and the outer edge of a continuous platform whose inner edge joins the wall face of the houses behind. The effect is powerfully questioning. Does this austere avenue, we wonder, lead to some great explosion of national piety, to some venerated mausoleum? It does not; and we perceive before we have traversed half its length that it stops as abruptly as it began. It is a monument and nothing more – nor less.

The Quadrant colonnades realised, in limited compass, an idea which had obsessed

Nash ever since his first design for the street, made in 1811, a design which had shown colonnades continuing through the whole length of it. These had been criticised in the strongest terms by Glenbervie and abandoned. But when in 1818 Nash undertook to build the Quadrant on his own account he reintroduced the theme and neither Huskisson (Glenbervie's successor) nor his colleagues attempted to dissuade him from it or to rule it out of order.

So it was built. One hundred and forty-five columns were cast in iron and raised on stone plinths to carry the Bath stone entablatures. Within the colonnades were shops and over the shops a mezzanine storey, intended as lodgings for the shopkeepers. To light the shopfronts Nash made discreet openings in the platform. Above the platform rose the remaining three storeys of the building, uniform and unadorned except for a trim cornice and blocking course against the sky.

The Quadrant colonnades were, as Glenbervie had foreseen, from every point of view except architectural magnificence, a disaster. They were gloomy and dirty; the shops attracted only inferior trades; and, as arcades and colonnades in great cities always do, they became promenades for prostitutes. The Commissioners, increasingly uneasy about public criticism, canvassed the shopkeepers and made their almost unanimous dislike of the colonnades an excuse for demolishing them. They came down in 1848 and the iron columns were auctioned. Amid feeble jesting about chimney ornaments and Roman Doric drains, a few were knocked down at £7 10s. apiece. Not everybody was pleased. 'One of the most striking features of modern London,' said the *Builder*, 'has been cut off its face, and a great public injury committed'.[17] Without the colonnades, the Quadrant became naked and monotonous, not much enlivened by the ornamental balconies which Pennethorne designed to hide the scars of amputation.

Beyond the Quadrant, the street assumed a new character. It entered the long shopkeeping stretch, with no terminal monument in sight till a twist to the right after Hanover Street brought Langham Place and the steeple of All Souls' church into view. The side-streets on the left having no correspondence with those on the right, architectural community between the two sides was impossible. The demand here being for houses with shopfronts and little else there was no opportunity, as there had been in Lower Regent Street, for picturesque improvisation involving a number of different building types. A dictated uniformity would have been reasonable but could have resulted in wearisome repetition. Complete *laissez-faire*, letting off the plots to a crowd of small builders, would have been destructive of the metropolitan character which the street was required to have. Nash took a middle course. His policy was to introduce, between each pair of side-streets, at least one long symmetrical front, covering anything from five to eighteen houses, the number and length of such fronts depending on how much land any builder would take. Their situation depended on the timing of the takes. That there were builders anxious to take large frontages made the policy workable. Of such builders, James Burton was, as we have seen, by far the most important.

This policy found justification in and was probably inspired by one of the most famous and admired of English streets – the High Street at Oxford. More than once Nash brought this famous thoroughfare into his reports.[18] Oxford's High Street is an amalgamation of architectural happenings through a period of three or four hundred years. What gives it distinction is that some of these happenings are buildings of considerable size and distinguished form: All Saints Church, Brazenose, All Souls and University Colleges, the Queen's College, New College and Magdalen College. They present themselves as the noble constituents of a street otherwise made up of more plebeian material, the latter, however, offsetting the former, giving them scale and importance. In the middle section of Regent Street the incidence of Nash's long architectural fronts had the same 'accidental' character as the colleges at Oxford and the same 'nobility' in relation to the smaller, miscellaneous, unpretending fronts between them.

There were, however, two parts of the street where Nash did impose a considered scenic arrangement. One was where a domed rotunda at the corner of Vigo Street (No. 115) was placed to catch the eye at the north end of the Quadrant (Plate 40B). The other was further north where he fixed the site of Regent Street's second church, St George's, exactly opposite the entry from Little Argyll Street (just as in Lower Regent Street he had placed St Philip's opposite Carlton Street). St George's was a powerful building designed by C. R. Cockerell with an Ionic portico in Bath stone extending over the pavement and twin towers rising beside it.[19] Only from Little Argyll Street could it be seen well and Nash made an additional concession by rounding off the corners of that street and decorating them with columns to underline the special relationship between church and street. St George's cost £16,180 and was consecrated in June 1825.

As to the long facades which made interesting perspectives from end to end of the street, they were nothing if not various in style, in composition and, indeed, in quality. Five of the biggest were undertakings by Burton with facades almost certainly supplied by Nash. Half a dozen more were by other builders and some were designed by other architects. Designs were often submitted to Nash, and if he thought them good enough he passed them. 'If a person presents a design for the elevation of a building and I do not see a material defect, it would be invidious for me to find fault with it; I return it as approved by me'.[20] This probably applied mostly to the smaller frontages. Of the grander compositions only two are known to have been designed by other architects.

Moving northward from the Quadrant, the first of these long facades was on the right (Nos 108–128), between Glasshouse Street and Leicester Street (now Regent Place). It was a Burton enterprise, fronted by Nash with a scheme of arched windows in three runs halted by four jutting bays. Next to this, still on the right, was another Burton block (Nos 132–154), with a facade unexpectedly pompous and conventional: a five-part composition with three porticos, much on the lines of some of the Regents Park terraces and rather unnaturally emphatic for a street. Opposite, however, on the left (Nos 133–167) was something wittier: a very long terrace of eighteen houses divided by twin pilasters with quaintly original caps between Nash's favourite shell-and-fan windows (Plate 42A). Elmes found this 'Frenchified in style and flimsy in detail',[21] but, in a shopping street, why not? This was a Burton building and so was the next on the left (Nos 171–195) between New Burlington and Conduit Streets. Here was an attempt to settle the shop-window problem by making giant Corinthian pilasters start from the pavement, with the shops squeezing in between them. This started a war of nerves between the pilasters and the shops and the shops soon won.

Northward again, on the right, was a block (Nos 156–170) built by Robins, the auctioneer, with John Soane as his architect. Perversely, this was a residential terrace, without shopwindows and with conspicuous domestic porches. In style it was no less perverse, Soane's austere reductionist idiom scolding every building within sight. Here we are at Chapel Court (now Tenison Court) on the far side of which the narrow stone front which Cockerell designed for the preserved church of St Thomas, King Street. Beyond was the block (Nos 178–186) built by Carbonell, the wine merchant, from the designs of his architect, Robert Abraham, and a facade probably by Nash (Nos 194–200) much on the lines of his York Gate elevations in Regents Park.

Meanwhile, on the left between Conduit Street and Maddox Street was a seven-part composition with a pilastered centre (Nos 203–221) behind which was a large hall called the Cosmorama – a place of entertainment analogous to the Diorama in Park Square. Between Maddox and Hanover Streets came a tidy little block (Nos 223–227) of three houses distinguished only by a reappearance of the shell-and-fan window.

Here we are at the point where the street straightens out to the north and the steeple of All Souls' comes into sight. On the right, opposite the entry to Hanover Street, was a massive undertaking by Baxter (Nos 224–240) with the most mannered facade in the street (Plate 41A). Elmes attributes it to Nash. It had every trick of what we think of as the 'Regency' style: recessed columns, 'Grecian' windows, scored surfaces and acroteria in the fashion of Soane. It took Elmes's perverse fancy and he made it a text for cataloguing the architect's stylistic misdemeanours while awarding him high honours as a contriver of the Picturesque.[22]

Beyond Hanover Street the portico of St. George's Church jutted over the pavement on the left, while on the right was the entry to Little Argyll Street with the rounded corners already mentioned. The furthest of these rounded corners belonged to one of the few buildings in the street designed in its entirety by Nash: the Harmonic Institution (Plate 41B). This was a public-spirited adventure by Joseph Welch and his partner, Hawes, and Nash gave them the design for nothing. It consisted of a music shop, a drawing-room, a ballroom and a lordly concert-hall with four tiers of boxes at one end and the orchestra at the other. Elmes supplies further details:

> The side walls . . . are decorated by fluted pilasters of the Corinthian order, and the apertures to the orchestra and boxes are terminated by four majestic columns of the same description. The cornice is ornamented by modilions,

137

the ceiling arched, forming the segment of a circle, and enriched with octangular Mosaic pannels, and with large embossed flowers in each pannel.[23]

The exterior of the building expressed its quasi-public nature. Its rounded corner was domed and the concert hall had a continuous balcony supported on 'terms' carved with female heads by the inevitable Bubb. For a few years the hall played a conspicuous part in the musical life of London. Spohr, Weber and Mendelssohn performed there. But in 1830 it was burnt down. Ordinary houses and shops covered the site.

At this point we enter Baxter's Oxford Circus development which, it will be recalled, started early in the progress of the street. It consisted of the Circus itself with long extensions, southwards into Regent Street and northwards into Upper Regent Street (Plate 42B). Architecturally it displayed a uniform procession of Corinthian pilasters with a very few conventional modulations. One has the impression that at the date it was begun (1815) Nash was contemplating a far more disciplined and less picturesque approach to street design than the approach he ultimately adopted in the critical years around 1820. If we bring together in our minds Waterloo Place, Piccadilly Circus, the Quadrant and Oxford Circus we have the clue to this alternative conception. Add to these the imposed symmetries in Lower Regent Street and the formal siting of the churches, and presume a more authoritarian policy to have been agreeable to the commissioners, and the image of a formal Regent Street emerges. It is not an unattractive one.

Baxter's buildings carried the shopkeeping area some way north. At the point where they stopped, Great Castle Street intervening, the street became once again exclusively residential, though it did not long remain so. Between Great Castle Street and Margaret Street, two identical blocks by Baxter (Nos 273–287 and 288–300) faced each other, their domestic character signalled by angular bay-windows in the end pavilions. Beyond Margaret Street, on the left, were two three-house blocks, in which the centre house was a paraphrase of Nash's own house in Dover Street. Between these two blocks was a row of low stable buildings – a concession to the light and air requirements of the houses on the east side of Cavendish Square. On the right was the opening to Little Portland Street, with balanced blocks on either side of it to compliment the symmetry opposite. Then came Langham Place and at the end of Langham Place the peristyle, cylindrical tower and conical spire of All Souls' church. To the left of this was the garden of Foley House, the property which Sir James Langham had been obliged to buy, in self-defence, in 1815. To the right stood the monumental London Carriage Repository.

Of All Souls' church something has been said in an earlier chapter. Its relation to the street belongs here. Churches with circular vestibules were not unknown: Archer's St Paul's, Deptford, was and is the most famous English example. A church 'pivoting' on its vestibule was not a familiar idea but here at Langham Place the circumstances evoked it. The site of the church was provided by the Crown, no doubt on Nash's recommendation. It allowed for a building with the conventional east-west orientation, its axis lying athwart the axis of Langham Place and Upper Regent Street. This was just where the street switched to the west to enter Portland Place but by no possibility could a rectangular church on that axis be made to present an acceptable elevation to Langham Place. The pivot-vestibule was the solution.

The church and the area round it vividly epitomise Nash's singular kind of cleverness. Look back, for a moment. Challenged by the Duke of Portland's threat to buy Foley House and block the street he had outbid the Duke and bought the property himself, setting against the price Lord Foley's debts to him and reselling what he could to the Crown. Challenged again by the inhibition from siting his street alongside Cavendish Square he had moved it to the east; then, in his turn, had challenged Sir James Langham to protect his amenities from the twisting street by buying the land (Nash's land) in front of his house. The final challenge was again to Nash: to turn the crookedness of his street into an architectural opportunity. This he effectively achieved by the siting and planning of All Souls' church, thus bringing to a conclusion a really rather remarkable chain of challenge and response.

It is time to recapitulate the purposes of the New Street Act of 1813. Of these the creation of a street leading from Pall Mall to Marylebone Park was the first and chief; but to accomplish the ultimate aim of the Act, which was to provide 'a more convenient communication from Mary-le-bone Park . . . to Charing Cross', five further developments were necessary. These were as follows. 1, widening the east end of Pall Mall; 2, continuing Pall Mall by a new street into St Martin's Lane, terminating at the portico of St Martin-in-the-Fields; 3, widening Cockspur Street from the south end of Haymarket to Charing Cross; 4, forming an open space on the site of the King's Mews; 5, continuing Charles Street to the Haymarket. Moreover, the powers given to the commissioners included 'diverting, altering, widening and improving such parts of the present Streets, as will form entrances into such new Streets or into the Streets, Squares and Places connected therewith'. A commendably liberal invitation to marginal initiatives.

All these provisions and their contingent architectural potentialities were in Nash's head as early as 1811. In the widening of Pall Mall and the prolongation of Charles Street he saw a peculiarly interesting possibility. This concerned the King's Opera House on the west side of the Haymarket. The buildings on the south of the theatre would be cleared to widen Pall Mall; those on the north would vanish with the formation of the eastern arm of Charles Street; those on the west would give place to the east side of Waterloo Place. Thus the theatre itself would be isolated. There was no question of demolishing it. Built in 1789 by the Polish architect, Novosielski, it had a noble auditorium, the first in England to adopt the horseshoe plan. The façade to the Haymarket was less satisfactory; it had been begun on a Palladian design but never finished and was something of an eyesore. Nash proposed to recast the whole block as an insulated monument, still comprising some houses but partaking generally of the character of a metropolitan opera house with a grand front to the Haymarket.

As it happens, each element in this proposal had its origin in suggestions made, long before, by Leverton or Fordyce. Moreover, Charles Holloway, the Crown lessee of the theatre, had been negotiating with Fordyce since 1807 for a further long lease, conditional on the enlargement of the Opera House. It was for Nash simply to gather up these trailing threads and bind them into his master-plan.[24] A bargain was struck with Holloway and Nash undertook the rebuilding around the theatre, sharing the commission with George Repton, now his chief assistant. The new building was distinguished by arcades and colonnades standing over the pavement on north, east and south, recalling somewhat the arcades of the Théâtre Feydeau in Paris. The theatrical character was further expressed by the two pavilions standing forward over the Haymarket colonnade with, between them, a long relief panel by Bubb, from sketches by Flaxman, illustrating the origins of music and the dance. For the arcades and colonnades supplementary legislation was necessary and a section authorising them was tucked into a 'general purposes' Act of 1817,[25] which Act at the same time allowed the stopping up of a grubby little street called Market Lane and its conversion into a pedestrian arcade. This, as the Royal Opera Arcade, still exists. The rest of the Opera House site is covered by New Zealand House and Her Majesty's Theatre.

Eastward of the Haymarket was an area of Crown property consisting of Great Suffolk Street running across it, east and west. With the widening of Cockspur Street, Great Suffolk Street (now called Suffolk Street) would be curtailed. As the leases here were due to fall in in 1819 the Commissioners decided to demolish the whole street, together with Little Suffolk Street (now Suffolk Place) and to offer the sites in the building market.[26] From this decision emerged an interesting group of buildings, planned and partly designed by Nash and which still largely survives. Part of this development is the Haymarket Theatre.

The old Haymarket Theatre stood behind a common brick house-front to which a slight timber portico had been fixed in or about 1766. The proprietor was David Edward Morris who we are told 'held a lucrative situation in the War Office'. He rented the theatre from one George Moore, whose Crown lease terminated in 1819. Morris then petitioned for a direct lease including property further south, exactly facing the entry of the new Charles Street. Here he built a new theatre, employing Nash as architect, in 1820–1.[27] Parliamentary powers were obtained to build a portico over the pavement[28] with the result which we see today, the Roman portico closing the vista from St James's Square and complimenting the St James's layout on the east, as does Wren's St James Piccadilly, with somewhat less emphasis, on the north.

Behind the portico and the Nash facade, with its frieze of circular windows to light the gallery, the interior has been rebuilt. Nash's auditorium was straight-sided with a slightly curved end. There were three tiers of boxes, their fronts a golden network against

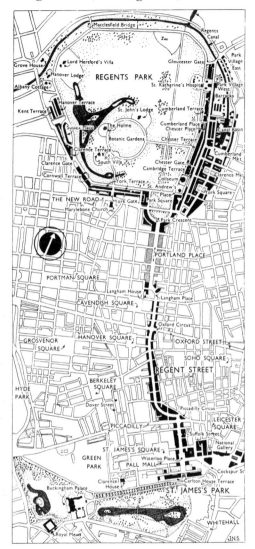

8. The Metropolitan Improvements of John
Nash.

a reddish-purple ground, their interiors maroon with crimson seats and curtains. The
proscenium was framed between two golden palmtrees.

The rebuilding of Suffolk Street and Suffolk Place proceeded from 1820, the year in
which the first sites were let. The whole of the east side was taken by Nash's cousin,
John Edwards. Edwards had no desire to build but took the land merely as a speculation
in ground-rents, a form of gambling to which he was much addicted, having scored

notable successes in this way on the Bedford and Foundling estates in ·Bloomsbury. His system was to take sites, advance money to builders at 5 per cent to get the thing going, lay on improved ground-rents and sell these at anything up to twenty years purchase. This he proposed to do in Suffolk Street and, not unnaturally, got his cousin Nash to act as his agent. As we shall see, this led to some embarrassing consequences.[29]

Suffolk Street and Suffolk Place were built up between 1821 and 1824. Nash designed at least two buildings in Suffolk Street and the whole of Suffolk Place, with its return fronts in the Haymarket. Of the Suffolk Street houses one was Price's Italian Warehouse, standing next to the University Club and adorned with Ionic columns and a set of vases to close the vista of Suffolk Place. This has been rebuilt. The other was the premises of the Society of Artists, whose Doric portico, standing over the three-arched entry, is now the chief feature of the street. The Society of Artists was founded in 1823 on the initiative of James Elmes, the architect and critic, whose observations on Regents Park and Regent Street we have had occasion to quote. He claimed to have had a share in the design, though he gives the street-front entirely to Nash.[30] The Society paid a very high ground-rent for their building, notwithstanding that it does not stand on the ground but on a vaulted basement, entered from Whitcomb Street and leased to a wine-merchant who also paid a respectable ground-rent. There was a suspcion that Nash profited rather substantially from this arrangement.

Of Suffolk Place, the north side only survives. It is a thoroughly indiosyncratic Nash design and the return front to the Haymarket contains almost the only 'shell-and-fan' window left in London. Next to this on the north is a rather simpler front with Soanean incisions on pilaster strips. Both these facades were duplicated on the south of the opening to Suffolk Place.

While Suffolk Street was rebuilding, the next stage in the design for connecting Regent Street to Whitehall was being worked out. The main feature of this scheme was to be a square on the site of the King's Mews. The Mews was a large, shapeless, untidy courtyard off Cockspur Street, consisting of stables and residences, some of timber, some of brick, going back two hundred years or more. Only one part of it was of any architectural consequence and that was the stone building along the north side designed by William Kent for George II and known as the Great Stable. This building commanded respect and was a factor in the replanning. Eventually, however, it was demolished.

The first plan by Nash, showing the old Mews courtyard redeveloped, belongs to 1813. In this no square is proposed but there is a symmetrical arrangement of streets in front of the Great Stable. Pall Mall is extended as far as the Great Stable, bends to conform with the frontage of that building then bends again to enter St Martin's Lane opposite the portico of St Martin-in-the-Fields. This is not a very pretty arrangement. In June 1819 Nash submitted a plan showing a square in front of the Great Stable with Pall Mall coming into it on the west and leaving it on the east.

It was in 1820 that the decision was taken to vacate the Mews and build a new establishment for royal stabling at Pimlico, close to Buckingham House.[31] The old buildings were to be demolished and the Great Stable surrendered for whatever public use might be found for it. It would dominate the new square which would occupy the whole site of the lower Mews. It was not an entirely happy place for a 'square', being too far west to bear significant relation to Whitehall and rather awkwardly shaped, the east side being longer than the west. However, this was the sort of square which was envisaged when in 1822 the commissioners leased the west side of it to two institutions, the Royal College of Physicians taking the north end and the Union Club the south.[32] Robert Smirke was the architect for the whole block, which still stands and is now wholly (with some alteration) occupied by Canada House. It was not till 1825 that the old Mews buildings were cleared and Smirke's facade emerged as a major component of what was obviously to be one of the most important squares in London.

The awkward proportions of the square as now proposed led to second thoughts. The commissioners instructed Nash to reconsider the whole project and to provide plans and estimates for enlarging the square eastwards and extending the process of improvement to the west end of the Strand. His new plan is included in the commissioners' Fifth Report of 1826 (Plate 43) and shows what we now recognise as Trafalgar Square, the name it was eventually to receive.[33] In this plan the square extends as far east as St Martin's Lane and forms a majestic open space at the top end of Whitehall. The southern end of St Martin's Lane vanishes into the square and St Martin's church is exposed in its full dignity at the square's north-east corner. South of St Martin's, a new block of building is proposed, balancing Smirke's block on the west. The west end of the Strand is implicated and a rearrangement of streets, based on the orientation of St Martin's, is proposed. For the implementation of this plan further legislation was required and a bill was presented to Parliament extending the powers contained in the New Street Act to 'Charing Cross, the Strand and Places adjacent'. The bill became law on 31 May 1826.

Nash saw this new square as essentially a *forum*, surrounded not by houses but by public buildings and institutions. The College of Physicians and the Union Club already had this character. Other allocations of sites, shown on his plan, were speculative. Assuming the eventual demolition of the Great Stable, he gave the north side to a National Gallery, proposing a long colonnaded building with a central portico. On the east he proposed to accommodate the Athenaeum, St Martin's vicarage, the Royal Society of Literature and the Golden Cross Hotel (which, as west London's chief coaching-house, already on the site, had to be retained in the rebuilding). Then, in the middle of the square, he proposed a Greek temple, an imitation of the Parthenon, facing down Whitehall. This was to be the seat of the Royal Academy of Arts. In the spaces to left and right he indicated sites for statues of George III and George IV.

The commissioners did not feel themselves committed to any such exclusive range of uses. In 1830 they leased the whole of the eastern block to a speculative architect, George Ledwell Taylor, who built it as a terrace of big houses, though it later became a hotel. In

1831 the commissioners instructed Nash to propose a design for houses and shops along the north side,[34] a scheme fortunately extinguished by the government's decision in the following year to use that site for a new building to house both the Royal Academy and the National Gallery.[35] The Athenaeum and the Royal Society of Literature dropped out. The vicarage of St Martin's found a site to the north of the church and the Golden Cross was rebuilt by William Tite on a triangular site facing the Strand.

Two-dimensionally speaking, Trafalgar Square is Nash's creation but of the buildings arising on his plan none was designed by him except the group to the north of St Martin's which includes the vestry-hall, the parish school and a pair of houses, one of which is still St Martin's vicarage and the other demolished. The square was never an architectural success but for that Nash is not to blame. His finest gesture was the liberation of St Martin's which, emerging from obscurity, became the noblest ornament of the new square. With its churchyard trimmed to a geometrical shape, it also set the pattern of the last phase of Nash's work here – the West Strand Improvements.

The east side of the square already took its direction from the west front of the church; it is not parallel with the west side, though the divergence is barely noticeable. Along the south side of the church Nash made Duncannon Street run into the Strand at a sharp angle; along its north side he made William IV Street do the same, with Adelaide Street connecting them along the east front of the church. Three triangular sites were thus created: one bounded by Trafalgar Square, the Strand and Duncannon Street, a second by the Strand, Adelaide Street and William IV Street, and a third by William IV Street, Chandos Place and Agar Street. The first of these triangles contained Taylor's terrace of houses towards the square and Tite's Golden Cross Hotel and was, in our time, completely rebuilt as South Africa House. The third was taken by the trustees of Charing Cross Hospital whose architect, Decimus Burton, built the building which still partly survives. The second and largest triangle has a frontage to the Strand (Fig. 9) and was built to consist of houses and shops with a covered gallery on the lines of the Royal Opera Arcade, running through it from the Strand to Adelaide Street. This, known as the Lowther Arcade, was demolished when Coutts's Bank rebuilt the centre part of the Strand front in 1902–4. That rebuilding has now (1979) been demolished and replaced by a spectacular glass curtain. The remainder of the block has been reconstructed inside a careful restoration of the surviving facades.

This last triangular block was developed by William Herbert, a builder who claimed to be 'architect and builder' of the block, though he certainly followed designs provided by Nash.[36] The interest of the block is in the way Nash treated the corner sites, turning them to picturesque account by finishing them as cylindrical towers rising to balustrades and domed attics on the Bramantesque *tempietto* model. Nash also designed the Lowther Arcade with its glass-domed bays. The details are not altogether characteristic of Nash and Herbert should perhaps have the credit for some entirely acceptable revisions.

The West Strand Improvements, completed in 1831, were John Nash's last executed contributions to the replanning of central London. They were not to be the last he

9. Nos 430 to 449 Strand, built by William Herbert to a general design by Nash. Wood-cut in the *Gentleman's Magazine*, 1831.

proposed. Included in the commissioners' Fifth Report is an engraved plan of a street commencing at the north-east corner of Trafalgar Square, on the line of St Martin's Lane and proceeding through Seven Dials and Monmouth Street to join a westward extension of Hart Street (Bloomsbury Way) leading to an open square opposite the British Museum, with St George's church standing free on the south side of it – a liberation comparable to what Nash had effected for St Martin's. A welcome improvement it would have been, if less obviously useful than Charing Cross Road, the unhandsome Victorian equivalent which connects directly with Tottenham Court Road and leaves the British Museum in a Bloomsbury sidestreet.[37]

The Commissioners also obtained from Nash a plan for continuing Coventry Street into Leicester Square, thence to Long Acre, Great Queen Street, through Lincoln's Inn Fields and into Holborn.[38] Some of this, notably Cranbourn Street, was carried out under the Office of Woods and Works, from 1840. In one respect, Nash's intentions seem a little unkind. Taken to its conclusion the scheme would have sent traffic rattling past the fragile arches of Sir John Soane's Museum.

11

Scenes in the Isle of Wight

For thirty-seven years of his life, from his second marriage in 1798 to his death in 1835, Nash maintained and enjoyed the status of a country gentleman in the Isle of Wight. East Cowes Castle was no mere rural refuge from the pressures of town, but a hospitable country seat; and the hospitality was extended to many of those who played a part in Nash's metropolitan world. Nash was never a man to draw a hard line between social and professional life. It came naturally to him to mix the two; he liked to mix them and there were advantages in that. East Cowes played a considerable part in the strategy of his career.

Nothing whatever remains of East Cowes Castle today. The site of the house itself is bare and the grounds are covered by small neat houses and bungalows of an unsurprising kind. We must reconstruct the building and its history as best we can. The best of the early views is Cooke's sketch (Plate 44A), first engraved in 1808,[1] which shows the part of the house looking north-west towards Cowes and the Solent. Behind, unseen in the view, was a thick square tower. By 1811 what Cooke shows us had been very much altered, if not rebuilt, with an added storey to the drawing-room and several new bays and oriels, while behind the drawing-room a second, octagonal, tower had shot up to a fiercely machicolated summit. At some date before 1824 a conservatory, 140 ft long, was added.

To give some idea of the house as it stood in its last days – still much as its builder left it – impressions from a visit in 1933 must be recaptured. Notwithstanding its castellated pretensions, the castle seemed, and in fact was, a small house, and while we need not agree with Lord Aberdeen's remark in a letter to Uvedale Price, that its smallness rendered it 'absolutely ludicrous', we can see what he meant.[2] It was small in scale and even cosy (Luscombe still has this charm). It was built mainly of coursed rubble which gave it a friendly, indigenous air. Its siting, on a terrace cut into ground which

146

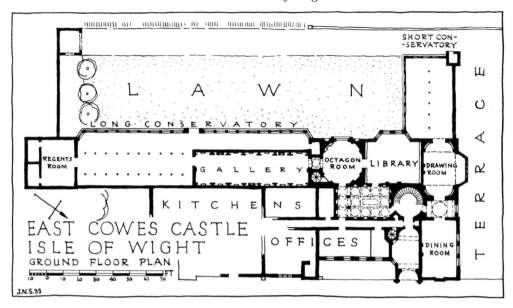

10. East Cowes Castle. Sketch-plan (1933).

dropped smoothly into a valley on the south-west, was perfect, or had been before an overgrowth of trees and shrubs obscured the prospects.

Entrance to the grounds from the road was past a small lodge, indistinguishable from one of the Blaise cottages. It still (1979) stands: the only memorial of Nash's habitation here. From this, a short drive (now blotted out) led to the severe and gaunt north-east front (Plate 44B). The doorway, within a shallow porch, was unwelcoming. Surprise and delight were reserved for the garden (south-west) aspect (Plate 45A), where the house seemed at first sight to consist of nothing but glass-filled arcades, a set of eight arches moving forward from the house and a set of nineteen in alignment with it, the two sets folding in towards each other at the base of the tower. The tower itself rose from this claustral setting without incongruity and with all the Walter Scott-like dignity of its kind.

The interior in 1933 remained much as it had been when Joseph Farington, holidaying in the island in September 1817, presented his card at the lodge and was told that he and his party might see the house and grounds.[3] Slightly supplementing his observations, we may follow in his steps (Fig. 10). From the porch Farington and his friends passed through a small, sombre vestibule into the circular staircase hall, its walls fluted, its domed covering enriched with a pattern like fish-scales, a chandelier hanging from a gilt foliated boss in the centre, and the stone stair, with thin S-shaped balusters, swarming up the wall. From here the party was directed (right) into a little domed anteroom, then (right again) into the dining-room, 'in which a table was very genteelly set for 7 persons'. This room had a fine cornice, consisting of a vertically-fluted cavetto, below this a tiny motif of curtains and tassels, painted red and gold, and, above, a scaly ovolo. The fireplace was of black marble with brass enrichments. The ceiling was, in 1933, still covered with early nineteenth-century wallpaper. 'This room, was ornamented,' says Farington, 'with several pictures – views of Houses designed by Mr. Nash.'

'The servant then told us,' he continues, 'we might pass through the opposite room, "the Drawing-room", in which was Mr. Nash with company, all of whom were seated when we entered, and we only passed through the middle of the room to the Conservatory. Mr. Nash bowed.' This room had apsidal recesses at each end and a great bay-window on the right, with a view to the Solent. Again there was a handsome cavetto cornice, though here with a reticulated enrichment, and the same curtain-and-tassel motif below. The chimney-piece, opposite the window, was of white marble with Egyptian figures holding up the mantel.

The conservatory, into which Farington and his friends now passed, formed an extension of the drawing-room and closed a vista through three rooms. Leaving this they were then shown the library, 'a handsome room well stored with books'. Here was a coved cornice of another type and a black marble chimney-piece like the one in the dining-room; but the room was altered and somewhat over-enriched after Nash's time. Farington will then have passed into the octagon room, occupying the lower part of the great tower, with eight wall arches carrying a flat radial-fluted ceiling. In later years a portrait of Sir Samuel Romilly hung in this room. Farington does not mention the billiard-room, evidently not yet built. He would not have failed to notice the ingenious lighting through a series of ten little hanging domes round a central lay-light. His tour ended, Farington gave the servant 2s., 'with which he appeared pleased'.

This was not Farington's only visit to East Cowes. In October 1821 he received a pressing invitation to stay and it was on that occasion that Nash recited to Farington the story of his life. Also on that occasion Nash showed him, with great pride, the kitchen garden.[4] This, in 1933, was still in perfect order but it has long since been in ruin. Formed on the slope of the hill, a hundred yards from the house, it consisted of five broad terraces built in brick with slate floors under the soil. The slate 'prevents any but good earth from lodging at the roots of the fruit trees. The roots, not being able to penetrate the [slate], shoot out horizontally'.

East Cowes was as perfect as Nash could make it. He spent much time there, ever active with pen, pencil and revolving thoughts, sending sketches and directions to the office and all the time enjoying the company of his guests. The castle was rarely without guests. Nash liked company, and his wife, according to Benjamin West, was a more than eager hostess.[5] A very short acquaintance with the Nashes could bring an invitation, offered in no conventional terms but kindly and pressing. A pleasant example survives at Windsor. It is to Robert Gray, keeper of the Prince Regent's privy purse, who had been seriously ill:

Allow me to repeat my invitation to you and Mrs. Gray . . . we have poney carts and an Irish jaunting Car a close carriage and a very gentle horse for you to ride – hot and cold Bathing, salt or fresh in the house – civil waiting and an attentive Landlord and Landlady – fine air sea breezes and graveld roads – where can you find a more commodious Inn? try it and believe me with a due sense of your kindness for which I am your debtor – my Dear sir,

faithfully yours

J. NASH.[6]

Nor were invitations only for important people. Assistants and pupils in the office were welcome at the castle, where they mixed with all manner of people, politicians and artists, lawyers and actors, with liberty to swim, to shoot and ride about the island and in the evenings to play cards or listen to music or philander in the fields and arbours under the high romantic battlements.

One such guest was George Repton who, notwithstanding the bitter rift between his father and Nash, was now the Chief Assistant at Dover Street. He was thirty and a bachelor when he met, at East Cowes, Lady Elizabeth Scott. She, rather more than thirty, was one of the two daughters of John Scott, Earl of Eldon, Lord Chancellor of England. George and Elizabeth formed an attachment and, in March 1817, eloped, George carrying the lady away from her father's official residence in Bedford Square.[7] Eldon was furious, and it made no difference that he, as a young man, had done much the same thing, snatching his bride out of the window of a house on Tyneside. Nevertheless, three years later, when Elizabeth's first child was born, all was forgiven.

This grave little scandal apart, the year 1817 was a glorious one for East Cowes, for on 13 July the Prince Regent came over from Brighton to dine at the Castle. Four hundred soldiers from Parkhurst barracks formed a guard of honour.[8] In August he arranged to come again; his chef spent several days at the castle and quantities of provisions were brought from Southampton. Then he changed his mind. 'The turtle being in a spoiling state', a hasty invitation went to all the gentry in the island and a hundred and twenty of them came; they danced, sat down at midnight to what should have been a royal banquet, then danced on till dawn.[9]

The Prince did come again, eventually, in September. He was becoming fond of sailing and in 1817 the *Royal George*, 320 tons, was built for him at Deptford. About this time, too, he bought from George Ward a house on the Parade at West Cowes. It is probably to one of these later years of the Regency that an unsent invitation card, a trifle which survived the wholesale destruction of Mrs Nash's papers after her death, belongs:[10]

Mr. and Mrs. Nash
request the honor of
Lady Melville and Family's

149

Company to a Déjeuné and Fête
on the Lawn at East Cowes Castle
at 2 o'Clock on and in Commemoration
of the Prince Regent's Birth Day.

The year 1818 was overcast by tragedy. Sir Samuel Romilly, whose encounters with Nash in the political crisis of 1813 have been recorded in an earlier chapter, came to stay at the castle and brought his invalid wife. In the castle she died. Romilly, already in a state of exhaustion, collapsed. He was moved to London by easy stages and reached his house in Russell Square. There, after a few distracted days, he cut his throat.[11]

In August 1819, the Prince was again at Cowes, when Lord Henry Seymour entertained him at Norris Castle. Lord Henry was not noted for high living but we are told that this particular event 'was attended with circumstances of unusual conviviality'.[12] During this visit John Edwards was invited to dine on the royal yacht, doubtless as a favour to Nash. There was yet another Royal visit in September 1820, this time by the newly-ascended but still uncrowned monarch. Again, Nash, George Ward and others of the island gentry dined aboard the *Royal George*.[13]

The beauties of East Cowes and the hospitable ways of its master are celebrated in letters, diaries and memoirs. At the castle Nash was seen at his most relaxed and companionable. 'Merry, amusing, naive,' young Cockerell called him, a galloping raconteur who now, at seventy, was beginning to tell the same story twice.[14] To diarists he was a real gift, as Porden discovered in 1812 and Farington in 1821.

A rather specially interesting diarist came with her husband for two days in 1824. The husband, Charles Arbuthnot, had succeeded Huskisson in the previous year as First Commissioner of Woods and Forests and was in the island to inspect some Crown property in Nash's company. Mrs Arbuthnot was enchanted by the situation of the castle and its lovely gardens, and captivated by its owner. 'Mr. Nash is a very clever, odd, amusing man,' she wrote, 'with a face like a monkey's but civil and good-humoured to the greatest degree.'[15] Of the house, significantly perhaps, she says nothing at all. The mixture of conservatories and battlements was not to everybody's taste.

Of Mrs Nash we hear little and Mrs Arbuthnot summed her up as 'a vulgar bore'. By Mrs Arbuthnot's standards she probably was, but the dismissal should not be regarded as absolute. Mrs Arbuthnot, a charming, witty and sensible woman, found herself, at East Cowes, somewhat out of her element. The company was aggressively new-rich. Sir William Curtis was there, who had made a fortune out of ship's biscuits and become a sort of elderly jester ('a fool whose bells have ceased to ring at all', wrote Byron) in the Carlton House circle.[16] Of the same breed was Nash's neighbour, George Ward, an upstart financier of immense wealth who had built up a property empire in the island.[17] Candidly admitting that these were 'clever, intelligent men and full of anecdote and conversation', Mrs Arbuthnot had not a word to say to them and was 'reduced to silence'. With such people, Mrs Nash was, no doubt, somewhat more at ease.

Further evidence concerning Mrs Nash comes in the rather dubious form of a broadside published soon after 1820 containing a cartoon and seven verses of doggerel.[18] The cartoon shows an unshaven George IV, half dressed, in the cabin of the *Royal George* embracing a very fat woman purporting to be Mrs Nash. 'I have great pleasure in visiting *this part* of my dominions,' reads a balloon floating from the King's mouth; and on the floor lies 'The Loyal Address of *Cows*'. As to the ballad, a very few lines suffice to give the gist:

> Now the Yacht is all ready, for the Isle of Wight I'll steer,
> With the lovely Mrs. N–sh I am all upon the go,
> I'll pack the husband off – for he has no business here,
> With his wife in pleasure's bark I will jovially row.

What was this all about? The print is a product of the gutter press, exposing the King as the adulterous betrayer of an innocent Queen, and was evidently set off by gossip circulating at the time of one of the Royal jaunts in the Solent. The essence of the cartoon is only properly apprehended when it is recalled that at the time of its publication the King was about sixty and Mrs Nash at least forty-five. The object is to make the couple, especially the King, look ridiculous and it succeeds. Whether George IV did indeed take liberties with his architect's wife and whether those liberties were accepted or not we are unlikely to discover. Nor shall we ever know how much real distress the print caused to Nash and his wife. Far greater ladies than Mrs Nash were treated with even less consideration by the traffickers in graphic libel. A more telling effect of the print and of whatever indiscretions may have prompted it was probably the planting of a sense of vicarious guilt in some who, though only remotely concerned with the events, lived into an age when the misbehaviour of monarchs and their women was not found amusing. Among these were Mrs Nash's relatives.

Of these relatives we first become aware through Farington's account of his two-day stay at the Castle in 1821. There were dinner-parties on both days and Farington gives table-plans.[19] On both occasions, Mrs Nash sat at one end of the table, Mr Nash in the middle of one side and at the other end, opposite Mrs Nash, a 'Miss Pennythorn'. On both occasions 'Mrs. Nash's aunt' was likewise present. She was, no doubt, Charlotte Gregory, Mrs Nash's mother's sister. Now, an aunt of these Gregory sisters had married a certain Thomas Pennethorne whose son, another Thomas, had at least seven children, one of whom was called Ann. She, now aged about twenty-one, was the young lady at the far end of the table.[20]

Nash's interest in his wife's Pennethorne cousins probably started when he took Ann's elder brother, Tom, into his office. Tom had great talent, it was said, but died before he was twenty. His place in the office was taken by a younger brother, James. Meanwhile, the other young Pennethornes, including two boys and two girls, continued to live mostly with their parents, Thomas and Elizabeth Pennethorne, in Worcester. The arrangements made for Ann, we may suppose, issued from Mrs Nash's need for a daughter-substitute. Having no children of her own she would welcome a companion who could help with the almost continuous entertaining at the Castle. For Ann this would provide both a genteel employment and an opportunity. With a variety of male company always on parade she might have been expected to make a good marriage and Nash no doubt had this in mind when he told Farington that he meant to give her £10,000 (his will did contain such a legacy, though contingent on Mrs Nash's dying before him).[21] But marry she never did. An affair with the curate of Whippingham ended abruptly with the curate, a Mr Sewell, running away with a bad conscience and an ambition, which he achieved, to be a great educationalist.[22] Ann stayed with Mrs Nash till the latter's death in 1851 and continued to live in the island till her own death in 1883. Her estimate of Mrs Nash was different from Lady Arbuthnot's. 'She was,' she said, when they buried the old lady, 'the kindest, best friend that anyone ever had.'[23]

James Pennethorne benefited in a different way from the family connection. Somewhat overshadowed at first by memories of the more brilliant Tom, he was trained in Nash's office, then endured the rigours of two years in Pugin's drawing school, followed by two years' study abroad, all at Nash's expense. In 1828 he became Nash's principal assistant and, on his retirement inherited some of his official practice. Eventually, a series of administrative changes brought him the post of salaried architect to Queen Victoria's government, in which he displayed great ability, retiring with a knighthood in 1869.[24]

Returning now to the offensive broadsheet and its implications, it seems that in the Pennethorne family the dark, unmentionable possibility of an amorous encounter between their cousin and benefactress and the wicked old King was darkly transmitted. There are stories of letters and, indeed, jewellery being committed to the flames by Ann Pennethorne because they bore the stains of this dreadful association.[25] Out of the darkness grew, in course of time, a legend in which Mrs Nash was elevated to the rank of King's mistress. Not only that, but in some fertile imaginations of later years was conceived the idea that the Pennethorne children or some of them might indeed have been the fruit of this obscure passion.[26] While this cannot be disproved it is in the highest degree unlikely. There is no reason to suppose that the children's parents were not the perfectly respectable couple living in Worcester where Mrs Pennethorne conducted an academy for young ladies.[27] The whole mystery, such as it is, starts and ends with what the author of the ballad knew, or thought he knew, and that is beyond retrieval.

There is no reason to suppose that the Nash ménage at East Cowes was anything but harmonious. If the wife strayed a little outside the matrimonial enclosure she did so in august company and it is by no means certain that the husband did not do the same on a rather less exalted level. An entry in the diary of a scholarly Oxford clergyman with a taste for scandal, the Rev. Robert Finch, in 1817, seems to point in this direction:

Nash the architect in London . . . is a great coxcomb. He is about 60 years of age [in 1817 he was in fact 65]. He is very fond of women, although he is married, and attempted even Mrs. Parker, his wife's sister. He lives in Dover Street in London, has a charming place in the Isle of Wight and drives four horses.[28]

This is mere gossip at very long range, but the allusion to Grace Parker does confirm a family tradition that Nash's original preference had been for Grace but that circumstances of one sort or another had moved him into the arms of Mary Anne. The preference seems to have been maintained. But Nash was not, in his later years, a fast liver. Benjamin West's view was that Mrs Nash made the pace. Late nights were not Nash's choice and he told West that if he had his way he would go to bed at nine. He was very moderate with the bottle and his favourite drink was punch. Notwithstanding the spacious living at Regent Street and East Cowes, he told West that 'he could live happily in a single room having his books about him'.[29] We need not take this too literally: a fancy for monkish seclusion is common enough in people of notoriously gregarious habits. To Farington he expressed a fatalistic indifference to his future. 'He could live or die. He could fall to low estate without repining.'[30] That, again, is easily said by a man of seventy who still has the world at his feet. But Nash had known failure in his youth, had taken huge risks all his life and was still taking them, so this confession is not so easily discounted. Nash was never lacking in fortitude or resilience. They were to be tested again before he died.

It may have been a misfortune for Nash and his wife that they had no children. If Nash had a son by his first, disastrous, marriage, we must assume that the boy died in infancy. He may still have hoped, at forty-six, to raise a family, with a male heir of his own name to whom the fragrant creations of East Cowes would be transmitted. Besides, he liked young people. His correspondence with Philipps of Cwmgwili contains many pleasant allusions to the Philipps children and he scolds his friend for being less than kind to the son whom he had packed off to make a career in the Navy.[31] For the lack of immediate kin, there were, however, compensations. For Nash himself there was his young cousin Edwards who, had he survived, would have inherited whatever Nash had to leave in property and honours. For Mrs Nash there were the Pennethornes, especially the companionable and devoted Ann. Endlessly involved in social relationships and professional enterprises, Nash had little inclination to magnify the shortcomings of nature into heavy misfortunes.

Nash was no mere commuter in the Isle of Wight. He grew roots there as if he expected heirs to follow him. Not content with the Castle and its grounds, he bought in 1806 the manor of Ningwood, on the north coast of the island, about five miles west of Cowes, a property worth £30,000.[32] It included the tiny hamlet of Hamstead, perched on the ultimate rise of the downs which lie between the main road and the Solent, a veritable brow of the island, with views so airy and distant as to give a sensation

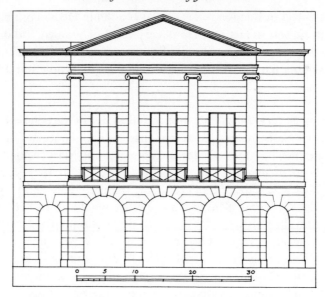

11. Newport Town Hall, Isle of Wight. (Redrawn from an original at Newport.)

usually to be had only at much greater heights. Here were an old house with a round tower and a farmhouse or grange with monastic antecedents. Nash converted the house into a picturesque cottage-style dwelling with a round tower and thatched roofs.[33] He used Hamstead as a shooting-box, farmed some of the land and had brick-ovens and lime-kilns there. Mrs Nash retired to Hamstead after her husband's death. Ann Pennethorne made it her home and was joined by her sister Sarah, her unmarried brother John and eventually by Sir James's unmarried daughter, Rose, who was there till her death in 1923. The Pennethornes did much rebuilding at Hamstead and of Nash's work nothing remains.

It was not only on his own property in the island that Nash designed and built. His help was solicited and freely given in the case of two public buildings in the island's chief town of Newport. The first of these was the Isle of Wight Institution (Plate 45B), a modest 'Lit. and Phil.' subscribed to by the island gentry, with a reading-room and museum. Built in 1811, it has a pilastered, pedimented front, more vigorously detailed than is usual with Nash and executed in Portland stone.[34] It is now the County Club. The second building was a combination of market-house and town hall, the market occupying the lower part and the upper storey containing in a very small space a council-chamber, town clerk's office, town hall and jury closet. This, built in 1814, is stucco-faced with an Ionic portico and colonnade (Fig. 11). Its symmetry is insulted by a Victorian clock-tower but it was always a rather meagre building. It faintly echoes the ambitious design for a county hall at Stafford which Nash made in 1794.[35]

Several houses in the island are attributed to Nash. He certainly designed the Gothic villa for Sir John Coxe-Hippisley which is now part of the Royal Corinthian Yacht Club. He built Doric lodges on his friend George Ward's estate at Northwood Park, one of which survives.[36] Altogether more remarkable was his handling of Ward's benefaction to West Cowes church in 1816. This took the form of a west tower whose lower part was to be in the nature of a Ward mausoleum. It is indeed so shaped, with conventional *antefixa* at the corners; over it rises the tower, a thin square shaft of masonry with the mausoleum theme repeated at the top, all very much in the 'modern French' spirit. The chamber in the base of the tower accommodates monuments to the Wards.

Two churches in the island were built from his designs, at Bembridge (1827) and East Cowes (1831–3). Both were excessively plain Gothic and must have been disgracefully cheap. Both have been rebuilt, but at East Cowes the tower remains. At its foot, the architect lies buried.

12

The King's Palace

In January 1820 the old King died and the Regent, at fifty-eight, became George IV. The Coronation was planned for 20 August but the sudden arrival from abroad of the new Queen rendered postponement convenient if not imperative. While the mob cheered her in the streets, grave counsel was taken at Court and in Parliament; the Bill of Pains and Penalties was debated in the House of Lords and made to seem like a trial; and when at the third reading it was dropped for lack of support the mob roared through London celebrating Caroline's 'acquittal'. Prudent citizens as well as partisans of the Queen illuminated their windows. Committed loyalists kept theirs dark and risked the hurtling brick. The windows of 29 Dover Street were not illuminated but, more by luck than by favour of the mob, remained unbroken.

In September George IV went sailing in the Solent and we hear of Nash dining on the *Royal George* at Cowes and going with the King to see the house he had bought from George Ward.[1] The postponed Coronation was now planned for 19 July 1821 and was to be a mighty spectacle. By tradition the ornament of such occasions was placed in the hands of the Officers of the Works. Under the new regime of the Board it might have been assigned to one of the three 'attached' architects and of these Nash, as the sovereign's private architect, would seem to have been the obvious choice. The Abbey and Westminster Hall, however, were in Soane's 'district' and Soane was accordingly invited. But he made a great fuss, pretended that the responsibility was too much for him and then, without positively declining, let things slide.[2] The result was that he found himself displaced by two officers of the Board, Robert Browne and Frederick Hiort, who between them brought the thing off triumphantly.[3] Nash had no hand in it.

The Coronation had the happy effect of turning the tide of popular favour once more towards the throne. Queen Caroline died while the King was in Ireland in August 1821 and her melancholy story was soon forgotten. George IV was now the symbol of a great, victorious and thriving nation and there could have been no better moment in English history for the realisation of what had for two hundred years been considered shame-fully wanting in the British scene – a metropolitan palace for the reigning monarch. St James's was always considered poverty-stricken. Whitehall never recovered from the fire of 1698 and had become an assortment of private mansions and government offices. Kensington Palace was over-modest. Carlton House, facing a public thoroughfare, was fine enough for an heir apparent but hardly for a King. The nearest thing to a palace in London was Buckingham House, built in 1715 by John Sheffield, Duke of Buckingham, and sold by his natural son, Sir Charles Sheffield, to George III in 1762. That King settled it on his consort and it became 'the Queen's Palace'.

But that did not make it really and truly a palace. There was always the feeling that a completely new building, royally conceived from the ground up on a new site (probably the Green Park) was the proper answer. Against this, however, was the inveterate hostility of Parliament to expenditure on an adequate scale. In 1820 Parliament was already sufficiently conscious of the new King's spending capacity and whenever, after his accession, a palace was talked of, assumed a defensive posture.

There had been talk of building a palace in 1819, when Lord Liverpool had put it to the Prince that no more than £150,000 could be found and that if more was wanted it would be necessary to get Parliament's authority to sell the site of St James's Palace, the Queen's Palace and other Crown properties. The Prince believed that nothing worth-while could be done under £450,000. So nothing was done. Finding himself King, however, the royal housing question became an obsession and on 12 July 1821, a week before the Coronation, he instructed Stephenson, the Surveyor-General, to put all plans relating to Buckingham House in the hands of Nash. Now this building was in Soane's 'district' and he was at that moment engaged on inspecting some alleged defects in the roofs. No doubt he had plans in his office; and the King's orders, transmitted to him rather casually at the end of a letter about something else came as an unpleasant shock and a premonition of what was to follow. Reiterated protests to Colonel Stephenson had no effect.[4]

For forty years Soane had been hugging the idea of some day building a palace. There was a design made in Italy when he was twenty-six which he especially cherished.[5] There was another design, made in 1817, for a palace, twice the size of the Bank of England and not unlike it, intended for Hyde Park.[6] This he showed at the Academy at the first opportunity after George III's death. Also in 1821 he made a design of a somewhat more realistic kind for a palace on Constitution Hill.[7] This he did not show till 1827, by which time it could only be acclaimed as a might-have-been. For by that time Nash was well away with what was to be called Buckingham Palace.

If Nash had snatched a palace commission from under Soane's nose, it can be believed that relations between the two old architects became a trifle strained. Soane, however, had the consolation of being able to start building, in the summer of 1822, the new Royal Entrance to the House of Lords. While this work was going on Nash visited the site and found Soane in a rage. What passed between them on that occasion we do not know but Soane, it seems, was maddened by the elusiveness of Sir Benjamin Bloomfield, the King's secretary, whom he considered as the agent of his dismissal, from Buckingham House. A few days later (18 September 1822) Nash wrote to Soane, from East Cowes, a letter which is a wonderful mixture of effervescent nonsense and real concern to put things right with his ruffled colleague. It is a letter which so illuminates the personality of the writer that it must be given in full. Soane was a Freemason and Nash teasingly takes the masonic theme as his text:[8]

BROTHER SOANE

You was in a Miff when I saw you at the head of your Masons. One of the Masonic rules, I am told is to acquire a meek and humble spirit. I fear therefore you are not qualified for Grand Master. Now, if you will but come here and copy me for a month you will certainly be appointed to a higher nich in your Lodge when you next meet and see poor Bloomfield with kinder aspect than you were wont to do, and do penance for the hard thoughts you expressed of him. He is as innocent of the crime you imputed to him, as you are of any crime – but, my Dear Soane, I did not mean to sermonize when I sat down to address you, but to say that I cannot come up as soon as Sunday and therefore thought it due to you to give you the earliest notice and absolve you from the appointment for Monday which you was so kind as to accede to. The Churches must therefore be without our architectural consecration till we meet, unless you and our colleagues will perform the ceremony and which I much wish you would do, as I am anxious the trowell shall be used on one of them (St. George's) before the winter sets in, which I smell every morning about 6 o'clock, an hour which I suppose finds you in the arms of some – oh! no impossible – and yet you are so thin – but it cannot be. It is against the Masonic Canon and such a thing would be neither square plomb or within Compasse. When I left you musing upon your wild-goose chase of Bloomfield it occurred to me that our appointments are perfectly Constitutional, I the King, you the Lords, and *your* Friend Smirke, the Commons, and the blood instantly rushed to my face seeing or fancying that you wanted to dethrone me. It then struck me that you wanted to be both King and Lords and in fancy I heard you cry out – 'Off with his head, so much for Buckingham', and I sighed 'why should he so long for my empty chair when a few years would give him that without offense which has occasioned in him so offensive an act,' for I am old, but feeling my head on my shoulders I marched off to Buckingham House. I had not gone 6 steps before I was stopped by the Black Rod, he demanded whether the south aperture of the arcade was to be stop'd up. I took him by the arm and pointing my finger said 'Lo! the architect of the fabrick,' and would have ushered him into the presence, 'shall I usher you,' said I, but, whether the term smelt too much of the shop or he thought I meant to insult him, I know not, but off he march'd. I recollected myself and had a Quarm, I beg your pardon, I mean qua*l*m, 'Something too much of this'.

I have scribbled so much that I am in doubt when we next we meet you will wear a face 'most in grief or anger . . .'. I hope neither, but lighted up by smiles, not such smiles as would seem 'to scorn your spirit that would be moved to smile at anything' but the smile of cordiality which be assured I feel for you, or if you strain a point and present yourself at our drawbridge I shall believe you actuated with the same spirit, and till you do so the sumptuous dinner you gave my trio at your elegant, doublefaced mansion will not sit quite easy on my stomach. The portcullis will arise at the touch of your masterly finger and the master spring to give you welcome.

> With you dear Soane,
> I've picked a bone,
> And fain I would requite it;
> Should you refuse
> I cannot choose
> Ah! let me not indite it
> But fist or stick
> A bone must pick
> With you and out must fight it.

Very bad, very bad. Off – Off – Well I am off, but one word more at parting. Mrs Nash and the 'Sweet Ann Page' desire me to say that they will expect you, and believe me I often think of you. As a proof, I have your figure now before my eyes, a thin black shadow standing on the foundation walls of the new arcade, with arms folded contemplating the mode of laying bricks. Oh that I had leisure for such contemplation, and that some friend could describe my thick, squat dwarf figure, with round head, snub nose and little eyes in such an act of contemplation, but I must be shot flying. All joking being at an end with my paper (luckily for you), I conclude in sober sadness a l'ordinaire, but with truth not appertaining to the custom, that I am, my dear Soane,

Very Sincerely Yours

JOHN NASH

J. Soane, Esq., Architect to the whole Peerage of England.

To unveil some of the obscurities of the letter it must be explained that the Monday meeting from which Nash excuses himself – the nominal pretext of the letter – was in

159

connection with the passing of plans for some of the new churches to be built under the Act of 1818 (St George's was one of the churches in Regent Street); that '*your* friend Smirke' is an ironic allusion to Soane's longstanding hostility to this successful younger man who had once been an unsatisfactory pupil in his office; that the name of the Yeoman Usher of the Black Rod in 1822 happened to be Robert *Quarm*; and that the question about stopping up the arcade refers to an arcade by Wyatt which adjoined the curved open-arched screen which Soane was about to build as part of the Royal Entrance. 'Sweet Ann Page' is, of course, Ann Pennethorne. The last paragraph seems to refer to current cartoons of Soane and Nash, the second apparently anticipating the famous later cartoon showing him poised like a weathervane on the spire of All Souls', Langham Place. The underlying sense of the letter is to turn the tables on Soane and make it seem that he and not Nash was the one trying to grasp the lion's share of opportunity.

Soane did not much care for the letter. He replied, however, in friendly enough terms, capped Nash's quotations and excused himself, on the grounds of pressure of business, from visiting at East Cowes. 'You, my dear friend', he wrote, 'may smile at my attention to professional pursuits, but I am convinced there are few persons more anxious of fame, and who would make greater sacrifices at the shrine of public approbation than yourself. Fame you possess, and you also have a friend who if ever the bitter shaft of envy and malice should reach you, that friend would 'kiss away the falling tear and smooth the pillow of sadness'.[9] The distance between the two correspondents is nicely measured by the subscriptions to their letters. Nash is 'very sincerely yours' to Soane: Soane is 'very truly yours' to Nash.

Between 1822 and 1825 nothing much is heard of alterations at Buckingham House and in 1823 George IV turned his attention to Windsor. Works at the cottage, transferred in 1815 from Woods and Forests to the Board of Works, were continually in hand. There was dry rot. Arrears of payments to tradesmen were giving endless trouble and Nash, heavily engaged with the Park, the Street, the Pavilion and a great deal else was consistently unhelpful.[10] Perhaps it was for this reason that, in 1823, George IV suddenly changed his architect. When the question of still further extensions to the cottage arose he entrusted the work to a man whom he knew to combine professional competence and punctuality with the inheritance of a famous architectural name, not conspicuously associated with either. He was Jeffry Wyatt, nephew of the celebrated Surveyor-General.[11]

Fourteen years younger than Nash, Wyatt had got himself a great reputation as a country-house architect while at the same time conducting a profitable business as a contractor. In the country-house field, which Nash had now abandoned, he could be said to be Nash's successor, building classical palaces, Gothic castles or Elizabethan mansions for the best people, from dukes downwards. In the matter of style he owed less to Nash than to his own famous uncle but it cannot be said that any of his work is irradiated by genius. Capable and reliable, he paid attention to his clients' needs and purses, which was more than could be said for some architects. George IV liked his gruff practicality and very possibly, when engaging him for the Cottage, had him in mind for an altogether more exalted task – the reconstruction of Windsor Castle itself.

Windsor Castle in 1823 presented, within its mouldering outlines, a picture of quaint rurality. Nothing much had been done to it since Charles II, with Hugh May as his architect, modernised the buildings containing the state apartments. George III had let James Wyatt loose on the interiors of these after 1800 but all exterior aspects remained dour. Windsor had nothing of the dramatic presence of Warwick or Alnwick and as a court residence was wildly inconvenient. Now, in 1823, George IV, advised by Charles Long, Lord Farnborough, conceived the idea of a comprehensive reconstruction which would not only make Windsor acceptable as an up-to-date palace but establish a new image. It was to be a castle not only in name but in form, feature and silhouette; a picturesque embodiment of patriotic sentiment and national glory.[12]

It would be expensive, but Parliament, without too much reluctance, voted £150,000 in April 1824. A delicate question was the choice of architect. The Board of Works triumvirate could not be bypassed but it was decided to bring Jeffry Wyatt within the range of selection and to invite all four architects – Nash, Soane, Smirke and Wyatt – to submit drawings. The King commissioned a 'committee of taste', which included Lord Farnborough, to pass judgement and advise on future plans and they started to meet in May 1824. They had before them plans by Nash, Smirke and Wyatt. Soane made excuses and produced nothing. Nash certainly made some designs, for Pugin and Mackenzie are recorded as working on them in April and May 1824, but only one – an interior of a new St George's Hall, freely modelled on the hall at Hampton Court – has survived. Whether the merits of Nash and Smirke were duly weighed against those of the outsider we do not know. 'There seems', wrote a contemporary, 'to be a degree of mystery hanging over that part of the business'.[13] But Wyatt was appointed and the King laid the first stone in August 1824. Whereupon Wyatt rendered himself slightly ridiculous to posterity by becoming, with the King's permission, Wyatville. In 1828, he became Sir Jeffry.

Nash's association with Windsor was now finished; Buckingham House and its future became his over-riding responsibility. A Bill for enabling the Crown lands revenues to be applied to the 'repair and improvement' of the building was introduced in the House of Commons in June 1825.[14] Nash had already made some tentative plans, but had been trying all the time to persuade the King to build on another site. Failing in this, he advised him to rebuild Buckingham House higher up in the garden, in a line with Pall Mall. He 'stated the lowness of the present site, and the northern aspect,' and thought at first that this proposition had some effect. But he was soon disillusioned, and the thing was finally settled in a conversation at Buckingham House or Kensington, at which Lord Farnborough was present.

'Long, now remember,' said the King good-humouredly, 'I tell Nash, before you, at his peril ever to advise me to build a Palace. I am too old to build a Palace. If the Public wish to have a Palace, I have no objection to build one, but I must have a pied-aterre. I do not like Carlton House standing in a street, and moreover I tell him that I will have it at Buckingham House; and if he pulls it down he shall rebuild it in the same place; there are early associations which endear me the spot.'

There was nothing more to be said, and from that moment the architect 'never presumed to press His Majesty on the subject of building a Palace, or of removing the site'.[15] So Buckingham Palace, like the cottage at Windsor, began as a pied-à-terre, a mere private residence to replace Carlton House, which had become very distasteful and even, it was said, rather unsafe.

It is clear that Nash's designs for the rebuilding were prepared and passed in a hurry. The plans were 'not yet quite finished' on 2 May 1825, no model was constructed and the design itself had some very rough edges. Work was actually begun before the bill had passed the House of Commons, and the members who voted money for the 'repair and improvement' of Buckingham House had no idea of the kind of building which they were authorising. However, they were told that the cost of the improvements 'might not be less than £200,000', and this did not seem to worry them, even though they had voted £150,000 for Windsor in the previous year.

Nash's first design for the Palace is preserved in a pair of engravings from drawings by Pugin (Plate 46A). Naturally, it follows to some extent the lines of the old house which consisted of a main block with forward-projecting wings. But the main block, now cased up in masonry, is provided with two orders, Corinthian above, Greek Doric below, the Corinthian expressed in a central *porte-cochère* and two pavilions and the Doric marching along on the ground, linking this Corinthian trio and then proceeding along the wings to make a frontal appearance where they return towards the Park. This is all very promising. One recalls Vanbrugh's marvellous play with two orders at Blenheim. But there are some oddities. The two pavilions carry box-like 'attic storeys' which seem grotesquely protuberant; a bald dome appears mysteriously a long way behind the portico; and the wings are broken into a number of different elements, the strangest of which are the two little upstairs lodges overlooking the Park.

As to the plan, this was not, at this stage very different from what was eventually built (Fig. 12).[16] It was predictable, perhaps, that Nash should introduce that famous feature of so many of his country houses and of the Brighton Pavilion – a spinal gallery. He found room for it within the carcase of the old house by sweeping away Buckingham's enfilade of state rooms along the west (garden) side. Then, beyond the gallery, he added an entirely new range of building fronting the garden, with a projecting semi-circular bay in the middle and four pavilions like the two on the courtyard side. It was the central bay which carried the dome seen behind the pediment. This rounded bay is still with us, but carrying a lower dome built after Nash's time.

Nash began to build Buckingham Palace in and around the shell of Buckingham House in June 1825, the official instructions as to procedure following on 5 August. It was agreed that, owing to the specially elaborate nature of the work, he should forgo his salary as 'attached architect' to the Board but take the full standard commission of 5 per

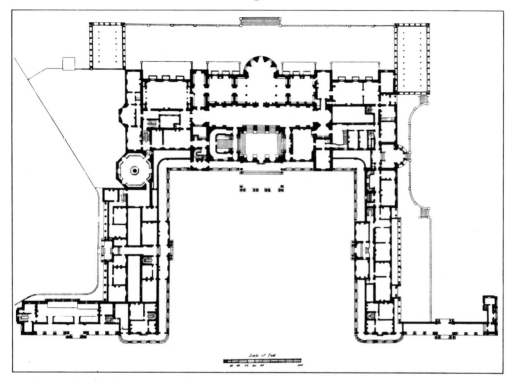

12. Buckingham Palace, as built by Nash, 1825–30. From W. H. Leeds, *Public Buildings of London*, 1838.

cent on the cost of the work instead of the 3 per cent prescribed by the Board. He threw himself into the work with a sense of extreme urgency. George IV wanted his palace and he wanted it soon. In August 1825 he turned sixty-three, not an age at which the future still seems limitless. Nash was even older. At seventy-three he reacted with the intensity of a loyal old servant striving to gratify every whim of his (relatively) young master. To speed the works he divided the site into three sections, each within separate hoardings, so that, in effect, three buildings were going up at the same time, each with its own clerk of works. A general clerk of works – William Nixon, who had served Nash well at Brighton – supervised the whole until his death in 1826. By 1828 the encasing walls, all in Bath stone, were at their full height, the whole building was covered in and the interior decorations were in hand.[17]

At this juncture, things began to go wrong. The thing most conspicuously wrong was, unhappily, the building itself, as seen from St James's Park. If the two wings had seemed a trifle eccentric in Pugin's drawing, in actuality they were a ludicrous jumble. Nash knew and the King knew that the sooner they came down the better. The Duke of Wellington had just succeeded Goderich as Prime Minister and early in 1828 Nash went to him and

163

announced the King's desire to demolish and rebuild the wings. The Duke replied coldly that 'it was no business of his; they could pull down as much as they liked'. But he knew well enough what the architect was after. 'If you expect me to put my hand to any additional expense, I'll be damned if I will.'[18] The truth was that by this time, the original estimate had been grossly exceeded.

The calamitous story of the financial administration of the works at Buckingham Palace was not to unfold till somewhat later but already in 1828 Parliament had shown anxiety about expenditure on public works in general. In February Henry Bankes, a member with an obsessional hostility to all public works, raised the matter in the Commons, linking extravagance and tastelessness as interdependent social evils. A few weeks later he moved for a Select Committee on the state of public buildings in the Office of Works. A committee of fifteen was appointed and began to sit on 25 March. Nash's turn to give evidence came on 3 April. Many of his architectural activities, past and present, were reviewed but Buckingham Palace loomed largest.[19]

Nash was relaxed, candid and perhaps even faintly amused by the proceedings. He made no bones about the failure of the wings: 'I was not at first aware that the effect would have been so bad, but now I think that any wings would take from the dignity of a palace . . . I am sorry to say I was disappointed in the effect of them.'

The committee then took up the subject of the dome over the projecting bay on the garden front and its ambiguous appearance from the Park. Nash confessed that he had not meant it to be so conspicuous from that side but defended it as an ornament of the garden front. As this was a matter which could not very well be argued, the committee changed their ground:

> 'Is any light conveyed from the top of the dome?'
> 'None at all.'
> 'Then it is purely an ornamental part of the building?'
> 'It forms the ceiling of the room underneath.'
> 'That is not one of the state rooms?'
> 'No, it is over one of the state rooms.'
> 'Will you inform the committee whether any useful part of the building is lighted by means of the dome?'
> 'There is no light from the dome, but the cavity of the dome is necessary to make the room underneath the dome of a proper height.'
> 'Is it a room of great utility?'
> 'No, nothing but a common bedroom.'[20]

In short, the only possible defence of the dome was, as Nash had said in the first place, that it contributed to the architectural effect of the garden front. There the matter was left and so, for the time being, was the dome. As for the offending wings, instead of being demolished they were built up to a uniform height and provided with terminal porticos giving an effect somewhat in the manner of the *ailes Gabriel* at Versailles. Between the wings an important feature, not shown in the design of 1825, was also begun in 1828. This was a Roman triumphal arch, intended to celebrate British victories on land and sea, and very obviously inspired by Napoleon's *arc du Carrousel* in the Tuileries gardens. At first proposed to be in Bath stone like the Palace, it was executed in white marble and became the Marble Arch.[21]

If neither Parliament nor the Public liked the palace and if even its architect confessed to serious shortcomings, George IV remained remarkably buoyant. 'Nash,' he said, in an interview at Carlton House in 1826, 'the state rooms you have made me are so handsome that I think I shall hold my courts there.' Nash protested that the building was not planned for such occasions. Not only was there no accommodation for a consort (which perhaps did not for the moment much matter) but none for the regiment of court officials on whom the correct motions of protocol depended. But the King would not listen. 'You know nothing about the matter; it will make an excellent Palace, and Lord St. Helens and myself have arranged the use of the several apartments.' He proceeded to show his architect how the principal rooms were to be appropriated. Nash raised every objection he could muster, but still the King would have his way. 'Lord St. Helens and I have arranged all that' was his only comment.[22]

So Buckingham House found its improbable destiny and became what nobody had ever intended it should be, the metropolitan palace of the Kings and Queens of England. It remained to decorate and furnish it in a style appropriate to its new character.

Nash was not and never had been a great interior designer. Nobody had found much to say in favour of his suite at Carlton House and to be faced now, at seventy-six, with the creation of a set of Royal apartments of the greatest possible dignity and richness might have daunted a Mansart or an Adam. But no self-conscious reflections of this kind deterred Nash. He produced the designs for all the grand interiors. They are dignified, they are rich and each has a marked stylistic character. The Green Drawing Room and the Throne Room (Plate 47B), occupying most of the courtyard side, arrive at ceremonial distinction with no more contrivance than a distribution of pilaster strips and enriched coves subtending panelled ceilings. The taste here tends towards Louis XVI. On the garden side, the White Drawing Room introduces a fanciful, almost rococo, pilaster order in which the capital contains the Garter star; the 'cove' here is reversed and becomes a convex projection under the ceiling. The Music Room which follows is the most English of the series, with a Corinthian order soberly marking out a domed square, then wheeling round the half-domed projecting bay. Then comes the truly majestic Blue Drawing Room with pairs of Corinthian columns standing against the walls in Palladian fashion and massive consoles swinging up from each pair in a surprising gust of baroque theatricality. Throughout these variations Nash's personal handling is discernible. His fondness for reticulated patterns (as at East Cowes), for lozenges in squares, squares in lozenges and circles inside or outside the one or the other, goes a long way to fill in spaces which might otherwise seem a trifle bare. The designs are worked out with a thoroughness not wholly characteristic of Nash and which may well owe something to the maturing abilities of young Pennethorne. Few of Nash's designs for these interiors survive but in the Victoria and Albert Museum is one for the Throne Room (Plate 47A): a little piece of paper, 16 cm × 22 cm, with a minimum of lines on it but enough for the clerks in the office to set up nearly all the necessary working-drawings. Nash never wasted energy.

In all the interiors, sculpture and craftsmanship play a part. Nash brought to the Palace works the best craftsmen and carvers he could find. The scrolled bronze balustrade of the Grand Staircase is a masterpiece by Samuel Parker and his, too, are the bronze capitals of many of the columns. George Seddon's parquetry in the Music Room and Bernasconi's flying Victories in the Throne Room are craftsmanship of the very highest class. In sculpture, Nash provided opportunities for Richard Westmacott, E. H. Bailey, Charles Rossi and William Pitts, as well as for William Croggon and his artificial stone. He would have had the co-operation of still better artists than these if Flaxman had not died in 1826 and if Chantrey had not declined to participate.[23]

One apartment in the palace (now completely altered) deserves notice for misplaced ingenuity. This was the Picture Gallery which stands between the two sets of state rooms. In designing this 135 ft long gallery Nash raided John Soane's recently finished Chancery Court at Westminster. In the ceiling there, Soane had introduced a highly idiosyncratic decorative device, a series of pendant arches forming compartments along the walls. Nash took this theme for his gallery but inserted a glass dome in each compartment, so that light fell immediately over where the pictures hung. Unfortunately, however, they lit the floor but not the pictures and William Seguier, the Surveyor of the King's Pictures, felt obliged to express the view that although the gallery was extremely fine the lighting was a complete failure.

The King's decision of 1825 to pull down Carlton House and transfer himself to Buckingham House had the curious effect of taking away from Regent Street the building which had, from the first, been its southern goal, whose presence had suggested the creation of Waterloo Place as a *place royale*, and whose axis fixed the position of Piccadilly Circus. With Carlton House gone there was nothing at the end of the street but a hole in the ground and a view across St James's Park to Westminster. The Act of 1826 which authorised the demolition of the building placed the site of the house and its gardens in the hands of the Commissioners of Woods, Forests and Land Revenues who were to arrange for its profitable development.[24] With the scenic appearance of this development, however, the King was personally concerned and when Nash was asked at the Committee of 1828 who had called on him to give the elevations of the new houses he replied rather grandly: 'The probability is that I received the directions from the person whom I may consider my patron and protector.' 'I presume,' he added with more tact, 'there is an order in the Treasury.'[25]

The development of this site brought under review the condition of St James's Park,

at that time a bare, sumpy tract with a canal streaking down the middle of it, unrelated
to Buckingham House or to anything else. In January 1827 the Treasury gave orders for
a general improvement. Nash now had before him a problem not wholly unlike that of
Marylebone Park. It was again a question of creating a picturesque scene out of
architecture, trees and water. Again, but now more acutely, there was the question of
transition from park to street. With Carlton House gone, what was to fill the space?

Nash saw at once that the last thing to do with the space was to block it. He
therefore proposed two great equal terraces standing to east and west and looking over the
Park, a duality inspired by the twin palaces of Gabriel's Place Louis XV (the Place de la
Concorde of today). Between these he would have placed, as a terminal feature to Regent
Street, a fountain within an open domed temple, the columns of the temple being, very
appropriately, the eight which had formed the portico of Carlton House.[26] The temple
would have been on a level slightly higher than Waterloo Place. But the Committee of
1828 were sceptical:

> 'Will the effect be good?', they enquired.
> 'I hope so; there will be a railing'.

The Committee asked whether the temple would not 'intercept the view between
Waterloo Place and the Park'.

> 'No, on the contrary, speaking as a painter, it will improve the view; and
> being an open Temple, you will see the Park between the columns in a most
> picturesque manner'.
> 'Did you ever see any example of a fountain with a cupola over it?'
> 'No'.[27]

With their growing distrust of the veteran architect's taste for bizarre experiments the
Committee was less than enthusiastic and when Nash drew an analogy between what he
proposed and a fountain in a conservatory their faith deserted them. So the fountain
proposal was stopped and, on the King's orders, a flight of steps leading down to the
Mall was introduced. A terminal feature for the street did arrive, however, five years
later when a Doric column of monumental dimensions was raised at the head of the steps
to commemorate the King's brother, Frederick Augustus, Duke of York, who had died in
1827. Although this was not designed by Nash but by Benjamin Dean Wyatt it originated
with an idea which had sprung into Nash's mind just about the time that Waterloo Place
received its name. As mentioned in a previous chapter, a design for such a column is in
existence.[28] It would have stood in front of Carlton House.

The two terraces facing St James's Park began to be built in 1827. An early plan shows
an additional terrace to the west covering the gardens of Marlborough House, which it was
proposed to demolish. Terraces and a crescent were also proposed for the Crown lands

on the south of the Park, where the Wellington Barracks were eventually built. The two terraces which were in fact built and which flank the Duke of York's steps are those known today as Carlton House Terraces, east and west (Plate 48). They consist of nine houses each, the end pairs (one house only on the extreme east, however) being of exceptional depth and height for terrace houses. Because of the change of level (some sixteen feet) between Waterloo Place and the Mall the basements of the houses look into areas on the north but are at ground level on the south. They are not, however, exposed on this side, for a fifty-foot extension advances towards the Mall, consisting of brick vaults on iron stanchions and carrying what was originally a gravelled platform or terrace for the use of the residents in the houses. This extension, with its strong horizontal line and stubborn Greek Doric order gives to the mansions behind a sublime patrician aloofness, while the mansions themselves are vested in the rigid magnificence of a thirty-six-foot Corinthian colonnade – a colonnade whose rhythm is unbroken even where a festive pediment, with ornaments by Bernasconi, rides in the centre. Nothing could be further from Nash's hesitant and confused design for Buckingham Palace. The Carlton House terraces are monumentally regal.

The terraces were Nash's conception and he supplied the designs and constructional details for the Mall elevations and the vaults. He also, as usual, had charge of letting the sites. Ground-rents were calculated at the high rate of four guineas per foot frontage. Sites in the west terrace went easily enough but not so easily in the east and Nash, in his anxiety to see the whole composition finished, took five sites (Nos 11–15), built the houses and offered them in the market at prime cost. In the event he sold them at less than this figure and made a loss.[29]

In the west terrace Nash designed No. 5 for Lord Caledon, No. 7 for William Hanning and No. 9 for James Alexander; in the east terrace, No. 10 for Sir Mathew White Ridley, and, of course, the five houses he built himself. The most important of all these houses is Lord Caledon's (now the Turf Club), the middle house in the east terrace.[30] It was the first to be built and was the model for the others, at least so far as the south front details were concerned. Nash deposited a bound copy of the drawings for No. 5 with the Commissioners of Woods so that owners employing other architects could ascertain the details with which they would be obliged to conform.[31] Among these other architects were J. P. Gandy-Deering who designed the palatial No. 1 and Decimus Burton who designed Nos 3 and 4. No. 18, the far eastern house, was not built till 1863–4 and was designed by William Burn.

On the ground to the west of the two great terraces, as soon as the idea of demolishing Marlborough House had been abandoned, Nash laid out the smaller group of seven houses constituting Carlton Gardens. Of these only four now remain. The two nearest the Mall were built for two men who were successively his masters at the Office of Woods: William Huskisson and Charles Arbuthnot.

The two Carlton House Terraces and Carlton Gardens covered the site of the gardens of the old palace. Meanwhile the demolition of Carlton House itself necessitated a new layout for the ground south of Waterloo Place. This resulted in the creation of two important new building sites at the east and west corners of Pall Mall. That on the east was taken by the United Service Club and that on the west by the Athenaeum, both in 1826. The United Service Club prudently engaged Nash as their architect. The Athenaeum, which had already considered two other sites in the improvement areas, retained young Decimus Burton. Nash made a design for the United Service Club and, in order to preserve the symmetry of Waterloo Place, ruled that the exterior of the Athenaeum should conform with his design. The Athenaeum accepted this. A highly confused situation then developed, the commissioners insisting upon strict symmetry, as recommended by their architect, the Athenaeum endeavouring to conform, but Nash vacillating, ignoring the commissioners and eventually declaring that he was 'persuaded of the bad effect of an attempt at perfect uniformity.' In the end, the two clubs resembled each other only in general bulk and outline, the Athenaeum gaining a rather special point when it received the commissioners' permission to install a restoration of the Panathenaic frieze under its cornice. In 1858 the United Service Club accentuated the architectural divergences between the two houses by renewing all the exterior ornaments in a rich Italian style. Their architect on this occasion was Decimus Burton.[32]

Nash's building (now occupied by the Institute of Directors) is chiefly notable for the enormous proportion of space occupied by the staircase. One possible reason for this is that the King offered the club the staircase from Carlton House. Its removal being presumably found impracticable, Nash filled the space on his plan with a stair ascending with spectacular extravagance to open galleries on three sides: an impressive and possibly unique arrangement.

While the terraces and the clubs were building, St James's Park itself was transformed. The Mall was widened southwards to bring its centre line on to the axis of the Palace. Nash still thought of it as a pedestrian promenade, which it had always been, but formed part of it into a carriage drive connecting with Constitution Hill. His layout for the Park (Plate 46B) was evidently suggested by a plan left by Capability Brown who had been appointed gardener at St James's in 1764; the Serpentine water with the great pool to the east containing a wooded island are Brown's ideas.[33] The planting is more in the manner of Repton, and indeed of Regents Park. It was superintended by Nash's own gardener from East Cowes with Nash choosing the trees and shrubs and setting in motion the clearing of the old canal and the stopping up or diverting of the various sewers which ran into it.[34] The old bridge which Nash had designed for the celebrations of 1814 and which had become an eyesore was removed; an iron railing was put round the Park and Birdcage Walk was levelled. The Park today with its winding paths and picturesque planting is still remarkably close to Nash's intentions.

As the palace, the terraces and the park moved toward conclusion, their creator began to be assailed by the kind of criticism which men who change their fellow citizens' environment all too readily attract. The grounds of this criticism were two-fold – taste and expense. Implied censure on both grounds had emerged in the report of the Select Committee of 1828. There was, not, however, in this the least reflection either on Nash's professional ability or his personal integrity. The Committee expressly stated that their criticisms of the designs of the attached architects went no further than the admissions of the architects themselves. Nash's admissions were, of course, fairly damaging; but what really stirred parliamentary indignation were the incidental revelations of the loose and unsatisfactory control of public money.

A Mr J. Wood brought up the subject in the Commons on 12 May 1829, and some inconclusive grumbling from one or two other speakers followed. A fortnight later, however, the member for Worcester, Colonel Davies, renewed the attack from a different angle altogether.[35] He broached the old subject of unwarrantable expense and criticised the 5 per cent which Nash was receiving for Buckingham Palace. Then he took a more direct and personal line, and, in plain terms, accused Nash of malversation and fraud.

Davies seems to have been a most disagreeable person, anxious to figure as a public avenger and confident that in Nash he had found the sort of victim he was looking for. He told the House that his information came from a most respectable source and assured them that he himself did not know Nash, even by sight. With an unnecessary affection of impartiality he observed that 'if these charges were made against a man who was innocent, they were most shameful'. But 'if they were true', he went on, 'the sharpest vengeance of the law ought to be inflicted on the minion who had so poured poison into the ear of his sovereign'.

The charges had nothing whatever to do with the ear of the sovereign. They concerned Suffolk Street and the land on the collateral cut in Regent's Park. In the former case Davies said that the transactions between Nash and Edwards (outlined in Chapter 10) had been a mere juggle, and that Nash had made immense profits out of the land purchased at his own valuation. The second charge proceeded on similar lines. Nash, he said, had taken land at a price far below what could have been obtained in the open market. Davies gave notice that he would move for a select committee.

There were, however, certain people in the House who had informed themselves of the real circumstances. The Chancellor of the Exchequer pointed out that the Suffolk Street property was taken on a valuation checked and modified by John Shaw, a highly esteemed surveyor. But Davies would allow no efficacy to this; Shaw, he said, was not even paid for his opinion and had evidently got his figures from Nash.

Charles Arbuthnot, a former First Commissioner of Woods and Forests and a client of Nash's, gave the lie to the whole story. 'Whatever faults Mr Nash might possess, he was quite sure that if there was one man less likely than another to lead himself to a fraudulent transaction, Mr Nash was that man.' William Huskisson, another sometime First Commissioner and client, was equally emphatic.

Then Sir Joseph Yorke, a genial sailor who knew nothing about Nash or his works, got up to give, as he said, 'a square view of the case'. The 'square view' led up to an assertion that 'all were agreed that this said Nash was a most suspicious character'. A few more speeches followed and the debate wound up with some remarks from Henry Baring, who, like Huskisson and Arbuthnot, lived in a Nash house in Carlton Gardens. Baring offered an oblique defence of his architect. 'From what he had heard of Mr Nash, he should be inclined to think that he was incapable of dishonesty; but he must say, that, as a manager of the public money and as an exhibitor of taste, he was sorry the public ever had anything to do with him.'

Davies carried his motion on 27 May. No time was lost, and three days later the Select Committee sat to take evidence. A Mr C. E. Rumbold was in the chair; Lord Lowther, the First Commissioner of Woods and Forests, Mr Arbuthnot, and others formed the committee. The proceedings lasted for ten days and twenty-five witnesses were examined.

One of the chief witnesses was, of course, John Edwards. He emerges from the verbatim reports as a frank and amiable man, delighted to talk about his business interests and to tell the committee everything they wanted to know and perhaps, indeed, a little more. He informed them that in the course of his life he had had a great deal to do with ground and ground-rents and had been very successful.

As to his dealings with Nash he was happy to give the Committee the minutest particulars. He was, he said, in the habit of taking his family to Wales in June and did so in 1820, soon after his application for the Suffolk Street sites had been accepted. Then, in December, he took the family abroad, asking Nash to look after things in his absence, which Nash 'most readily and kindly' undertook to do. Returning in June 1821 he was disappointed to learn that there were no takers for the land. However, towards the end of the year application came in from two clubs and two or three individuals, none of whom were speculative builders requiring loans; Edwards told the Committee:

> In January 1822 Mr Nash came to my house in Buckinghamshire. I expressed myself delighted that I had no occasion to advance money to builders and that it had gone off so well: He said 'Yes, but you must advance money [on the sites not yet applied for] if you mean to realize your speculation, and the only way is to cover the ground as rapidly as you can by building on it. I said, 'Mr Nash, that is not my view of the thing; I never meant to be a builder.' My wife came in at that time and she listened to the conversation between us, and she said, 'for God's sake, Edwards, do not have anything to do with building' and Mr Nash said 'I assure you I would not on any account propose that he should do anything I would not do myself,' and, said he, 'If you do not like the concern I will take it off your hands.' Said I, 'It is now afloat completely, and it will be a good thing.' 'Yes,' said he, 'it will, but I mean to lay out a large sum of money, to make it a good thing in building, which you will not do.' Said I, 'What will you give me for it?' He said, 'I will tell you what; I will give you £4,500 for it.' He made that offer with all the warmth of heart and in the liberal way in which he does everything and I said, 'Most readily I accept'.[36]

It was at that time that the two cousins were building their houses in Regent Street. Nash was conducting the work and the cost was to be shared. The £4,500 was debited to Nash on that account.

Other witnesses called before the Committee included Alexander Milne, the secretary to the Commissioners of Woods, Shaw, the surveyor, who explained that he and Nash were 'not on speaking terms' at the time of the complicity alleged by Davies, and a variety of architects, surveyors and leaseholders connected with the Suffolk Street buildings.

Nash himself was not called. He read the proceedings in the newspapers.[37] He had made a good impression by agitating for an inquiry as soon as Davies had launched his attack, and as the evidence accumulated it became more and more difficult for his integrity to be impugned. Certainly there were one or two awkward features. One was the absence of correspondence between him and Edwards; but this was plausibly explained, since they were relatives and in any case lived next door to each other. And there was a question of erroneous measurement along the Pall Mall boundary; but this carried little weight when it was proved that no financial gain or loss could have accrued to anyone, even in the unlikely event of the error remaining undiscovered.

The charges relating to the Regents Canal basin were easily disposed of. Lord Macclesfield, chairman of the Canal company, related how, when the company was in severe difficulties over letting – or rather, not letting – the land, Nash had suddenly announced at a meeting, 'I will take it myself.' Which he did, to the directors' great relief and his own considerable disadvantage.

The committee presented a report in which Nash was entirely exonerated on every charge. But they added a rider suggesting that it would be as well if official architects were prevented from interesting themselves in property for which they might be called upon to give a valuation.

The Select Committee brought their report to the Bar of the House on 19 June.[38] Davies was mortified and indignant. The evidence, he said, had been misinterpreted and he himself stood 'criminated as a false accuser'. He threatened to bring up the subject in the following session. After a short debate during which strangers were excluded, Sir Joseph Yorke rose once more to review the situation. He accepted the committee's verdict, but considered that Nash was 'excessively anxious to amass a fortune for his posterity,' whatever that might mean. 'He was certainly a great speculator,' Sir Joseph continued, 'for his extreme age had not prevented him placing a great stake on the event of this speculation, although hastening rapidly to "that bourne from whence no traveller returns".'

No sooner was the report published than Nash printed and circulated a further vigorous defence of his conduct, not only in the affairs which had been before Parliament but throughout his career.[39] 'I am anxious,' he wrote, 'to go beyond a mere acquittal of the charges or insinuations brought against me by Colonel Davies, . . . and to show the motives which induced me to embark personally, not only in the concerns which have already formed matter of investigation, but in every other transaction connected with the Crown property in which I have been induced to engage.'

Reviewing the conclusions of the Select Committee, he manages to get in a few hard thrusts at the Honourable Member for Worcester. Then he describes the circumstances of the building of Regent Street and recalls to what extent of personal risk the 'hope of the fulfilment of a favourite design' induced him to go. Finally he lays before the reader a frank admission that, while 'claiming no greater dislike for fair emolument' than his professional brethren, he nevertheless has been ruled all along by a passion for seeing his own designs carried out. The last paragraph runs:

> I admit that the anxiety to complete my designs, which has induced me at various times to incur an uncalled-for degree of personal responsibility, may require some explanation. I therefore readily and cheerfully give it; and if my friends are as well satisfied with my justification on these later matters as they declare themselves to have been by the unqualified acquital of the Parliamentary Committee touching the former ones, my object is attained. I may perhaps be excused for trespassing upon their time in endeavouring to shew the difference between a zealous, – I will say enthusiastic, – affection for my profession, united to an ernest desire to complete the plans in progress for the improvement of the metropolis; and a grasping anxiety for unfair emoluments with which I have been so unjustly charged.

That Nash's friends were completely assured of his integrity cannot be doubted. The pages of his diaries bear witness to the esteem in which he was held by people of every kind: people as different as Waterloo veterans, promising young lawyers and successful painters, none of whom would have cared to mix in the society of one who was not acquitted by common consent as well as by parliamentary finding. As for the King, he felt a deep resentment that a protégé of his should be persecuted as a public enemy and a probable rogue; and as soon as the committee's findings were known he proposed to set a royal seal of approval on the acquittal by making Nash a baronet. He wrote to his Prime Minister accordingly:[40]

ROYAL LODGE, 14th June, 1829

MY DEAR FRIEND,

I now write to you upon a matter in which I feel very much interested. The Report of the Committee of the House of Commons upon Mr Nash's business has been delivered in, and as I am informed by one of that Committee (not one of those who had any previous predilection towards him) '*without the slightest stain or imputation upon or against his character,*' I do therefore desire that you will direct his being *gazetted by himself* on *Tuesday next, the 16th of this month*, as a Baronet, with the remainder at his death (as he, Nash, has no family of his own,) to his nephew Mr Edwards, a gentleman of excellent character, large property, who sat in the last Parliament, and who has proved himself a thorough supporter of government, and a most *loyal man*, besides being well known to *me personally*. Mr Nash has been most infamously used, and there is but one opinion about it; and therefore it is not only an act of justice to *him* but to *my own dignity*, that *this* should *forthwith* be *done*. For if those who go through the furnace for *me* and for *my service, are not protected*, the *favour* of the *Sovereign becomes worse than nugatory*.

Your very sincere friend
G.R.

The Duke of Wellington was not a man to be hustled by a royal command, however peremptory, into doing something of which he disapproved. And he disapproved strongly of a baronetcy for Nash. His reply was firm. The report of the committee, he said, had not yet been before the House, and he concluded that His Majesty 'would not wish to confer an honour upon an individual while his conduct is, as far as the public knows, still under inquiry'. And, by way of postponing the event still further, he suggested that the completion of Buckingham Palace was the proper moment for the honour:[41]

> Mr Nash has now charge of the great works being carried on at Buckingham House which will not be finished as far as he is concerned till Christmas next. They will come under the discussion of Parliament more than once and I cannot but be apprehensive that your Majesty would expose your Government, and even Mr Nash himself, to much additional observation and inconvenience if your Majesty were to confer upon that gentleman any mark of your Majesty's favour until the great work were finished and Mr Nash should have closed and passed his accounts.

Wellington sent the King's letter on to Sir William Knighton, the royal secretary, with further observations on the subject. There were, he said, a hundred men, in the navy, the army and the civil service, with better claims. To grant a hereditary title to an architect, with remainder to a retired attorney whose son was now in the father's business, would create fierce resentment. It would harm the government and harm the King.[42]

The Duke had his way. He was the only man to whose rule the sovereign invariably submitted. So Mr Nash's honour was not gazetted and Mr Nash he remained.

13

The Clouded Years: the End

Vindicated by Parliament, his accusers humiliated, his sovereign radiating gratitude and esteem, Nash seemed to stand in 1829 at a summit of success. There he might have stood and stayed but for the calamitous state of affairs at Buckingham Palace. As the Duke of Wellington knew, as Goulburn at the Treasury knew and as a great many others suspected, expenditure in that quarter had become utterly out of hand. Nothing, in the long run, could save its architect from exposure as a grossly negligent if not downright dishonest servant of the Crown. It was a matter of time; and time, in this affair, meant the rapidly shrinking lifespan of George IV.

In May 1829, while the horizon was still relatively unclouded, we have a glimpse of Nash at his Regent Street house. It is preserved for us in a letter written by the wife of a young novelist, Edward Bulwer, the future Lord Lytton. The Bulwers were looking for a London house and one that came to their notice was 29 Dover Street. Nash had left it when he moved to Regent Street in 1823; it was then let or leased by him to a tenant who promptly went bankrupt and was now empty.[1] The Bulwers fancied it. Edward Bulwer had bargained with the architect but without much success. Mrs Bulwer takes up the story:

> Edward wanted him, before we took it, to alter the outside, enlarge the library, make a bathroom and another window to the Boudoir, for all which £500 a year instead of four, the original rent – which for an unfurnished house is high, let the house be ever so fine; but Nash being very obstinate I went with Edward the morning I left town to see if both together we could manage him better. We found that worthy sitting in his own splendid library, or rather gallery, which is half a mile long and done in mosaic [sic] in imitation of the Vatican at Rome. What Edward proposed was to give him

£500 for the first five years and £450 after, but Nash was more obstinate than ever – declaring with an oath that he would not abate a farthing, and then changed the subject altogether. At last he said suddenly – 'Pray, Sir, are you any relation to that very wonderful young man who wrote that delightful novel Pelham?'. 'Allow me, Mr Nash,' said I, to introduce you to that very wonderful young man, *in propria persona*. Upon which Nash got up and made him a low bow, saying, 'Well, then, Sir, for Pelham's sake, you must have the house on your own terms, and I'll make it one of the handsomest houses in town for you, with the best library; and if you ever again write anything half as good as Pelham, I shall be proud to think that I planned the room you wrote it in.' After this fine speech he offered him castes from all his statues, showed us all over his house, or rather Palace, and finished by throwing open the doors of another suite of rooms in which Mrs Nash sat ensconced, saying 'My dear, I have brought you the author of Pelham and his wife for you to look at,' upon which we put out our paws, wagged our tongues (in default of tails) and walked to and fro in the most docile manner possible to be stared at as the first Pelham and Pelhamess who had ever been caught alive in this country. At this juncture of affairs old Nash began fumbling in his pockets (which he has a great trick of doing). 'Oh, never mind,' said I, 'paying now I'll take the bronze chimney-piece to my Boudoir instead,' 'Very well,' said he, laughing, 'so you shall – and anything else you like.' Well, will you believe it after all this he has gone back and wants to screw us down for a continuance of the £500 a year. I do hope that, much as Edward likes the house, he will have nothing more to do with it.[2]

Nor did he; a few days later the Bulwers decided on a house in Hertford Street.
Pelham, Bulwer's first novel, combines the elements of a thriller with some rather ornate satire on contemporary manners, a sketch *sous clef* of Beau Brummel in retirement at Calais, and disquisitions on literature, politics and life in general as seen by a young dandy of the 1820s. Bulwer followed it in 1830 with *Paul Clifford*. There we find a satirical interlude at the 'flash public-house' kept by Gentleman George, one of whose intimates is 'one confounded dog of a bricklayer who runs him up terrible bills – a fellow called "Cunning Nat", who is equally adroit in spoiling ground and improving *ground rent*.'[3] The broken promise was avenged.

In the middle of January 1830 Sir Thomas Lawrence, President of the Royal Academy and the most applauded portrait-painter of his time, died. Nash had sat to him at various times between 1825 and 1827 for the portrait commissioned by Jesus College, Oxford, in recognition of his help in some negotiations about College property at the south end of the new London Bridge.[4] It was exhibited at the Royal Academy in the latter year. He had also obtained from Lawrence, with royal permission, a portrait of George IV for the gallery at 14 Regent Street, a portrait in which the King sits very alertly on a sofa as if suddenly diverted from the inspection of designs for the Brighton Pavilion which lie beside him.[5]

Lawrence was buried in St Paul's Cathedral on 21 January. There was a great assembly in the ice-cold cathedral. Nash was there. Soon afterwards he fell ill. He described the trouble, many months later, as 'a sudden rush of blood to the head, occasioned, as the physicians say, by standing on the marble pavement in St. Paul's cathedral . . . the effect of which was, at first, privation of sight, and ever since, pain and giddiness in the head.'[6] From this attack, presumably some kind of stroke, Nash never wholly recovered.

For a great part of 1830 he seems to have been more or less incapacitated. Much of his time was spent at East Cowes, while Pennethorne and Browne, his managing clerk, looked after the office and supervised the ornamental works then in full tide at the Palace. How much either of them knew about the money side of it and the long and intricate history of the estimates we may wonder. In April Nash received a letter from John Stewart, Assistant Secretary at the Treasury, demanding an explanation of expenditures in excess of the final estimate he had given to the Chancellor in May 1829. For nearly six months the letter lay unanswered. In the course of that time a blow fell from which Nash's public reputation never recovered and which cast an impenetrable shadow over his private life. This was the death of George IV.

The King's death at Windsor Castle on 26 June removed Nash's last bulwark against abusive Whigs in the Commons and nagging officials in the Treasury. It also removed – and this was far more bitter – any surviving hope that the baronetcy proposed just a year before but postponed by the obstinacy of the Duke of Wellington would ever be gazetted. The prospect of that honour had sunk deep into Nash's imagination. He craved it, not for the mere pomp of being 'Sir John' for his few remaining years but because of the deep satisfaction it offered of becoming, by the remaindering of the honour to the Edwards line, the founder of a titled family. So compulsive was the desire, once established, that when he heard that the King's condition was critical he took up his pen and wrote to the Royal secretary, his friend Sir William Knighton. It was a difficult letter to write, for its purport, crudely stated, was to enlist Knighton's help in extracting from the dying monarch a definitive act of creation. The letter is, indeed, clouded with embarrassment and feverishly ungrammatical. It never comes to the point, though to Knighton the point would be inescapable. The crucial part of the letter, which no scheme of punctuation would exempt from disorder, runs as follows:

> I will hope that in distinguishing between the grovelling feeling of selfishness and desire to raise to a flame the spark kindled by my dear Sovereign and which has become essential to my welfare seeing that HM empowered me to communicate His gracious purpose to Mr Edwards of including him – you well know what were my sentiments on the subject of honours which must

have ended with my life but when those honours were to be extended to my only relative a new scheme of life presented itself and I viewed myself as the founder of a family with honours that it became my duty to endeavour to perpetuate & my whole scheme of life as regarded the few years I have to live became changed.[7]

The letter concludes with a request for an appointment with Knighton at the following weekend. And there is a postscript, which the writer's state of emotional exhaustion as well as his state of health renders entirely understandable: 'I am quite giddy'. It was all in vain. No *fiat* issued from the royal death-bed and whatever 'new scheme of life' Nash was planning was brought to nothing.

By September, however, his health had improved and he was wrestling with the problem of the palace estimates. Replying, at long last, on 29 September, to the Treasury's challenge of 6 April, he was obliged to confess that there was a total excess of £46,000 on the estimate of May 1829.[8] He enclosed a series of statements which, while they served to explain the various directions in which the excesses had occurred, did nothing to explain *why* they had occurred, which was what the Treasury wanted to know. There was nothing in this communication which the Treasury could accept. It was now clear to them that Nash had incurred expenditure on a large scale without authority, in defiance of repeated warnings and in spite of his own assurances. So far as the Treasury was concerned this was the end of the road and on 15 September their Lordships issued a minute, summarising their conclusions and conveying their orders in the following terms:

> Upon the whole . . . My Lords see in the papers before them no justification of Mr Nash's conduct. The estimate submitted to and sanctioned by Parliament, has been exceeded to a large amount; the progress of such excess has been concealed from My Lords, and their earlier interposition therefore prevented. My Lords feel it incumbent upon them to mark their sense of such conduct by every means in their power. My Lords have already directed Mr Nash's commission to be withdrawn. They are therefore pleased to direct, that a case be submitted without delay to the Attorney and Solicitor-General, for their opinion how far Mr Nash is, under all the circumstances, pecuniarily liable for the whole or any part of the expense incurred in defiance of the orders of My Lords. My Lords are further pleased to suspend Mr Nash from the office held by him of Architect to the Board of Works.[9]

The Minute further directed that work at Buckingham Palace should be immediately stopped and the tradesmen's bills be paid up to date.

Nash's dismissal from the Board of Works was communicated to him in a curt letter of 22 October from Colonel Stephenson, the Surveyor-General. On 26 October he wrote to the Treasury expressing 'Very great surprise and sorrow' at his dismissal. 'I am entirely ignorant of the cause which has induced Your Lordships to direct such a step to be taken,' he wrote, and begged to be supplied with a copy of the Minute of 15 October.[10] Having seen the document he wrote to Stewart of the Treasury stating and elaborating the two main causes of the excessive expenditure. The first was, quite simply, 'the express commands of his late Majesty'. The second was that he had been prevented from exercising his own judgement in the mode of contracting. He had been compelled to follow the Board's system of contract by prices and measurement until 1828, by which time two-thirds of the building was complete. Only then had he been at liberty to make contracts in gross, his preferred method.[11]

Neither of these excuses was of the slightest avail. As to the first, Nash had given an undertaking in 1828 to put nothing in hand without Treasury sanction. His position here was certainly very delicate, perhaps more so than his accusers ever allowed. When George IV gave an order he expected it to be obeyed and there were occasions when, as Nash told Stewart, there appeared no course open to him but that of implicit obedience. Perhaps what made the situation peculiarly sensitive was Nash's very real personal devotion to the King, which forbade any sort of shuffling behind his back. Coupled with this was, no doubt, a conviction that under the sovereign's personal patronage he was, in the last resort, invulnerable. To indict Nash during George IV's lifetime would certainly have been difficult. Now, after his death, it was all too easy.

In the matter of the contracting systems Nash had no real case. He was no doubt right in his claim that contracting in gross was more economical than the older method; but most of the excesses of which his critics complained had been incurred after 1828 and it was not really possible to spread the blame retrospectively to conditions, however unsatisfactory, prevailing before that date.

In November 1830 Wellington's ministry fell and a Whig government came in, headed by Lord Grey, with Lord Althorp at the Treasury. Obviously the Palace affair would have to come before Parliament and in February Althorp moved for a Select Committee. On 3 March it began to sit, under the chairmanship of Robert Gordon. Nash, with Pennethorne and Browne to help him, was the first to give evidence. He was examined again on 10 March. He was not, on this occasion, a very satisfactory witness, his answers to questions showing a tendency, not wholly involuntary, to miss by a subtle margin the point at issue. There were five further sessions in March, one in April and one in July, at which evidence was given by tradesmen, architects, engineers and administrators.

The committee was concerned not only with the history of the successive estimates but with the whole conduct of the work, including the supply of materials and the structural stability of the building. It was well-known that Nash himself owned brick-kilns near Southall and had supplied more bricks for the palace than anybody else. The committee inquired into the possibility of pressure having been exerted to use the architect's bricks. Several tradesmen admitted having bought the bricks (at a slightly higher price than others) in the expectation of favours in return, but no trace of such favours was admitted or discovered.[12]

The question of structural defects in the completed building was altogether more formidable. The first hint of such deficiencies seems to have been given by William Whitehead, a master-bricklayer, who suggested that the walls of the rounded bay towards the garden, which he was building, were not strong enough to carry the dome. On his suggestion they were strengthened and the dome modified but rumours of instability persisted and the select committee felt it necessary to appoint a special committee of architects to go thoroughly into the matter and prepare a report. The committee consisted, inevitably, of Nash's former colleagues, Soane and Smirke, to whom were added Wyatville and H. H. Seward, the assistant Surveyor-General. They, in their turn, found themselves in considerable difficulties because of what they called 'the extensive and very peculiar use of iron'.[13] As the building was both structurally and decoratively complete the iron elements were not easily inspected and the drawings supplied by Nash's office were far from adequate. Moreover the behaviour of iron was a subject on which few architects would care to give a confident opinion and they therefore shifted the responsibility on to three expert advisers, George Rennie and John U. Rastrick, both engineers, and Joseph Bramah, a well-known founder. Each made his own report, based on such evidence as could be gathered without actually pulling the palace to pieces and testing deflections *in situ*. Rastrick's report was the most critical and, according to him, there was hardly a piece of iron in the building which could be relied upon. He referred to Nash as 'an ignorant person' and made particular game of the iron 'cradles', introduced under segmental arches, which he said merely negatived the effect of the arch as such without contributing any other useful function. Rennie and Bramah were more cautious in their condemnations but all agreed that it would not be prudent to occupy the palace until the floors of certain of the first-floor rooms had been subject to tests.

Some of the girders were, in fact, tested and, fortunately, proved entirely satisfactory. Nash triumphantly mocked the theoretical condemnation of others. 'All admit,' he wrote, 'that the iron which they have thought proper to try has withstood the test, and yet they *doubt* and *apprehend*.' The Committee were taking no risks and proposed various devices for 'securing' the building. This goaded Nash to an infuriated outburst:

> It must be obvious to every one that the arrangement of the Plan and the Elevations of a Design have their origin in the *conveniences required,* and the *taste* of the Proprietor; and that it is the *province of the Architect to find the* MEANS of carrying them into effect; *thence* arose the construction in question; and it must be evident that if I had not had recourse to it, *I could not have given His Majesty the room he required*; the question I presume is, simply, whether the construction I have adopted renders the Building insecure; at present there are no appearances of weakness of any kind; they *insinuate*

weaknesses, but they *prove* none; nor *can they show any*, or *prove* that any additional security is required. I have said that none is required, and that the Building is in every part perfectly secure; *and I call upon them to make any fair or just experiments they may think proper to justify the opinions they have given*; at present every part of their Report is founded on *conjecture*, on *opinions merely* ASSERTED, not PROVED: or where attempted to be founded on facts, *the facts* STATED *are* NOT BORNE OUT.[14]

Nash tried to persuade the committee to apply the one obvious and ultimate test, which was to pack every floor of the building with soldiers and watch the result, temporary strutting being introduced to allay the apprehensions of the doubters. But they ignored the suggestion. They were unhappy about Nash's handling of the iron from beginning to end. The contract for it had been loosely handled without fair competition open to the trade. The main contractors, R. & W. Crawshay, had sub-contracted to a founder in Staffordshire who went bankrupt, and left for America, and Crawshays could give no firm assurances about testing. The actual merits or demerits of Nash's ironwork at the palace remain obscure to this day. He had, as he declared himself, been one of the pioneers of cast-iron construction but his use of it was wholly empirical and, by the 1820s, probably old-fashioned.

The findings of the Select Committee were laid before Parliament on 14 October 1831. Nash was blamed for the gross inaccuracies of his estimate of May 1829 and for making improvident contracts with tradesmen, notably with Crawshays for the ironwork. The committee considered it improper that an architect should sell his own materials to tradesmen although they found that in this particular instance the public had sustained no loss in the transaction. They criticised the ambiguous arrangements which Nash had made with a marble contractor, Joseph Browne, whom he had despatched to Italy to obtain a supply of Ravaccione marble for the Marble Arch without making it clear to him that he was acting merely as an agent and not as the contractor for the work.

The committee concurred with the criticisms contained in the Treasury Minute of 15 October 1830, except that they could find no proof that Nash had wilfully concealed the excesses of the estimate from the Treasury. Moreover, while they charged Nash with 'inexcusable irregularity and great negligence', they took the view that successive governments had also been to blame for not informing themselves more exactly about the estimates which they brought before Parliament. These findings took some of the rigour out of the Treasury's indictment. They showed that, in spite of everything, there was more of negligence than knavery in Nash's behaviour and that any pecuniary liability would be difficult to establish. Of the threat of prosecution no more was heard.[15]

Finally, the committee reported that they had taken the advice of Edward Blore, an architect hitherto unconnected with Royal works, as to the feasibility of completing the palace for the use of the new sovereign, William IV, and his consort. Blore had given a rough estimate of £75,000. In November the Treasury ordered the completion of

Nash's work and committed the alteration of the building to Blore, the ultimate responsibility being at the same time moved from the Office of Works and given to the chief Commissioner of Woods, Lord Duncannon.[16]

The cost of converting Buckingham House into Buckingham Palace, estimated in 1826 at £252,690, had increased to £331,973 in 1827, to £432,926 in 1828 and to £496,169 in 1829, and now stood at £613,269, exclusive of the alterations contemplated. These involved substantial modifications of Nash's design, Blore removing the dome and the box-like tops of the pavilions, filling in the spaces between the centre part of the garden front and the north and south pavilions and adding a continuous attic. To say that he spoilt the garden front might be to accord more merit to Nash's design than it deserved; what he certainly did was to remove whatever was idiosyncratic and picturesque. It was not till 1847 that he made the most devastating alteration of all, which was to close the courtyard with a new block on the east, dismissing the Marble Arch to somewhere near its present site and shutting off the whole of Nash's palace from public view.[17]

So far as the public was concerned, Blore's frontispiece relegated Nash to a pre-Victorian limbo, but in fact the Nash story was not quite finished. In 1852 one further addition was made to the Palace – the great ballroom at the Pimlico end. The commission for this was given to James Pennethorne. In 1830 he had been Nash's assistant. Now, twenty-two years later, he was the government's chief architect. It must have been a curious experience for him to pick up the themes of the sad old Georgian story and re-orchestrate them in a Victorian and Albertian epilogue. But this he did with complete confidence. His classical ballroom was still the classicism of Nash, but refined and enriched with an expertise and sensibility entirely his own.[18]

Pennethorne's ballroom remains (though altered in 1902), but Blore's eastern block does not. Built, rather unwisely, of Caen stone, it soon began to disintegrate and by the turn of the century was an eyesore. In 1911 its rebuilding was undertaken as part of the Queen Victoria Memorial and Sir Aston Webb closed the architectural history of the Palace with the impeccably grand, unsmiling frontispiece we all know.

Buckingham Palace, as completed by Nash in 1830, was not an architectural success, but neither was it a total failure. It contained some noble ideas; the trouble was their hasty and superficial interpretation. The constraints of the old Buckingham carcase may have been partly to blame. The scale of the old house was that of a country gentleman's residence, not that of a metropolitan palace; and the one does not become the other by a mere application of porticos and pilasters, statues and trophies. Nor, it must be admitted, was Nash's genius really of the kind to evoke the eloquence of the classical language in a composition requiring scholarly resource and deep concentration.

With so many weaknesses in the architecture and so much scandal in the administration it was inevitable that the palace should become an object of universal contempt. Creevey pronounced it 'the Devil's own' in 1828 and, after a tour of inspection in 1835, suggested that 'instead of being called 'Buckingham Palace' it should be the 'Brunswick Hotel'.[19] In 1830 a certain I. Hume issued an illustrated doggerel called 'The House that

N – built' with a picture of Nash squatting at the foot of the dome, licking his lips over a long bill.[20] Somebody else produced a lampoon in the form of 'a letter addressed by a French architect in London to his friend in Paris':

> De Buck-and-Ham Palace which is building for de English King in de spirit of John Bull plum-pudding and roast beef taste, for which de English are so famous . . . the name of de architect is Mistaire Hash, de King's architect. De palace, ven complete, will be called after von famous English dish, de Toad-in-de-Hole.[21]

Colonel Trench, the would-be improver of Thames side, seriously suggested in the House of Commons in 1831 that the palace should be given over to some other national purpose such as a national gallery or a record office and the saving thereby affected put towards the building of a worthy royal residence elsewhere.[22]

One periodical did indeed take a less contemptuous line. The May 1830 issue of *Fraser's Magazine* contained a long and intelligent appreciation of the building and its architect, written possibly by Allan Cunningham, whose biographies of the English architects have earned him respect among historians. Cunningham took the palace very seriously, as one of the major endeavours of its kind in Europe of the time. He defended its extravagance, believing that the encouragement of a school of artists and artificers by the building of a first-rate palace was no less beneficial to society than bounties to herring fisheries or the manufacturers of Irish linen. He praised Nash as a planner, especially (and very properly) commending the combination of hall, gallery and staircase on the ground floor. In describing the state rooms he was particularly struck by the design of the ceilings, attributing their Baroque character (as we should call it) to the influence of the Bibienas and confirming that in the Baroque touches Nash gave to his interiors he anticipated the Victorian revival of the style.[23]

During the years when the Palace was building Nash undertook few commissions elsewhere. In London he was mainly concerned with the future of the new square at Charing Cross, the West Strand improvements and the development of the Park Villages. At St James's Palace he built a house for the Duke of Clarence.[24] Outside London he provided a few gratuitous designs. One of these was for a monument to General Picton who was killed at Waterloo. It was to be erected at Carmarthen. The design was a small version of a project – one of several – for a vast Waterloo monument made about this time.[25] It consisted of a Greek Doric column on a massive base, supporting a statue of the General, and adorned with trophies and bas-reliefs. Begun in 1825, it was complete by 1828 and in that year Nash re-visited the town where so much of his early life had been spent. Now a celebrity, the Town Council presented him with an 'Honorary Gold Box laid in Oak' and engraved his name on the monument, describing him as 'our countryman' John Nash Esq. F.R.S., architect to the King'.[26] Nash was never a Fellow of the Royal Society and we must assume either that the inscription was added in his absence or that he turned a blind eye to save his hosts embarrassment. Although it cost £3,000, the monument did not survive for long and today a plain obelisk occupies the site.

After the gruelling experiences of 1831 Nash spent more and more time at East Cowes. In September 1831 the foundation-stone of the new church was laid by the twelve-year-old girl who, six years later, succeeded her uncle as Queen Victoria and was the first sovereign to hold court in Buckingham Palace.

For 1832 the diaries of both Nash and Pennethorne survive.[27] In Nash's diary the island entries reflect the social and sociable life in and around the castle: a vestry meeting at Shalfleet, an excursion to the Sandrock Hotel, trips to the farm at Hamstead where improvements were continuously in hand, a picnic at Carisbrooke and entertainments at the castle. Among the latter was a concert by Litolff, then a prodigy of fourteen, who came with his father in August: 'a first-rate pianist', wrote Nash.[28] Callers are noted almost daily and they include peers and a bishop, admirals, politicians, lawyers. The only architect to be received there in 1832 was C. R. Cockerell, for whom Nash, his father's fellow-pupil, had a special liking, not unreciprocated.

London entries record dinner-parties and theatres. Here are some characteristic extracts for March to May 1832, when the Nashes were living at 14 Regent Street:

> March 2. London – called at the office of woods and walked round to look at several of the new buildings – we dined at Mr. Vaughan's.
>
> March 12. London – drove up to the Regents Park and the Village with Mrs Nash – we dined with Mrs Fitzroy.
>
> March 13. London – drove down to Percy Cross to call upon Lord Ravensworth – the Vaughans, Lyons, Miss Tierney, Chas. Romilly and Genl. Carey dined with us.

Nash was never free from illness after his stroke in 1830. His doctor, probably the same Johnson who was physician to William IV, appears now and then – sometimes as a card companion.

> March 22. London – called on Dr. Johnson and was cupped – drove to the village – went to the play at the Adelphi – the Reform Bill passed the Commons by a majority of 110.

Here we seem to have a dinner party of lawyers and their wives:

> April 27 . . . the Herries, Pembertons, Vaughans, Lyons, Pollocks and Jones dined with us.[29]

And here is an entry reminding us that Nash was a foundation member of the Athenaeum:

May 18. London – called upon Lord Wenlock – read the Papers at the Athenaeum – went to Evans the booksellers – and in the Evening to the German opera – Lord Grey announced that he and his colleagues had resumed office.

Pennethorne's diary for the same year is more concerned with business, of which, however, there does not seem to have been an overwhelming amount. There are meetings with the plaster-worker, Bernasconi, about one of the florid pediments at Carlton House Terrace and with Blore about the Palace, meetings about the Ophthalmia building in Albany Street, still on Nash's hands, and about developments at the Park Villages. From time to time Pennethorne is summoned to East Cowes and takes the night mail, arriving for breakfast. He notes that on 24 May Mrs Vaughan (i.e. Mrs John Edwards Vaughan) gave a ball for 700 people, presumably in the great triple drawing-room at 16 Regent Street. Christmas 1832 he spent at East Cowes, leaving London on the 'Eclipse' coach, arriving at Southampton at 7.30 and sleeping at the Coach and Horses. In the morning he met 'Turner' (almost certainly J. M. W. Turner, who had been visiting at Petworth). They had a rough crossing, by steam, and spent the rest of the week at the castle where they were entertained on one evening by 'young Kean' (no doubt Charles John, the great tragedian's son). On New Year's Eve 'Mr G. Ward' (G. H. Ward) a prospective parliamentary candidate, came to dinner and was, says Pennethorne, 'violent on the Tory side'.

For 1833 and 1834 no diaries survive. The former year was marked by the sudden death in August, at the age of sixty-one, of John Edwards Vaughan, the man whom Nash had called his 'only relative' and who was certainly his oldest and closest friend. He died in his Regent Street house and was buried with his parents in the old burial ground at Lambeth on 15 August. It was perhaps the shock of losing this near kinsman and nearest neighbour which induced Nash to leave London in the following year. In 1834 14 Regent Street was stripped. The gallery was dismantled and removed, lock, stock and barrel, to East Cowes where it was rebuilt inside the long conservatory. At the same time Nash formally retired from practice. Not that there was much from which to retire. With his suspension from the Board of Works he had no public duties, and the Board had, in any case, ceased to exist, having been merged in 1832 with Woods, Forests and Land Revenues. With that office Nash's long association had come to a natural end. He wrote, nevertheless, on 22 March to its former secretary, Alexander Milne, now promoted to Second Commissioner for the united Offices, informing him that he had left London and that his practice was now in the hands of Pennethorne, whom he earnestly recommended to the commissioners' patronage.[30]

East Cowes was a place perfectly fitted for unruffled retirement. Unruffled, however, Nash's retirement was not. His debts had for long been a matter for speculation and gossip. As long before as 1821 Westall, the painter, had told Farington that reports had reached him 'from three different quarters' that Nash owed £800,000, if not a million, and was 'at a stand in money matters'.[31] This was soon after his major speculations in the Quadrant and the Regents Canal scheme. The figure is an absurd exaggeration. The fact that in the same year he found it 'inconvenient' to repay a debt of £800 to the Canal Company puts the scale of his liabilities into more realistic perspective.[32] Anyway, he was clearly not 'at a stand' and for the next ten years he was spending freely on his new house and its furnishings and on improvements at East Cowes. In 1833, however, there was a crisis. What exactly happened is not clear, but at the root of it seems to have been an unfortunate financial arrangement with one of the Wards.

At the beginning of 1833 Nash was in debt to the extent of between £16,000 and £17,000 to the banking firm of Vere, Sapt, Banbury and Co. of Lombard Street.[33] John Robert Ward, a son of his old friend, George Ward who had died in 1829, and younger brother of George Henry Ward, was a partner in the firm and it was through him that the loan had been arranged on easy terms with repayment over a long period. Unfortunately, however, John Ward met with financial disaster in 1833, whereupon he was dropped from the partnership and the firm pressed Nash for almost immediate repayment. To meet their demands he was obliged to sell real estate in a falling market at a sacrifice which he estimated at £4,000. Nevertheless, by July 1834 he had paid off all capital and interest except for a sum just short of £500 and this was amply secured by title deeds in the bankers' hands.

However, at this date Nash was under pressure from another quarter for a matter of £3,000. He therefore wrote to Vere, Sapt requesting a loan of this amount at 5 per cent to be repaid over three years. The security he offered was a rather curious one and suggests that he was being driven into a corner. He had, at some period, bought himself an annuity of £3,000 a year. He now offered Vere, Sapt power of attorney to receive this income, retaining £1,000 to liquidate the debt and handing over the remaining £2,000 to his account. In addition, in case he should not survive the three years, he offered to secure the loan against the real estate already mortgaged in connection with the earlier loan.

The result of this application does not emerge, and there is no further evidence of the nature and extent of Nash's embarrassments, except, indeed, a story handed down in the Pennethorne family, which casts a rather melancholy sidelight on the business. The story is that a substantial part of Nash's fortune vanished through the fraudulent act of a person whom Nash regarded as a friend and whom for that reason he declined to prosecute when the fraud was detected. The person concerned is supposed to have committed suicide.[34] This person may possibly have been John Robert Ward. Ward's 'defalcation' (the word used by Nash in his letter to Vere, Sapt) may have been fraudulent or it may not. Of Ward we know only that he died shortly before 10 April 1834 at the age of thirty-nine, leaving an unwitnessed will dated five years earlier when he had clearly been in a state of affluence.[35]

Ward's defalcation not only placed Nash in a critical situation in respect of the initial loan of something over £16,000 but (so Nash states in his letter) deprived him of an income of £2,000 a year from an unspecified source. What becomes obvious is that in 1834 Nash was extremely short of money. The reason can be stated in his own words: 'my capital was embarked in Houses, and in materials for Building, both of which, at the present epoch, were most difficult to turn into cash.'

In October Nash made a new will, evidently designed to meet his changed circumstances.[36] It was generally supposed that, after providing for Mrs Nash and Ann Pennethorne, he would leave everything to John Edwards' son, Nash Vaughan Edwards Vaughan. The will of 1833, however, leaves the whole of his estate absolutely to Mrs Nash, the intention being, no doubt, that whatever ill winds might blow after his own death she would have the maximum security available.[37] His annuity did not extend beyond his own life.

At the end of 1834 Nash was still tolerably well and active for a man of eighty-two. In the first three months of 1835 his diary (the second of the two which survive) records frequent business conferences with Charles Nixon, who seems at this time to have been his manager or agent, much as Morgan was in earlier days. He was perhaps a relative of William Nixon, his trusted clerk-of-works at Brighton and the Palace. Local affairs still engaged Nash's interest. On 12 January he went to Newport to attend the nomination of Sir Richard Simeon and G. H. Ward as candidates at the approaching election and three days later he was in Cowes before breakfast to vote for Ward (who was not returned). There were, as always, frequent callers. One was Sir George Seymour, William IV's Master of the Robes, who had inherited Norris Castle from his uncle, Lord Henry. Another was Lord Yarborough, the owner of Appuldurcombe. Another, a Mr Philipps, was presumably one of the Cwmgwili family. In February there was no clergyman to take duty at the little church and Nash signed a letter of remonstrance. A new curate, a Mr Baugh, turned up on 1 March and stayed at the castle till he found lodgings. John Pennethorne, James's younger brother, makes an appearance at the castle. He had lately returned from the middle east where, at Athens, he had been the first to notice the optical corrections in Greek architecture – a discovery comically remote from the ideas of Greek architecture entertained at East Cowes Castle.

Towards the end of March Nash was losing strength. Exercise was limited to a stroll along the conservatory. On 28 March he was 'very poorly and faint'. On the following day he transacted business for the last time. It was to execute the assignment of the Opthalmia to Sir Felix Booth.[38]

On 1 May John Wittet Lyon, Nash's solicitor, arrived, no doubt in response to an urgent summons. The diary, precise and orderly as ever, tells the rest.

> May 2. Cowes – Saw Mr Lyon and shook hands with him – sat up at night to have the bed made.
> May 3. Cowes – much the same as yesterday.

May 4. Cowes – took a little castor oil in the morning – sat up in the evening to have the bed made and to be shaved.

May 5. Cowes – not able to get out of bed without assistance. Sleepy all day. Mrs Nash ill.

May 6. Cowes – very ill indeed all day.

May 7. Cowes – very ill.

May 8. Cowes – very ill – no appetite.

May 9. Cowes – very ill.

May 10. Cowes – very ill.

May 11. Cowes – much worse.

Death came two days later.

The burial took place on 20 May 1835 in the churchyard at East Cowes. The coffin, it is said, was carried across the fields from the castle on the previous night because of a rumour that local creditors were planning to make the disagreeable gesture of 'arresting' the corpse.[39] A stone monument in the conventional form of a sarcophagus (Fig. 13) was built over the grave. It has an early Victorian look and was perhaps not placed till after 1851 when Mrs Nash's remains were laid with her husband's. The inscription records merely the names, dates of decease and ages of John Nash Esq., of East Cowes Castle, and Mary Ann Nash his wife. It is, to all appearances, the memorial, quite simply, of an island squire.

The executors named in Nash's will were Mrs Nash, George Henry Ward and James Pennethorne. They lost no time in converting some of the property into cash to satisfy the most urgent calls on the estate. The pictures from East Cowes Castle, which included three splendid works by Turner, painted in the island, two by West and copies of old masters by Richard Evans, were auctioned by Christie and Manson on 11 July, fetching £1,061.[40] The books, medals, drawings and engravings were sold by Evans, the bookseller, on 15 July and brought £1,423.[41] The land and castle of East Cowes were put on the market and sold within the year to the Earl of Shannon, whose heir had lately married the daughter of Sir George Seymour of Norris Castle. The reported figure was £20,000.[42] Of the total claims outstanding at this time we have no idea but the executors managed things pretty well, for on 29 December 1841 the following appeared among the titbits which helped to fill up the columns of *The Times*:

> BETTER LATE THAN NEVER. The executors of Mr John Nash, the architect of Regent Street, who died on the 13th. of May; 1835, at his castle in the Isle of Wight, have given notice of their being in a situation to pay his debts in full. We believe they amount to £15,000. Not bad Christmas news to those interested.[43]

13. The tomb of John Nash and his wife, East Cowes churchyard.

The Hamstead property was not sold. Mrs Nash moved there after the sale of the castle and she and Ann Pennethorne lived there for the rest of their days.

The death of the once famous architect did not pass unnoticed but informed and sympathetic tributes were rare indeed. Nash had faded from public view after George IV's death, an event in itself widely unregretted, and the last glimpse of him was disfigured by the shadows of parliamentary censure. The *Annual Register* bluntly recorded what many believed to be the truth: 'As a speculative builder, this gentleman amassed a large fortune; but as an architect he did not achieve anything that will confer upon him lasting reputation.'[44] Only one newspaper thought the subject worth serious and sensitive notice. This was *John Bull*, the satirical and, in earlier years, somewhat scurrilous, Tory paper, edited by Theodore Hook. The notice was evidently, from its editorial tone, written by Hook himself. He had probably known Nash since the Regency days, not only at Carlton House but at East Cowes where Hook's elder brother, as Rector of Whippingham, was the local parson.[45] In his article he stoutly defends Nash against his persecutors – 'certain political patriots, desirous of exhibiting their animosity against the late King'. Nash, he writes, was the loyal servant of a kind and generous master whom he never betrayed by justifying himself at his master's expense. Criticism of the structural stability of the palace had proved completely unfounded, as unfounded as the indictments of the architect's professional integrity in other circumstances. His architecture might or might not be wholly admirable – that was a matter of taste. But on what he had done for London there could be no two opinions:

> Let the readers recollect the huddled mass of wretched streets and houses which twenty years ago covered the site of Regent Street, the Quadrant and Waterloo Place; let the reader recollect the still more wretched courts and

alleys, dens of infamy and haunts of thieves, which maze-like spread themselves from St. Martin's Church to the neighbourhood of Covent Garden; let him now look upon the range of buildings and the handsome streets which occupy their places . . . Let the reader, we say, turn his eyes to that magnificent adjunct of London, the Regent's Park, now one of the healthiest and gayest of the public walks and drives, a creation of the mind of Mr Nash.

Hook then turned to Nash's love of the arts, praised his encouragement of artists and his own liberal patronage. Finally, of the man himself he wrote:

In private life Nash was a warm and sincere friend; his mind, active and comprehensive as it was, was singularly natural and simple; his conception was quick and clear; his thoughts were original, and his conversation was both instructive and pre-eminently agreeable. He was, in fact, a most extraordinary man.[46]

This is not only kind but true. 'Natural and simple' is right. In action, Nash could be devious and ruthless – a subtle, swift and dangerous warrior. But when action came to rest, there was this likeable, natural, humane, humorous, simple and sometimes even naive personality, which appealed strongly to people of many sorts and in many situations, from the throne downwards.

For twenty years after his death a dense blanket of indifference obscured Nash's memory. Then, on 18 May 1857, a meeting was held at the Royal Institute of British Architects. It was the occasion when a special medal was presented to James Pennethorne in acknowledgment of his successful completion of the west wing of Somerset House. In the speechmaking which followed, Nash was remembered as Pennethorne's master. The President, Earl de Grey, who had known him, spoke kindly of him. Mr William Tite, MP, said that although his architecture was 'anything but bold' (a curious observation) 'his style of dealing with the improvements of the metropolis was so, and deserved the gratitude of this generation'. Professor Cockerell recalled that Nash and his own father had both been pupils of Sir Robert Taylor and 'rejoiced to see the merit of that school acknowledged'. Nash, he said, was 'a courageous little man. It was a matter of regret that no biography of him had appeared'.[47]

1. John Nash. From a painting, probably by Richard Evans (in the possession of Major Allan Cameron of Lochiel).

2A.   Nos 17 Bloomsbury
Square and 68–71 Great Russell
Street, London, 1777–8. The
porch and attic storey were
added in 1860. (Photograph,
1935.)

2B.   Carmarthen Gaol,
1789–92. Demolished 1938. The
original entrance was in the
middle; the opening under the
right-hand arch is more recent.
(Photograph, 1933.)

3A. Hereford Gaol, 1792–6.
Demolished c. 1930.

3B. St David's Cathedral. The
west front, at the time of
Sir Gilbert Scott's restoration.
The photograph shows Nash's
work of 1791–2.

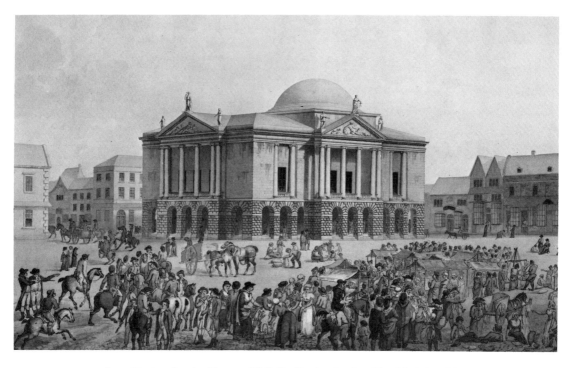

4A.   Design for the County Hall, Stafford, submitted by Nash in 1794
but not accepted.

4B.   The iron bridge at Stanford-on-Teme, Worcs., which collapsed
shortly after erection in 1795. Drawing in the collection of the Society
of Antiquaries, said to be after an original by Nash.

5A. Ffynone, Pembrokeshire, during the reconstruction of 1904.

5B. Llysnewydd, Cardiganshire, demolished c. 1970. (Photograph
c. 1870, before the later Victorian alterations.)

6A.   Hafod House, Cardiganshire, as remodelled and extended by Nash for Thomas Johnes, 1793. The view shows the octagon library and, on the right, the conservatory. Watercolour by an unidentified artist. (In the possession of Miss Anne Lloyd-Johnes.)

6B.   Castle House, Aberystwyth, built by Nash for Uvedale Price, c. 1796–7. Engraving by an unidentified artist (Victoria and Albert Museum).

7A and 7B.   Miniatures of Mary Anne Bradley and John Nash at about the time of their marriage in 1798. The miniature of Mrs Nash is attributed to Anne Mee. (In the possession of Mr Peter Laing.)

7C.   A conservatory for the Prince of Wales; probably the drawing exhibited by Nash in the Royal Academy exhibition, 1798. (Royal Library, Windsor Castle.)

NORTH FRONT.

CORSHAM HOUSE,
Wiltshire.

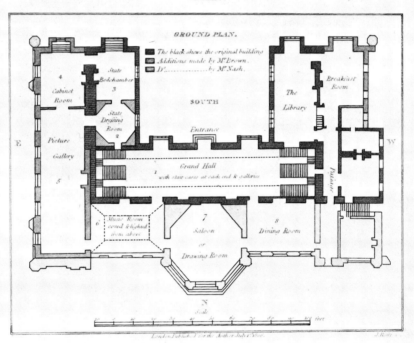

GROUND PLAN.

The black shows the original building
Additions made by Mr Brown
Dᵒ. . . . . by Mr Nash.

8. Corsham Court, Wiltshire, as remodelled for Paul Cobb Methuen in 1797–8. Nash's Grand Hall (shaded dark) is contained in the shell of the old building. The Music Room, octagon Saloon and Dining Room (shaded light) are additions by Nash in collaboration with John Adey Repton. (J. Britton, *Historical Account of Corsham*, 1806.)

Drawn by J.P.Neale.   Engraved by T.Higham

9.   Corsham, Wiltshire, the Grand Hall. The iron supports to the
galleries and the balustrades were made at Coalbrookdale. Engraving by
T. Higham after J. P. Neale.

10A.   Southgate Grove, Middlesex, built for Walker Gray, 1797; the
north front. (G. Richardson, *New Vitruvius Britannicus*, 1802.)

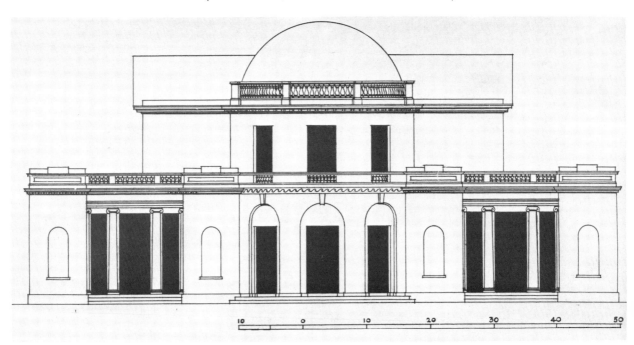

10B.   Casina, Dulwich, built for Richard Shawe, 1797. Demolished
1906. The south-east elevation, redrawn from an original among the
Repton drawings in the RIBA collection.

11A. Downton Castle, Herefordshire. Engraving by J. Powell after
T. Hearne, 1801.

11B. Luscombe Castle, Devon, built for Charles Hoare, 1800–4; view
from the east. Engraving by I. Smith in T. H. Williams, *Picturesque
Excursions in Devonshire: the Environs of Exeter*, 1815.

12A. Cronkhill, near Shrewsbury, built for Francis Walford, c. 1802 (NMR).

12B. Longner Hall, Salop., built for Robert Burton, c. 1805. Drawing preserved at Longner (NMR).

13. Longner Hall, Shropshire; the staircase (NMR).

14A.   Killymoon Castle, Co. Tyrone, built for Col. William Stewart,
c. 1801–3. Drawing in G. S. Repton's sketch-book (RIBA).

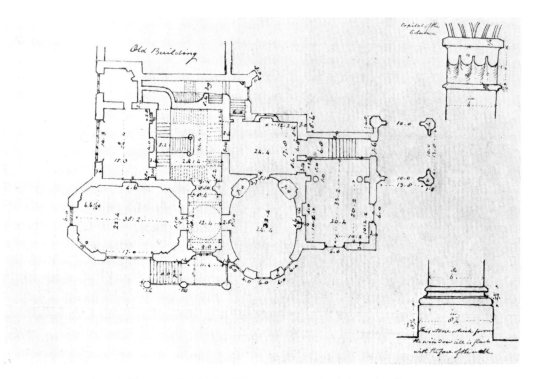

14B.   Killymoon Castle, Co. Tyrone; plan and window details.
Drawing in G. S. Repton's sketch-book (RIBA).

15A. Aqualate Hall, Staffordshire, enlarged for Sir John F. Boughey, Bt., 1808. View from south-west. Destroyed by fire, 1910. (Victoria and Albert Museum.)

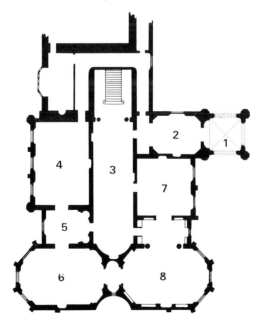

15B. Aqualate Hall, Staffordshire. Plan from G. S. Repton's sketch-book (Brighton Art Gallery).

1. Porch
2. Hall
3. Gallery
4. Dining-room
5. Ante-room
6. Drawing-room
7. Study
8. Library

16. Caerhays Castle, Cornwall, built for J. B. Trevanion, c. 1808. View from south-east.

17A. Childwall Hall, Lancashire, built for Bamber Gascoyne,
1806–13; view from south-east. Demolished 1949. (Photograph, 1933.)

17B. West Grinstead Park, built for Walter Burrell, c. 1809. Drawing
in G. S. Repton's sketch-book (Brighton Art Gallery).

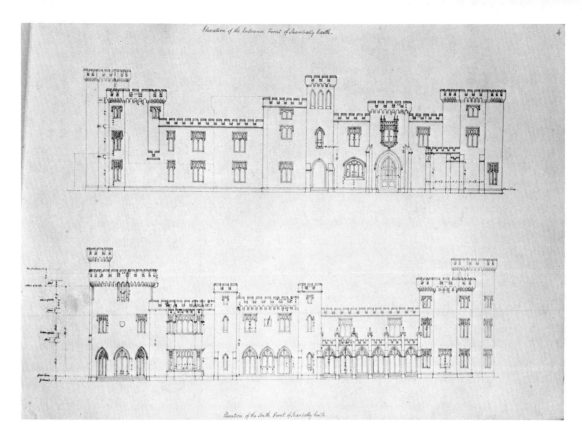

Elevation of the South Front of Shanbally Castle

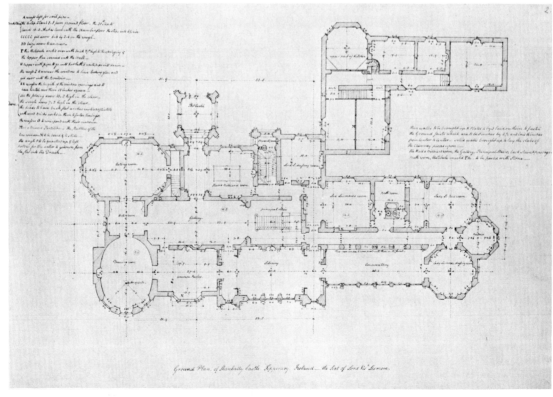

Ground Plan of Shanbally Castle Tipperary Ireland the Seat of Lord Vt Lismore

18A and 18B. Shanbally Castle, built from designs by Nash for
Viscount Lismore, 1818–19. Demolished 1960. Plan and elevations in
G. S. Repton's sketch-book (RIBA).

19A.   Rockingham House, Co. Roscommon, built for Viscount Lorton,
1810. Destroyed by fire, 1957. Drawing in the author's possession.

19B.   Witley Court, Worcestershire. Built for Lord Foley, c. 1810.
(Drawing in RIBA.)

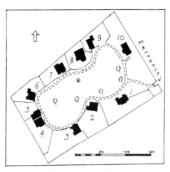

20A. Blaise Hamlet, Bristol. Site plan.

Cottage No. 1

Cottage No. 2

Cottage No. 3

Cottages Nos 4 and 5

Cottage No. 6

Cottage No. 7

Cottage No. 8

20B. Cottages at Blaise Hamlet, Bristol, built for John Scandrett
Harford, 1811. Lithographs by Joseph Horner (RIBA).

Cottage No. 9

Cottage No. 10

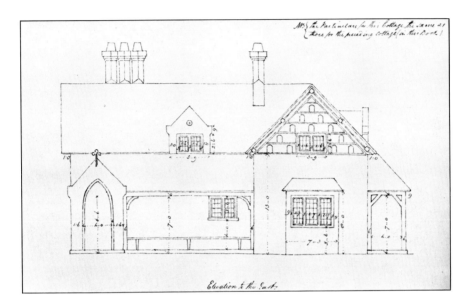

21A and 21B.   Blaise Hamlet, Bristol. Plan and elevation of the double
cottage (Nos 4 and 5 on the Plan). Drawings in G. S. Repton's sketch-
book (Brighton Art Gallery).

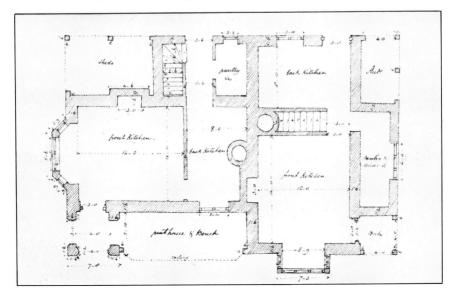

22.   Plan for Marylebone Park, signed and dated 'John Nash, Dover Street, March 1811' (PRO).

23A. Section of panorama illustrating Nash's proposals for Marylebone Park, 1811. This section shows the road leading south from the central circus to the New Road (Marylebone Road) (PRO).

23B. Adjoining section of the same panorama, showing a crescent of houses on the left, the southward termination of the artificial water and terraces in the distance (PRO).

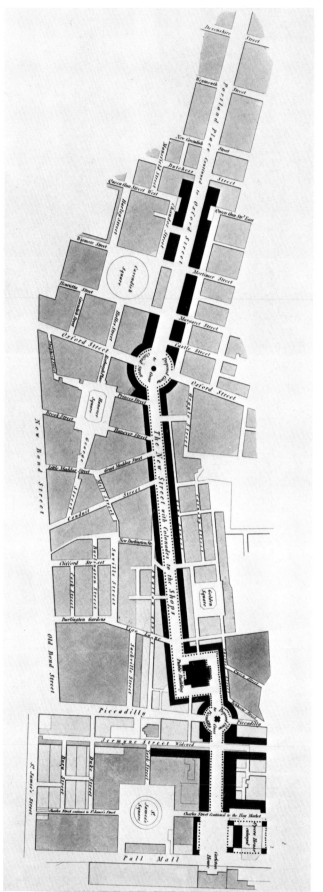

24. 'Plan of a New Street from Charing Cross to Portland Place.' From the First Report of the Commissioners of Woods, Forests and Land Revenues, 1812.

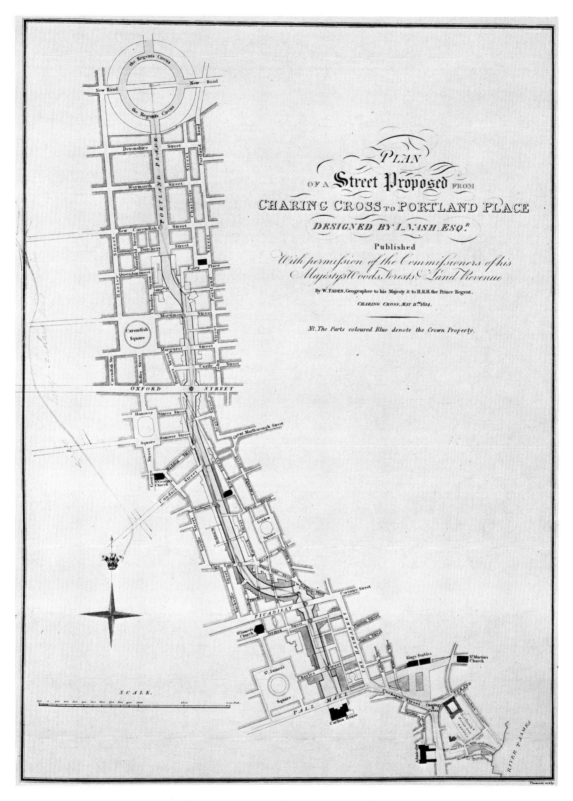

25. Map of the New Street, published by W. Faden, 11 May 1814
(BM, Crace Maps).

26A. The Royal Lodge in Windsor Great Park, begun in 1813.
Engraving after a drawing by Delamotte, 1824 (Royal Library,
Windsor Castle).

26B. Carlton House. The Gothic Dining Room, designed by Nash in
1813. (W. H. Pyne, *History of the Royal Residences*, 1819.)

27A. Pagoda and Bridge in St James's Park, built for the celebrations of 1814. Engraving by Rawle, after J. P. Neale, for *The Beauties of England and Wales*.

27B. The Royal Pavilion, Brighton, from the north-east (A. F. Kersting).

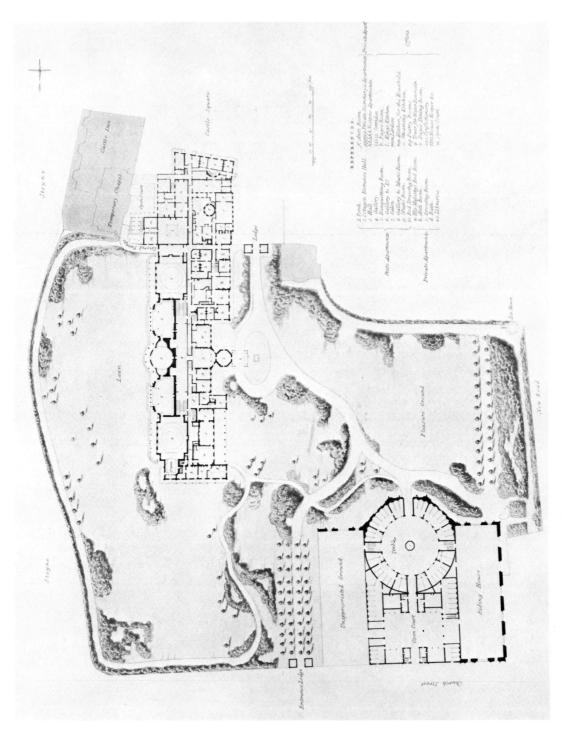

28. Plan of the Royal Pavilion estate, Brighton, showing (left) the stables and riding house built by William Porden in 1804–8 and (centre) the Royal Pavilion as remodelled and extended by Nash between 1815 and 1821. (John Nash, *The Royal Pavilion*.)

29A.   The Royal Pavilion, Brighton; entrance front. (John Nash, *The Royal Pavilion.*)

29B.   The Royal Pavilion, Brighton. Section through the south drawing-room, banqueting-room and kitchen. (John Nash, *The Royal Pavilion.*)

30B. St Mary's Church, Haggerston, built for the Commissioners for New Churches, 1826–7. Engraving by W. Deeble after T. H. Shepherd.

30A. All Souls' Church, Langham Place, built for the Commissioners for New Churches, 1822–5. Engraving by J. Tingle after T. H. Shepherd.

NASHIONAL TASTE!!!

(Dedicated, without permission, to the Church Commissioners —

Providence sends meat.   Parliament sends Funds —
The Devil sends cooks —   But, who sends the Architects?—!!!

31.   Satirical print by 'Q in the corner', published by G. Humphrey,
7 April 1824.

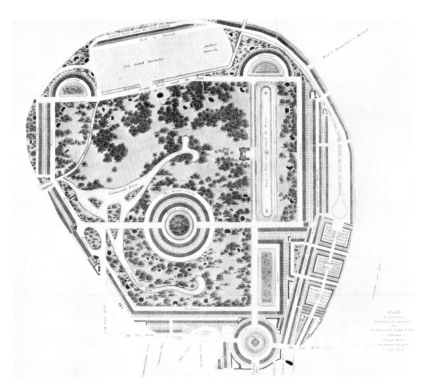

32A.   Plan of 'Marylebone Park Farm'. From the First Report of the
Commissioners of Woods, Forests and Land Revenues, 1812, showing
proposals for leasing.

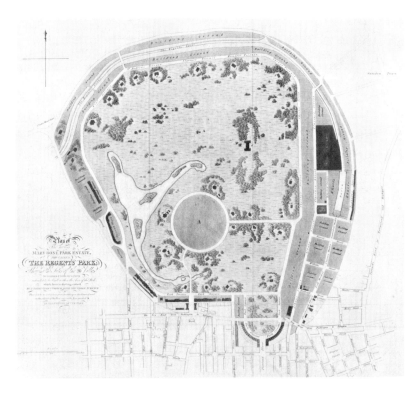

32B.   Plan of the 'Marylebone Park Estate (the Regent's Park)', from the
Fourth Report of the Commissioners of Woods, Forests and Land
Revenues, 1823, showing the sites of 26 villas.

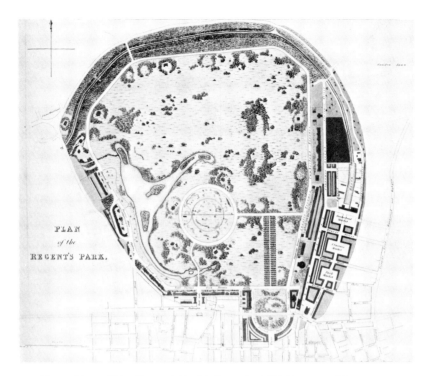

33A.   Plan of 'the Regent's Park', from the Fifth Report of the
Commissioners of Woods, Forests and Land Revenues, 1826, showing
the terraces and villas built or in progress at that date.

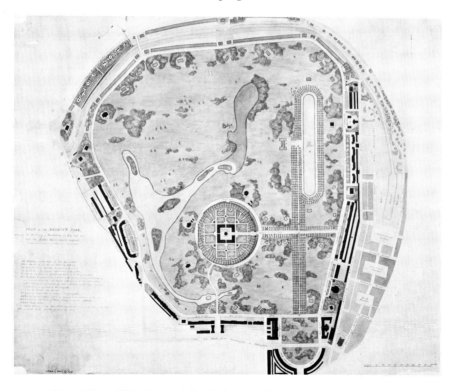

33B.   Plan of 'the Regent's Park' showing buildings erected by 1828
with proposals for extending the artificial water and the avenues. The
formal 'basin' and the 'guinguette', omitted in the plan of 1826, are here
restored. An overlay on the circus shows a quadrangle and chapel for the
proposed King's College (PRO).

34A.   Park Crescent, Regent's Park, begun 1812, interrupted by the
failure of Charles Mayor in 1815 and resumed in 1819. Engraving by
J. Redaway after T. H. Shepherd.

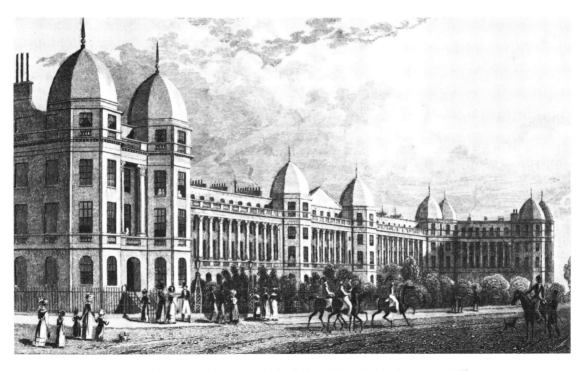

34B.   Sussex Place, Regent's Park, designed by Nash in 1822 and built
by William Smith. Engraving by W. R. Smith after T. H. Shepherd.

35A. York Terrace, Regent's Park. The overall design is by Nash, 1822. The west block was built by James Burton, the east by W. M. Nurse. Engraving by T. Barber after T. H. Shepherd.

35B. York Gate, Regent's Park, with the parish church of St Marylebone. Engraving by H. Wallis after T. H. Shepherd.

36A. Chester Terrace, Regent's Park, designed by Nash and begun by James Burton in 1825. Criticism of the detached wings led to the addition of the ornamental arches, one of which is seen here (NMR).

36B. Cumberland Terrace, Regent's Park, designed by Nash and built by W. M. Nurse, with James Thomson as executive architect (NMR).

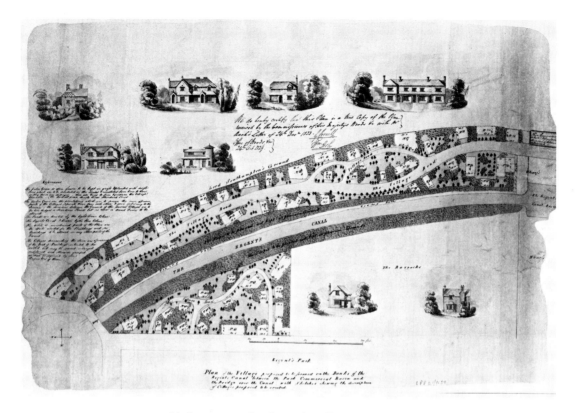

37A.   Nash's first project for the Park Villages, December 1823. The houses are sited on continuous open lawns. (PRO).

37B.   Park Village East and the Commercial Cut. Engraving by W. Radcliff after T. H. Shepherd.

38A. Waterloo Place, built 1815–16, looking towards Piccadilly Circus. Engraving by W. Tombleton after T. H. Shepherd.

38B. Regent Street, looking south from Piccadilly Circus; built between 1815 and 1820. The Nash–Edwards houses are seen on the left and the tower of St Philip's church on the right. Engraving by J. Bluck after T. H. Shepherd.

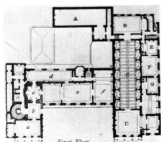

39A. Nos 14 (right) and 16 Regent Street, the houses of John Nash and John Edwards respectively, built in 1820–3. Drawing by Pugin (in the possession of Mr Peter Laing).

39B. Nos 14 and 16 Regent Street; first floor plan.
Letters A to G distinguish Nash's house from letters a to f which mark John Edwards' house.

39C. No. 14 Regent Street; the gallery. Engraving by T. Kearnan after F. Arundale for Britton and Pugin, *Public Buildings of London*, 1827.

40A. The County Fire Office and the Quadrant, built from 1819 onwards. The architect of the Office was Robert Abraham. Engraving by J. Bluck after T. H. Shepherd for Ackermann's *Repository of Arts*, 1822.

40B. The Quadrant, looking north-west. Engraving by W. Wallis after T. H. Shepherd.

41A. Nos 224–40 Regent Street, designed by Nash and built by
Samuel Baxter, 1822. Engraving by W. Wallis after T. H. Shepherd.

41B. The Harmonic Institution, built by Nash for Welch and Hawes
in 1819, on the corner of Little Argyll Street. Opposite, on the right, is
the portico of St George's church. Engraving by W. Wallis after
T. H. Shepherd.

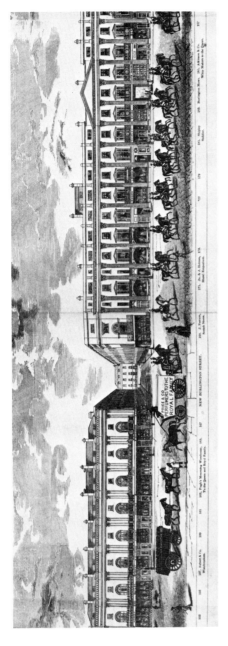

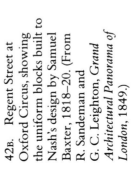

42A. Regent Street. The west side with the blocks to south and north of New Burlington Street. On the left, part of Nos 133–67; on the right, part of Nos 171–95. The blocks were built by James Burton in 1820 and 1822 respectively. (From R. Sandeman and G. C. Leighton, *Grand Architectural Panorama of London*, 1849.)

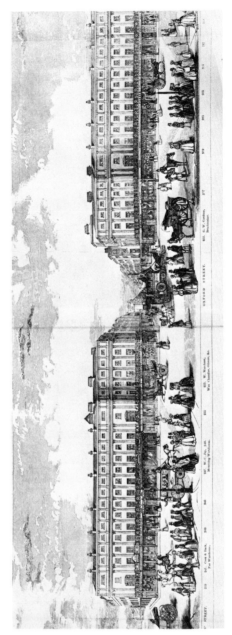

42B. Regent Street at Oxford Circus, showing the uniform blocks built to Nash's design by Samuel Baxter, 1818–20. (From R. Sandeman and G. C. Leighton, *Grand Architectural Panorama of London*, 1849.)

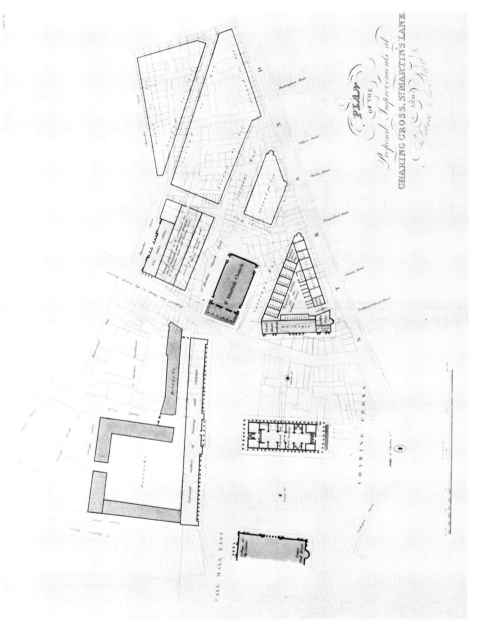

43. 'Plan of the Proposed Improvements at Charing Cross, St. Martin's Lane, and Entrance to the Strand.' From the Fifth Report of the Commissioners of Woods, Forests and Land Revenues, 1826. The plan shows (left) the area later to become Trafalgar Square, with a 'Parthenon' in the centre facing down Whitehall and intended to accommodate the Royal Academy. North of this is the proposed 'National Gallery of Painting and Sculpture'. On the right is the area between St Martin's Lane and the Strand with new streets developed round St Martin-in-the-Fields.

44A.   East Cowes Castle, from the north-west. Engraving by William Cooke, 1808.

44B.   East Cowes Castle, from the north-east. Engraving from T. Barber, *Picturesque Illustrations of the Isle of Wight*, c. 1834.

45A.   East Cowes Castle, from the lawn. (Photograph, 1933).

45B.   The Isle of Wight Institution, Newport, built in 1811, now the County Club. At the far end of the High Street is seen the portico of the Town Hall, built in 1814. Engraving from drawing by G. Brannon, 1821.

46A. Buckingham Palace, as first designed and partly built, 1825–8.
Engraving by W. Wallis, after A. Pugin, 1829.

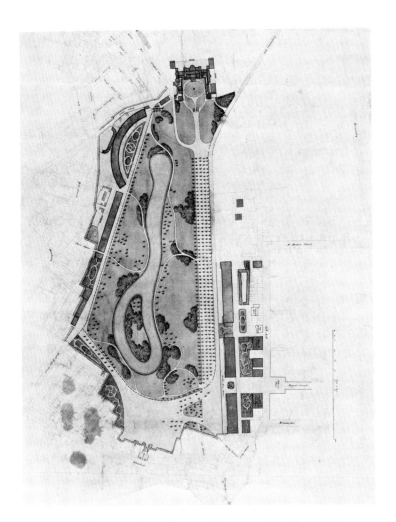

46B. St James's Park. Plan of proposed layout, 1828. The Mall is shown
as a pedestrian way, planted with five rows of trees. The two Carlton
House Terraces are shown as executed but with a fountain in place of
steps between them. A longer terrace is proposed on the west, covering
the site of Marlborough House and garden. To the south-west a large
crescent is proposed (PRO).

47A. Buckingham Palace. Design by Nash for the Throne Room
(Victoria and Albert Museum).

47B. Buckingham Palace. The Throne Room (NMR).

48. Carlton House Terrace. Designed by Nash and built between 1827 and 1833. The Duke of York's column was built to the design of Benjamin Dean Wyatt in 1831–4.

Appendix I

List of Works

The most complete referenced list of Nash's works is contained in the entry under 'John Nash' in Howard Colvin, *Biographical Dictionary of British Architects* (1978). The following list includes all the buildings named in Colvin's work regrouped, however, under headings appropriate to the biographical treatment in the foregoing chapters. Colvin's references are included only when sources are not given in notes to the text.

1 EARLY WORKS, 1778–96

Living in Lambeth

No. 17 Bloomsbury Square and adjoining houses in Great Russell Street, London, 1778 (pp. 6–7).

Living in Carmarthen

Carmarthen Church; new roof and ceiling, 1785 (p. 10). Demolished.

Golden Grove, Carmarthen; bath, c. 1787 (p. 5). Dem.

Clytha Castle, Mon., for William Jones (Monmouthshire Record Office, M413/2114), 1790.

Trev-Gevail Bridge, Cards., 1792–3 (Nat. Library of Wales, Cards., QS Order Book, 17 July 1793).

Ffynone, Pembs., 1792–6 (p. 18).

Hafod House, Cards., alterations, library and conservatory, 1794 (p. 20). Dem.

Abergavenny, Mon., Market House, 1794–5 (pp. 16–17). Dem.

Llanayron, Cards., c. 1794 (p. 19).

Whitson Court, Mon., for William Phillips, c. 1794. (James Baker, *Guide through Wales*, i, 1795, p. 200).

Llysnewydd, Cards., c. 1795 (p. 18). Dem.

Temple Druid, Maenclochog, Pembs., for Henry Bulkeley (sale advt. in *Cambrian*, 8 Sept. 1821), c. 1795.

Dolaucothi, Carm., remodelled for John Johnes (Dolaucothi papers, National Library of Wales), 1795.

Sion House, Tenby, Pembs., for William Routh, c. 1795. Dem.

Cardigan Priory, c. 1795. Dem.

Castle House, Aberystwyth, c. 1795 (pp. 21–2). Dem.

Kentchurch Court, Heref., remodelled, c. 1795 (p. 33).

The Park, Harrow-on-the-Hill, Middlesex, for Richard Page (GLC Record Office B/TRL/9, pp. 20–1, 24–6), c. 1795–1803.

Hereford, County Gaol, 1795–6 (p. 15). Dem.

Aberystwyth, Cardiganshire, bridge over R. Rheidol, c. 1797–1800; destroyed by flood 1886 (Nat. Library of Wales, Cards., QS Order Book, 13 Oct. 1792, 8 Oct. 1794).

2 COUNTRY HOUSES IN ENGLAND AND IRELAND, 1796–1818

Living at 28 and (after 1797) 29 Dover Street, London

Corsham Court, Wilts., remodelling with new north front, 1797–8 (pp. 33–6). Dem.

High Lee Hall, Cheshire, alterations and additions,

1797 and later (pp. 52–3). Dem.

Southgate Grove, Middlesex, 1797 (pp. 36–7).

Casina, Dulwich, 1797 (p. 37). Dem.

Bank Farm or Point Pleasant, Kingston-on-Thames,

1797 (p. 37). Dem.

Sundridge Park, near Bromley, Kent (with Humphry Repton), 1799 (p. 37).

Helmingham Hall, Suffolk, 1800. Alterations for the 6th Earl of Dysart (A. Oswald in *C. Life*, 23 Aug. 1956).

Chalfont House, Bucks., exterior remodelled for Thomas Hibbert (*The Gardener's Magazine*, ed. J. C. Loudon, iv, 1828, pp. 119–20), c. 1800.

Barr Hall, Great Barr, Staffs., alterations to house and Gothic entrance to churchyard, for Joseph Scott (S. Shaw, *History of Staffordshire*, ii, pp. 103 and 106), c. 1800. Dem., except the house.

Luscombe Castle, Dawlish, Devon, 1800–4 (pp. 38–9).

Killymoon Castle, Co. Tyrone, c. 1801–3 (pp. 44–5).

Cronkhill, near Shrewsbury, c. 1802 (pp. 41–2).

Hollycombe, near Linch, Sussex, for Sir Charles Taylor, c. 1805. Rebuilt. (T. W. Horsfield, *History of Sussex*, ii, 1835, p. 103). Drawings in Repton sketch-book, RIBA

Moccas, Herefs., Bridge Lodge and Daw's Lodge, c. 1805 (p. 54).

Merly House, Dorset, stables for Ralph Willet (Repton Sketch-book, RIBA), c. 1805.

Harpton Court, Radnorshire, for Frankland Lewis (*Sale Cat.*, 1835), c. 1805.

Longner Hall, Salop., c. 1805 (p. 42).

The Warrens, Bramshaw, near Lyndhurst, for Mr Eyre (Repton Sketch-book, RIBA), c. 1805.

Witley Court, Worcs., remodelling, c. 1805 (pp. 49–50).

Sandridge Park, Stoke Gabriel, Devon, c. 1805 (p. 42). Dem.

Hale Hall, Lancs., south front, for John Blackburne, 1806 (p. 50). Dem.

Garnstone Castle, Herefs., c. 1806 (p. 45). Dem.

Barnsley Park, Glos., lodge, conservatory and interior of library for Sir James Musgrave, Bt. (C. Hussey in *C. Life*, 2–9 Sept. 1954), 1806–10.

Childwall Hall, Lancs., 1806–13 (p. 45). Dem.

Lissan Rectory, Co. Derry, 1807 (p. 42).

Kilwaughter Castle, Co. Antrim, 1807 (p. 45).

Attingham Hall, Salop., picture gallery and staircase, 1807–10 (p. 4).

Parnham Hall, Dorset, additions for Sir William Oglander, Bt., 1807–11 (Dorset County Record Office MW/M8. *C. Life*, 29 Aug. 1908).

Goodwood, Sussex. Additions for the Fourth Duke of Richmond, c. 1808.

Aqualate Hall, Staffs., 1808 (p. 45). Dem.

Southborough Place, Ashcombe Avenue, Surbiton, Surrey, 1808 (p. 42).

Caerhays Castle, St Michael Caerhays, Cornwall. c. 1808 (p. 46).

Caledon, Co. Tyrone, interior decorations and colonnade for 2nd Earl of Caledon, 1808–13 (*C. Life*, 17, 24 and 31 Oct. 1957).

Caledon church spire, 1808.

Ingestre Hall, Staffs., remodelling, for 2nd Earl of Talbot, 1808–13. Dem.

Ravensworth Castle, Co. Durham, begun 1808 (p. 46). Dem.

Knepp Castle, West Grinstead, Sussex, c. 1809 (p. 47).

West Grinstead Park, Sussex, c. 1809 (p. 47).

Betley Court, Staffs., alterations to drawing-room for Sir Thomas Fletcher, 1809–10 (F. R. Twemlow, *The Twemlows*, 1910, p. 218).

Rockingham House, Co. Roscommon, 1810 (p. 49). Dem.

Preshaw House, Hants., additions for Walter Long, 1810 (G. F. Prosser, *Select Illustrations of Hampshire*, 1833).

Charborough Park, Dorset, alterations for Richard Erle Drax Grosvenor, c. 1810 (RCHM, *Dorset* ii, 163–8).

Blaise Hamlet, Henbury, Glos., 1810–11 (pp. 54–5).

Lough Cutra Castle, Co. Galway, 1811 (p. 48).

Hopton Court, Salop., portico and additional storey for Thomas Botfield, 1811–13 (B. Botfield, *Stemmata Botevilliana*, 1858, p. ccxxii).

Rheola, near Neath, Glam., enlarged for John Edwards, c. 1812.

Shane's Castle, Co. Antrim, partial rebuilding after fire for 2nd Viscount O'Neil, 1816 (*Davies (1966)*, pl. 29).

Gracefield Lodge, Co. Kildare, for Mrs Kavanagh, 1817 (J. N. Brewer, *The Beauties of Ireland* ii, 1826, p. 105).

Shanbally Castle, Co. Tipperary, 1818–19 (pp. 48–9). Dem.

The following are undated

Northerwood, near Lyndhurst, Hants., 'improved' (G. F. Prosser, *Select Illustrations of Hampshire*, 1833).

Worcester Park, near Ewell, Surrey, enlarged (G. F. Prosser, *Select Illustrations of Surrey*, 1828). Dem.

Appendix I. List of Works

3 WORKS FOR THE PRINCE REGENT, 1811–20

Living at 29 Dover Street, London

a. *As architect to the Office of Woods, Forests and Land Revenues*
The Royal Lodge, Windsor Great Park, 1813–16 (p. 95). Dem.

b. *As private architect to the Prince*
Carlton House, Pall Mall, London. Suite of rooms on lower ground floor, 1813–14 (p. 97). Dem.

The Royal Pavilion, Brighton, remodelled and extended, 1815–21 (pp. 103–8).

c. *As Deputy Surveyor-General to the Office of Works*
Polygon Room in Carlton House garden (p. 98). Removed to Woolwich.
Bridge and pagoda in St James's Park for the festivities of 1814 (pp. 98–9). Dem.

4 WORKS IN LONDON FOR THE OFFICE OF WOODS, FORESTS AND LAND REVENUES, 1810–33

Living at 29 Dover Street till 1822; thereafter at 14 Regent Street

a. *As salaried architect, in partnership with James Morgan*
Plans for Marylebone Park and the New Street (pp. 63 et seq.).

b. *As architect under agreement (contract from 1815) with the commissioners*
Designs for terraces, lodges, etc., in Regents Park, including the following: Park Crescent, 1812 (re-built 1963–5, with facsimile elevations); Sussex Place, 1822; Hanover Terrace, 1822; York Terraces, East and West, and York Gate, 1822; Park Square, Ulster Terrace and St Andrew's Place, 1823–6; Cambridge Terrace, 1824; Chester Terrace, 1825; Cumberland Terrace, 1826; Kent Terrace, 1826; Lodges at Hanover Gate and Gloucester Gate; Houses in Park Village, East and West. (See ch. 9).

Designs for elevations in Regent Street, including the following: Waterloo Place, 1815; Oxford Circus, 1815; Piccadilly Circus, 1818; the Quadrant, 1819. Attributions for other elevations in the street are uncertain (see ch. 10). All dem.

Elevations in Suffolk Street and Suffolk Place, 1820; Carlton House Terrace and Carlton Gardens, 1827–33 (pp. 168–9); the Strand, William IV Street and Adelaide Street, including the Lowther Arcade, 1830 (pp. 143–5).

5 LONDON WORKS INDEPENDENTLY COMMISSIONED

a. *On the Crown Estate*
Langham House, for Sir James Langham, 1813–15 (p. 83). Dem.
Warren's Hotel, No. 1 Regent Street, 1815 (p. 13). Dem.
Royal Opera House, Haymarket, 1816–18 (pp. 139–40). Dem.
Ophthalmia Hospital, Albany Street, 1818 (p. 129). Dem.
No. 15 Regent Street, for C. T. Blicke, 1819 (p. 132). Dem.
Harmonic Institution, No. 246 Regent Street, 1819 (p. 137). Dem.
Nos. 14–16 Regent Street, for himself and John Edwards, 1820–1 (pp. 132–3). Dem.
Suffolk Street Gallery, 1823 (p. 142).
Adult Orphan Asylum, Regents Park, 1824 (p. 122). Dem.
United Service Club, 1826–8 (p. 169).
St Martin's Vicarage, Vestry Hall and National School, c. 1830 (p. 144).

b. *Elsewhere than on the Crown Estate*
No. 29 Dover Street, for himself, 1798 (pp. 29–31). Dem.
Highgate Archway, 1812 (pp. 73–4). Dem.
Picture Gallery, Newman Street, for the sons of Benjamin West, 1820–21. Dem.

6 ROYAL BUILDINGS, 1820–30

a. *As Attached Architect to the Board of Works*
The Royal Mews, Pimlico, 1822–4 (p. 143).
Clarence House, St James's, 1825–8 (p. 183).
Ascot Racecourse, Royal Stand, 1822 (*King's Works*, vi, p. 257). Dem.

b. *As private architect to George IV, with responsibility to Parliament*
Buckingham Palace, 1825–30 (see ch 12).

7 WORKS FOR THE COMMISSIONERS FOR BUILDING NEW CHURCHES

All Souls' Church, Langham Place, London, 1822–5 (pp. 112–13).

St Mary's Church, Haggerston, London, 1826–7 (p. 113). Dem.

8 WORKS IN THE ISLE OF WIGHT

East Cowes Castle, for himself, 1798 onwards (pp. 31–3 and 146–8). Dem.
Hamstead Farm, *c.* 1806 (pp. 153–4). Dem.
Isle of Wight Institution, Newport, 1811 (p. 154).
Market House and Town Hall, Newport, 1814–16 (p. 154).
West Cowes Church, tower, 1816 (p. 155).

Villa for Sir J. Hippisley Coxe, Bt., West Cowes, *c.* 1825 (p. 155).
Bembridge Church, 1827 (p. 155). Dem.
East Cowes Church, 1831–3 (p. 155). Dem., except tower.
Northwood House, West Cowes; lodges for George Ward (undated).

9 MISCELLANEOUS WORKS

Chichester, Market House, North Street, 1807–8 (T. W. Horsfield, *History of Sussex*, ii, 1835, p. 11).
Oxford, Jesus College, alterations, 1815–18 (J. Ingram, *Memorials of Oxford*, iii, 1837, p. 15).
Oxford, Exeter College (with G. S. Repton), repair of hall (J. Ingram, *Memorials of Oxford*, i, 1837, pp. 12–13).

Picton Monument, Carmarthen, 1825–7 (p. 183). Dem.
Winchester, St Cross Hospital restoration, 1827–9.
Leamington, Warwickshire, layout of estate of E. Willes, 1827 (R. Chaplin, 'The Rise of Royal Leamington Spa', *Warwickshire History*, ii (2), 1972, p. 22).

Appendix II

Portraits

1 Miniature, probably painted about the time of the subject's second marriage, 1798. Framed with miniatures of Mary Anne Bradley (Mrs Nash) and Grace Bradley (Mrs Parker). In the possession of Peter Laing, Esq. *Plate 7B.*

2 Oil-painting showing Nash seated at a table on which is a plan of an unidentified building. Regent Street, with part of No. 14, in the background. Probably by Richard Evans, who exhibited a portrait of Nash at the Royal Academy in 1826. Passed down in the Edwards family and now in the possession of Major and Mrs Allan Cameron of Lochiel. Front cover and *Plate 1.*

3 Oil-painting similar to the above, passed down in the Pennethorne family and now in the possession of R. Liddon Few, Esq.

4 Wax miniatures (profile) by J. A. Couriguér, c. 1825. Three of these are believed to exist. One is in the National Portrait Gallery. Another, illustrated as frontispiece in *Summerson* (1935), is in the possession of R. Liddon Few, Esq.

5 Oil-painting by Sir Thomas Lawrence, painted for Jesus College, Oxford, where it hangs in the hall (see p. 176). Exh. RA, 1827. Reproduced as frontispiece in *Davis* (1966).

6 Miniature bronze bust, a pair with similar bust of Mrs Nash. In the possession of R. Liddon Few, Esq.

7 Whole-length profile sketch in brown ink by Edwin Landseer, c. 1830. Nash stands with one hand in trouser pocket and holds his hat behind him. Caricaturish in style. National Portrait Gallery.

8 Marble bust by William Behnes. Exh. RA, 1831. In the possession of Peter Laing, Esq. Plaster cast in RIBA. Modern copy in stone by Cecil Thomas in the portico of All Souls', Langham Place.

Notes

I THE FIRST FORTY YEARS

1 C. Knight (publisher), *The English Cyclopaedia: Biography* (1854–70): article, 'Nash, John'. B. Ferrey, *Recollections of A. W. N. Pugin* (1861), pp. 13–15. J. Britton, *Autobiography* (1850), Part i, pp. 345–6. *Builder*, vol, xiii (1855), pp. 585–7; xiv (1856), pp. 441–2.

2 HLRO, Main Papers, 20 May 1787.

3 *The Universal British Directory of Trade and Commerce*, 1790. Later references are extracted from the collection of London directories in the GLC Library, County Hall.

4 PRO, PROB 11/1614.

5 A copy of the entry in the Lambeth register, annexed to an election notice of 1818, is in National Library of Wales MS. 6575 E.

6 Ferrey (1861), p. 15.

7 Knight, (1854–70), *loc. cit.*

8 D. Watkin, *C. R. Cockerell* (1974), p. 42. *Builder*, xiii (1856), p. 442.

9 St Martin-in-the-Fields Rate Books, Westminster Public Library, Buckingham Palace Road.

10 *Survey of London*, xx, p. 65, but the identification of the house is doubtful. Watkin (1974), p. 61. A. E. Richardson and C. L. Gill, *London Houses from 1660 to 1820* (1911), p. 63, pl. xlvii.

11 CRES 2/847.

12 For Taylor see *Colvin* and authorities there cited.

13 Farington Typescript, p. 8078.

14 *Ibid.*

15 Ferrey (1861), p. 10. *Builder*, xiii (1856), p. 442.

16 Porden MS. Entry for 3 July 1812.

17 *Ibid.*

18 Farington Typescript, p. 8081.

19 Baptismal Register of St Mary Newington, GLC Record Office.

20 *Colvin, s.v.* 'Blackburn, W.'

21 In E. Laws, *Collectanea Pembrokeana*, in the National Library of Wales, lithographs of Tenby by Reinagle, published by Hullmandel, are tentatively attributed to 'Nash, builder of houses in Heywood Lane and son of the London architect'. No supporting evidence has been found.

22 The bond is in the Bedford Office (Title Deeds, vol. 5, Midd., St George's and St Pancras, Bundle 17).

23 St George, Bloomsbury, Rate Books in the Holborn Public Library, Theobalds Road.

24 J. Swarbrick, *Robert Adam and his Brothers* (1915), pp. 278, 280.

25 PRO, C 12/921 (11).

26 The events here narrated are based on *Journals of the House of Lords*, xxxvii (1783–87), pp. 605, 623, 639–41, and HLRO, Main Papers, 28 Feb. 1787, etc.

27 L. Shelford, *The Law of Marriage and Divorce* (1841), pp. 373–9.

28 *Gent's Mag.*, Liv (1), p. 155 (Feb. 1784).

29 PRO B4/22; B 16/6.

30 Porden MS. *loc. cit.*

31 *Colvin, s.v.* 'Saxon, Samuel'.

32 W. Spurrell, *Carmarthen and its Neighbourhood* (2nd ed. 1879), pp. 32, 129.

33 *Builder*, xiii. (1856), p. 442 n.

34 Order Book of Carmarthen Corporation, in Carmarthenshire Record Office. Nash appears to have held this property till 1811.

35 Spurrell (1879), p. 51 n.

36 *Journals of the House of Lords*, xxxvii (1783–97), pp. 605 ff.

37 *The World*, 30 March 1787. This passage was kindly brought to my attention by Mr Frank Kelsall.

38 See p. 18, *post*.

39 Cwmgwili MS. 234.

40 Cwmgwili MS. 259.

2 THE CARMARTHEN YEARS: FROM PRISONS TO THE PICTURESQUE

1 Nash to Soane, quoted in full, pp. 158–9, *post*.

2 See p. 150, n. 15.

3 B. Burke, *Landed Gentry* (1894), ii, p. 2,091.

4 Cwmgwili MSS 390A, 424, 433, 441, 493, etc.

5 J. Howard, *State of the Prisons in England and Wales* (1777–80), p. 468, App., p. 189.

6 Howard (1777–80)., App., p. 189.

7 p. 6, n. 20.

8 Cwmgwili MS. 234.

9 *An Act for Building a New Gaol and House of Correction for Carmarthen*, etc., 32 Geo. III, cap. 104.

10 Howard (1777–80), App., p. 189.

11 J. Price, *Historical Account of the City of Hereford* (1796), p. 72. J. Duncomb, *Collection towards the History and Antiquities of Hereford* (1804), i, p. 425.

12 This feature is shown in a print in the Hereford Public Library.

13 W. B. Jones and E. A. Freeman, *History and Antiquities of St. David's* (1856), pp. 175–6, where excerpts from Nash's specification are given. *Gent's Mag.*, lxxiv (1804, ii), pp. 833–4. I. Wyn Jones, 'John Nash at St. David's', *Archit. Rev.*, Oct. 1952, pp. 263–4. *Davis (1960)*, reproduces elevation and section by Nash (pls 133 and 134).

14 T. Ruddock, *Arch Bridges and their Builders 1735–1835* (1979), p. 124.

15 Vestry Minute Books preserved in the Town Hall, Abergavenny. The Act of 1794 (33 Geo. III cap. 106). was 'for paving and otherwise improving the Town'.

16 The whereabouts of this drawing is unknown. A photograph is in the author's possession.

17 p. 57, *post*.

18 *The Life and Times of Mrs Sherwood* (ed. F. J. Harvey Darton, 1910), p. 171.

19 *1831 Report*, p. 285.

20 *The Glenbervie Journals* (ed. W. Sichel, 1910), p. 149.

21 S. Smiles, *Life of Telford* (1867), pp. 171–7.

22 Society of Antiquaries, Prattington Coll., Box iv (2).

23 Price (1796), p. 72. The author of a descriptive poem published in 1794 or 1795 alludes to Nash as 'an eminent architect in Carmarthen'. *Carmarthen Antiq. Soc. Trans.*, ix, p. 75.

24 P. Smith, *Houses of the Welsh Countryside* (1975), p. 323.

25 *Ibid.*, Fig. 188, p. 127.

26 Sketch elevation in *Davis (1966)*, p. 28.

27 E. Inglis-Jones, *Peacocks in Paradise* (1950).

28 D. Watkin, *C. R. Cockerell* (1974), p. 5.

29 H. M. Vaughan, *Some Letters of Thomas Johnes of Hafod* (Cymmrodorion Soc. Publication, 1925), p. 213.

30 E. Inglis-Jones, 'An Eccentric's Castle House', *C. Life*, 4 July 1952, p. 33.

31 The original of this letter is now in the Pierpont Morgan Library, New York, but access is temporarily restricted and I have been unable to check the text printed here.

32 *Davis (1966)* reproduces, pl. 4, a drawing, c. 1810, in the National Library of Wales.

33 The outlines of the building can be distinguished in a plan of proposals for the University College of Wales, Aberystwyth. *Builder*, 18 Feb. 1887.

34 U. Price, *An Essay on the Picturesque* (1794), p. 188.

35 *Ibid.*, p. 28.

36 N. Pevsner, 'Richard Payne Knight', *The Art Bulletin*, iv, 4 (Dec. 1949). A. Rowan, 'Downton Castle', *The Country Seat* (ed. H. Colvin and J. Harris, 1970), pp. 170–173.

37 Nash to P. C. Methuen, Sept. 1799, quoted in D. Stroud, *Humphry Repton* (1962), p. 96.

38 Nash to J. G. Philipps, 16 June 1796. Cwmgwili MS. 424.

39 C. Price, *The English Theatre in Wales* (1948), pp. 82–92.

40 A. Mathews, *Memoirs of Charles Mathews* (2nd ed., 1839), i, p. 168.

41 B. Ferrey, *Recollections of A. W. N. Pugin* (1861), p. 2.

42 I owe this information to Mr H. M. Colvin, who found the entry after his *Biog. Dict.* had gone to press.

43 See MS. note on Foulon in the grangerised *A.P.S. Dictionary* in the Soane Museum.

44 C. J. Mathews, *Life of C. J. M.* (ed. C. Dickens, 1879).

45 Unpublished thesis by I. Wyn Jones, *The Work of John Nash in Wales*.

46 Morgan's will (PRO, PROB 11/2242/856) is dated 21 Dec. 1855 and was proved in the following November.

47 Cwmgwili MS. 433.

48 Cwmgwili MS. 441.

49 Cwmgwili MS. 392.

50 *Bolton*, p. 196.

51 Cwmgwili MS. 424.

52 *Gent's Mag.*, lxix (2), 1799, p. 1087.

53 *Ibid.*, lxxvii (2), 1807, p. 1171.

54 The drawing-room in the Bloomsbury Square house has a ceiling of conspicuously original design, containing the radial-fluted motif which Nash used at Ffynone, East Cowes and elsewhere. Such a ceiling would certainly not be installed before the house was sold and may therefore have been designed by Nash for John Edwards.

55 *Gent's Mag.*, ciii (2), 1833, p. 380.

56 Wills of William Vaughan (PRO, PROB 11/1759), and John Edwards Vaughan (PRO, PROB 11/1825). B. Burke, *Landed Gentry* (1894), ii, p. 2091.

57 E. Jenkins, 'Rheola'. *Neath Antiquarian Soc. Trans.* (1978), pp. 61–8.

58 Patent No. 2165 (1797). Printed, 1856.

59 J. W. Willis-Bund, 'Worcestershire Bridges', *Assoc. Architectural Soc. Reports*, xxxi (1911–12), p. 285.

3 DOVER STREET AND COWES: THE REPTON CONNECTION

1 Cwmgwili MS. 441.

2 Cwmgwili MS. 456.

3 Ratebooks of St George, Hanover Square, Westminster Public Library. The name of James Morgan, probably acting as a trustee for Nash, is entered as the ratepayer through the whole period of Nash's occupancy of the house.

4 A letter from Thomas Pennethorne to his son James Pennethorne, 25 May 1837, among the Pennethorne papers, states that 'Mr Nash's mother (Gregory) married Mr Bradley, a coal merchant of Abingdon Street, Westminster'.

5 PRO, B6/6.

6 *Gent's Mag.*, 1799, ii, p. 619

7 Genealogy of the Pennethorne family among the Pennethorne papers.

8 Marriage register, St George's, Hanover Square.

9 Information kindly supplied by Miss Alison Kelly.

10 A. Dale, *James Wyatt* (1956), pp. 160–1, pls 57–8.

11 J. Cornforth, 'Kentchurch Court', *C. Life*, 15 Dec. 1966.

12 D. Stroud, *Capability Brown* (2nd ed., 1975), pp. 86–90.

13 D. Stroud, *Humphry Repton* (1962). J. C. Loudon, *The Landscape Gardening and Landscape Architecture of the late Humphry Repton, Esq.* (1840), in which Repton's published works are collected, with biographical notice by J. C. L.

14 C. Hussey, *English Country Houses: Early Georgian* (1955), pp. 228–33. *Neale*, 2nd ser., ii; J. Britton, *Historical Account of Corsham House* (1806).

15 *Loudon*, p. 289.

16 The papers relating to the building of the house are preserved at Corsham Court.

17 Farington Typescript, p. 1384.

18 *Loudon*, p. 284.

19 E. T. Hall, *Dulwich History and Romance* (2nd ed., 1922), p. 44.

20 J. Hassell, *Views of Noblemen and Gentlemen's Seats*, 1804, etc. contains a badly distorted view, reproduced in *Davis (1960)*, pl. 57. J. Dallaway, *Anecdotes of the Arts in England* (1800), p. 159.

21 View in Peacock's *Polite Repository*, April 1797. *Davis (1960)*, pl. 103.

22 *Loudon*, p. 141. View in W. Angus, *Seats of the Nobility and Gentry* (1797).

23 *Colvin*, p. 958.

24 C. Hussey, *English Country Houses: Late Georgian* (1958), pp. 55–65.

25 The Red Book is preserved at Luscombe.

26 *Loudon*, p. 121.

27 Windsor, RA, quoted in D. Stroud, *Humphry*

Repton (1962), p. 605.

28 Windsor, RA, 17090.

29 T. S. R. Boase, 'An Oxford College and the Gothic Revival', *Jnl. of the Warburg and Courtauld Institutes*, xviii (1955).

30 C. Hussey, *English Country Houses: Mid Georgian* (1956), pp. 195–202.

31 M. Rix in *C. Life*, 21 Oct. 1954.

32 He died in 1856. His monument, which may be described as a Grecian pillar-box, is in the churchyard at Atcham.

33 The Red Book is preserved at Longner.

4 CASTLES AND COTTAGES: WOODS AND FORESTS

1 Stewart Papers in Public Record Office of Northern Ireland, especially D3167/2/159, 172, 174, 181.

2 *Davis (1966)*, pl. 28.

3 *Neale*, 2nd ser., iv (1828). *Davis (1960)*, pls. 27–8.

4 *Neale*, 2nd ser., ii (1825).

5 E. M. Jope, 'Lissan Rectory and the Buildings in the North of Ireland designed by John Nash', *Ulster Jnl. of Archaeology*, xix (1956), pp. 121–7. *Davis (1960)*, pl. 44.

6 G. E. C., *Complete Peerage*. W. Fordyce, *History of Durham* (1857), ii, p. 641.

7 Add. MS. 37918, f. 251.

8 RIBA, Cat., L–N, Nash, J. [4], 1 and 2.

9 *Illustrated London News*, ix, p. 45 (1846). *Davis (1960)*, pls. 11–14.

10 Introduction to Report on Boughey papers in the William Salt Library, Stafford, in National Register of Archives. The papers include correspondence with Nash, 1805–9. Engraving of the house by S. Bourne, in the William Salt Library, is reproduced in *Davis (1960)*, pl. 43 and *Davis (1966)*, pl. 24.

11 E. Twycross, *The Mansions of England: Cornwall* (1846), p. 52. A. L. Rowse, *The Byrons and Trevanions* (1978), pp. 186, 196, 198–9. *Davis (1960)*, pls. 64–5, 124. *Davis (1966)*, pl. 23.

12 *Davis (1960)*, pls. 72–4. J. Harris, *Catalogue of British Drawings in American Collections* (1971), p. 150.

13 *Davis (1960)*, pls. 8–10. D. G. C. Elwes and C. J. Robinson, *Castles and Mansions of W. Sussex* (1867), p. 108.

14 G. E. C., *Complete Peerage*.

15 Architectural Pubn. Soc., *Dictionary*, s.v. 'Pain, J. and G. R.'.

16 Letter to *The Times*, 14 May 1935, p. 17. D. Guinness and W. Ryan, *Irish Houses and Castles* (1971), pp. 177–80. *Davis (1960)*, pls. 81–4.

17 *Davis (1960)*, pls. 18–24.

18 The building accounts are in Nat. Lib. Ireland, MS. 3775.

19 G. E. C., *Complete Peerage*.

20 *Davis (1960)*, pl. 46.

21 *C. Life*, 8 and 15 June 1945.

22 J. Harris, 'C. R. Cockerell's "Ichnographica Domestica"', *Architectural History*, xiv (1971), p. 28.

23 Bodleian Library, Oxford. Papers of the Wykeham-Musgrave family.

24 Two are in the RIBA Collection, one is in the Brighton Art Gallery.

25 U. Price, *An Essay on the Picturesque* (1794), p. 134.

26 N. Temple, 'In Search of the Picturesque', *Architectural Rev.*, Aug. 1976, pp. 96–100.

27 Cornwall-Legh papers in the John Rylands Library, Manchester.

28 *Davis (1960)*, pls 122–3.

29 I am indebted to Mr C. R. Harris of Francis Edwards Ltd, for bringing this letter to my attention and allowing me to copy this passage.

30 D. Stroud, *Humphry Repton* (1962), p. 98.

31 Watkin (1974), p. 81.

32 Bristol Record Office, Harford Papers, P52/1–8.

33 *Ibid.*

34 Bristol Record Office, MS. 28048/P52/10.

35 *Tour in England, Ireland and France by a German Prince* (1832), ii, p. 204.

36 *Nine Lithographic Views of the Cottages composing Blaise Hamlet* (n.d.). Drawn on stone by J. D. Harding from sketches by O'Neil. There are incomplete copies in the Blaise Castle Museum and the Central Library, Bristol. A complete copy is in the Paul Mellon Collection.

37 Soane's warrant of appointment, LR4/16.
38 Soane Museum, Correspondence. Soane to Lords of the Treasury, 3 June 1799 2, xiv (J).
39 LR4/20/4.
40 E. Lascelles, *The Life of C. J. Fox* (1936), pp. 89–91.
41 *1828 Report*, p. 105.
42 RIBA Cat., O–R, Repton, G. S. [47].
43 Sale Catalogue, 1835, in Soane Museum.

5 MARYLEBONE PARK

1 A. Saunders, *Regents Park: a Study of the Development from 1086 to the Present Day* (1969), Chs 1–2.
2 *1st to 17th Reports of Commissioners appointed to enquire into the . . . Woods, Forests and Land Revenues of the Crown etc.*, 2 vols. (1787–93).
3 34 George III, cap. 75.
4 *Gent's Mag.*, 1809, ii, p. 685.
5 Saunders (1969), pp. 75–6. Add. MSS 33056, f. 211; 35128, f. 480.
6 *1st Report SGLR* (Reprint of 1812), App.3A, pp. 16–17.
7 *Ibid.*, p. 17.
8 J. White, *Some Account of the Proposed Improvements etc.* (2nd ed. 1815), pt. 1, pp. 17–26.
9 *4th Report SGLR*, pp. 28–9.
10 *Ibid.*, App. 15, p. 89.
11 *Ibid.*, App. 15, p. 90.
12 Under 50 George III, cap. 65.
13 Article, 'Sylvester Douglas, Baron Glenbervie', *DNB. The Glenbervie Journals* (ed. W. Sichel, 1910), p. 156.
14 LR4/20/5.
15 *1st Report SGLR*, App. 18A, p. 50.
16 CRES 2/1736.
17 CRES 2/742.
18 *Ibid.*
19 *1st Report CWFLR*, App. 12, p. 74.
20 *Ibid.*, pp. 10, 79.
21 *1st Report CWFLR*, App. 12G, p. 113.
22 F. M. L. Thompson, *Hampstead: Building a Borough, 1650–1964* (1974), p. 114.
23 *1st Report CWFLR*, App. 12G, pp. 113–4.
24 PRO, MPEE/58.
25 D. Stroud, *George Dance* (1971), p. 166.
26 J. Summerson, 'The Beginnings of Regents Park', *Architectural History*, XX (1977), pp. 56–62.
27 PRO, MR 1045 and 1047. A letter rom Nash apologising for their late submission is in CRES 2/1736.
28 R.C. Papers, Book I.
29 *1st Report CWFLR*, App. 12G, p. 113.
30 *Ibid.*, App. 12B, p. 87.
31 White (1815) p. 33.
32 *1st Report CWFLR*, App. 12I, p. 116.
33 *Ibid.*, App. 12H, pp. 115–6.
34 *The Glenbervie Journals,* as above, p. 152; 21 October 1811: 'I had before I left London to go to the Isle of Wight an interview with the Prince Regent on the subject of Marylebone Park.' Sichel omits Glenbervie's account of the interview, whose subject he dismisses as 'this now uninteresting affair in which Spencer Perceval was involved'. The present whereabouts of the MS. is unknown.
35 Thomas Moore to James Corry, 24 Oct. 1811. *Memoirs . . . of Thomas Moore* (ed. J. Russell, 1856), viii, p. 97.
36 R. C. Papers, Book I.
37 White (1815), p. 91.
38 *Parl. Debs.*, xxiii, 71–3.
39 R. C. Papers, Book I.
40 No. 34 Albany Street seems to be the last survivor of these houses.
41 *3rd Report CWFLR*, p. 10; *4th Report*, pp. 24, 48, 50, 60. CRES 2/752.
42 R. C. Papers, Book I.
43 CRES 2/744 contains all the relevant correspondence.
44 F. W. Simms, *Practical Tunnelling* (2nd ed., 1859), p. 172, where it is suggested that Nash was, in fact, the designer of the tunnel which collapsed. J. Thorne, *Handbook to the Environs of London* (1876), i, pp. 355–6.
45 CRES 2/742.

6 THE NEW STREET

1 For the building history of Soho see *Survey of London*, xxxiii and xxxiv (1966).

2 J. Gwynn, *London and Westminster Improved* (1766).

3 *1st Report SGLR*, pp. 12, 44.

4 A plan purporting to include the main features of this is given in White (1815).

5 *4th Report SGLR*, pp. 28–9.

6 *1st Report CWFLR*, App. 12A, pp. 88–90.

7 *1828 Report*, p. 74.

8 *1st Report CWFLR*, p. 89.

9 CRES 26/17.

10 *1st Report CWFLR*, p. 90.

11 C. J. Matthews, *Life of C. J. M.* (1879), i, p. 195.

12 Mr John Harris kindly drew my attention to this drawing, which is in his possession.

13 *1st Report CWFLR*, App. 3.

14 A plan of the sewers is given in White, (1815).

15 *1st Report CWFLR*, App. 12F, p. 107.

16 *Ibid.*, App. 12B, p. 97.

17 *2nd Report CWFLR*, App. 22A, pp. 114–8.

18 *Ibid.*, App. 22A, p. 116.

19 *Ibid.*, App. 25B, p. 123.

20 *Parl. Debs*, xxvi, 642, 643.

21 CRES 26/1, pp. 1 ff.

22 *Ibid.*, p. 6.

23 *Ibid.*, p. 119.

24 *Ibid.*, p. 22.

25 *Morning Chronicle*, 14 Nov. 1817.

26 CRES 26/2, p. 136; 3, p. 98.

27 CRES 26/2, pp. 57, 71, 451.

28 CRES 26/3, pp. 2, 37, 113, 234.

29 CRES 26/3, p. 8.

30 *Ibid.*

31 CRES 38/1283, 1284. The profits arising from the development were to pay off a debt of £10,000 to Lady Mary Bowlby, contracted by Foley on the security of Foley House.

32 C. H. Smith, 'The Site of Foley House and the Crookedness of Langham Place', *Builder*, 1863, pp. 703–4. J. Timbs, *Curiosities of London* (1868), p. 711. *Statement*, 1829.

33 LR1/255, f. 6.

34 *Builder*, 1863, pp. 703–4. CRES 38/1289.

35 *The Diaries of Sylvester Douglas, Lord Glenbervie* (ed. F. Bickley, 1928), ii, p. 211.

36 *Statement*, 1829.

37 *The Diaries of Sylvester Douglas*, as above, ii, p. 199.

38 *3rd Report CWFLR*, p. 13.

39 *Ibid.*, pp. 12–14.

40 *1829 Report*, pp. 12–13.

41 J. Summerson, *Georgian London* (3rd ed. 1978), pp. 169–73.

42 *1829 Report*, p. 55.

43 *1828 Report*, p. 73.

44 CRES 26/4, p. 463.

45 *1828 Report, loc. cit.*

46 CRES 26/4, pp. 264, 463.

47 *1829 Report*, p. 50.

48 CRES 26/5, p. 95.

49 *Ibid.*, p. 207. Lamp-irons with elongated baluster profiles, rising from pedestals, are shown in early views and a few survive at St Andrew's Place and Cornwall Terrace, Regents Park.

50 *1828 Report*, p. 104.

51 *Ibid.*

52 *Ibid.*, p. 73.

53 *Ibid.*, p. 107.

54 *1833 Report*, p. 109.

7 THE REGENT'S ARCHITECT

1 S. Romilly, *Memoirs* (edited by his sons, 2nd ed., 1840), iii, p. 86.

2 In what follows, I am deeply indebted to Roger Fulford's lucid and entertaining work, *George the Fourth* (1935).

3 A. Aspinall (ed.), *The Letters of King George IV, 1812–1830* (1938), letter No. 163.

4 Romilly (1840), pp. 86–7.

5 *Ibid.*, pp. 88–9.

6 *Ibid.*, pp. 93–4.

7 Lord Yarmouth to MacMahon, Windsor, RA, 42701–2.

8 LR 2/20, vol. X, f. 40.

9 Windsor, RA, 42701–2.

10 LR 2/20, vol. X.

11 *Ibid.*, f. 83.

12 O. Morshead, *George IV and Royal Lodge* (1965), p. 12.

13 P. Fitzgerald, *Life of George IV* (1882), ii, p. 157.

14 Morshead (1965), pp. 18–39.

15 WORKS 4/23, p. 114.

16 *King's Works*, vi, pp. 49–54, 97–100.

17 *Ibid.*, p. 101–2.

18 *Ibid.*, p. 109.

19 Britton and Pugin, ii, pp. 193–201. *Survey of London*, XX, pp. 69–76, pls 54–64. D. Stroud, *Henry Holland* (1950), Ch. 6.

20 W. H. Pyne, *History of the Royal Residences* (1819), iii.

21 *Annual Register*, 1814, p. 64.

22 *Gent's Mag.*, 1814, ii, p. 179.

23 Illustrated in R. Ackermann, *Repository*, xii (1814), 225, 286; Papworth, *Select Views* (1816), p. 13; J. Britton, *Beauties of England and Wales*, X, pp. 108–9.

24 *Absalom Watkin: Extracts from his Journal* (ed. A. E. Watkin, 1920), p. 65.

25 J. Timbs, *Curiosities of London* (1868), p. 653, quoting *Quarterly Review*.

26 *Bolton*, p. 245.

27 *Architectural History*, xi (1968), p. 46, n. 20.

28 Both designs are reproduced in H. Clifford Smith, *Buckingham Palace* (1931), pls 24 and 25.

29 WORKS 4/21, p. 341.

30 Writ, dated 3 September 1812. Windsor, RA, 34543.

31 Windsor, RA, 34576.

32 *Parl. Debs.*, XXX, 846.

8 THE BRIGHTON PAVILION: THE BOARD OF WORKS

1 For the early history of the Pavilion see the following works: E. W. Brayley, *A History of the Palace* (1838); J. G. Bishop, *The Brighton Pavilion* (1875); H. D. Roberts, *A History of the Royal Pavilion, Brighton* (1939); C. Musgrave, *Royal Pavilion: an Episode in the Romantic* (1959).

2 Brayley (1838), p. 2.

3 D. Stroud, *Henry Holland* (1966), pp. 89–90, pl. 67.

4 Musgrave (1959) pl. 11.

5 *Loudon*, pp. 367–9.

6 H. Repton, *Designs for the Pavilion at Brighton* (1806), reprinted in *Loudon*.

7 *Loudon*, p. 19.

8 Roberts (1939), pp. 86–7.

9 Musgrave (1959), p. 63, quoting a draft account by Nash of the rebuilding of the Pavilion.

10 They were made in London by William Slark and Son and cost £1874 15s. Windsor, RA 33347.

11 See the engraving reproduced in Roberts (1939), p. 100.

12 Bishop (1875), pp. 66–8.

13 Musgrave (1959), p. 67.

14 *Ibid.*, pp. 106–9.

15 Roberts (1939), pp. 113–4.

16 Windsor, RA, 33973–4.

17 *Ibid.*

18 *Ibid.*

19 Sir W. Knighton to Danvers, 9 Feb. 1823: 'I think it will be right to allow him his commission.' Windsor, RA, 33960.

20 Windsor, RA, 34066.

21 Windsor, RA, 33414.

22 Architectural Publication Society, *Dictionary of Architecture*, s.v. 'Hamelin's Cement'.

23 *Ibid.*, s.v. 'Stanhope, Lord'.

24 *Builder*, i (1843), p. 289.

25 Windsor, RA, 34069.

26 *1831 Report*, p. 273.

27 Bishop (1875), pp. 71–5.

28 Windsor, RA, 31710.

29 Pugin's account with Nash is in the Shide Ledger, ff. 3–15.

30 WORKS 4/21, p. 381.

31 *King's Works*, vi, pp. 105–9.

32 *Ibid.*, pp. 109–10.

33 *Ibid.*, pp. 127 ff.

34 *Ibid.*, p. 129.

35 *Ibid.*, p. 106.

36 *Ibid.*, p. 111.

37 WORKS 4/23, pp. 98, 232, 314.

38 M. Port, *Six Hundred New Churches* (1961).

Notes

39 WORKS 4/23, p. 61.

40 R. Liscombe, 'Economy, Character and Durability: Specimen Designs for the Church Commissioners, 1818', *Architectural History*, xiii (1970), pp. 43–57, pls 27–35.

41 Plan and elevation in *Britton and Pugin*, ii, pp. 99–101.

42 Port (1961) p. 47.

43 *Parl. Debs.*, N.S., xi, 35.

44 D. Watkin, *C. R. Cockerell* (1974), p. 68.

45 T. F. Bumpus, *London Churches Ancient and Modern* [1909], p. 126.

9 BUILDING THE PARK

1 CRES 2/742.

2 CRES 2/745. D. Stroud, *Capability Brown* (1975), p. 35.

3 *2nd Report CWFLR*, p. 17.

4 *Ibid.*, App. 20, p. 113.

5 R. C. Papers, Book I.

6 *Ibid.*

7 This statement occurs in a draft history of the canal among the R. C. Papers, but is scored through in the original.

8 Letters from Nash to Drinkwater, secretary of the company, 15 Sept. and 13 Oct., in R. C. Papers, Book II.

9 *Compendium* (1831) in R. C. Papers.

10 *Morning Herald,* 2 Aug. 1820

11 *The Times,* 2 Aug. 1820.

12 *Statement* (1829).

13 In 1831 a *Compendium* and map were printed and circulated to shareholders. Nash's letter to Drinkwater (East Cowes, July 1831), acknowledging his copy, contains an invitation to the island, and ends with a postscript: 'the vellum map Mrs. Nash has appropriated to herself, saying that it is too handsome for me'. R. C. Papers, Book IV.

14 *Britton and Pugin*, i, pp. 83–88. J. M. Crook, 'The Villas in Regents Park (1)', *C Life,* 4 July 1968, pp. 22–25.

15 CRES 2/758.

16 J. M. Crook, 'The Villas in Regents Park (2)', *C. Life,* 11 July 1968, pp. 84–7.

17 William Smith, builder of Sussex Place, paid him £200. *Shide Ledger*, f. 156.

18 *Britton and Pugin*, ii, pp. 233–4.

19 CRES 2/767.

20 CRES 2/770.

21 *Britton and Pugin*, ii, p. 229.

22 *Ibid.*, pp. 233–4. CRES 2/775.

23 *Elmes*, p. 48.

24 CRES 2/772.

25 Probably the perspective reproduced in *Architectural Review,* 1905, p. 109.

26 J. White, *Some Account of the Proposed Improvements* (2nd. ed., 1815), pp. 94–5 and lxxvi–lxxxii.

27 *Britton and Pugin*, i, pp. 167–179.

28 CRES 2/771 and 774.

29 Nash to Milne, 17 April 1822, in CRES 2/771.

30 *Britton and Pugin*, i, pp. 66–71.

31 H. B. Wheatley, *London Past and Present* (1891), i, p. 9. *6th Report CWFLR*, p. 5.

32 Wheatley (1891), i, p. 446. CRES 2/777.

33 CRES 2/780.

34 Nash to Milne, 3 Mar. 1825, in CRES 2/1737.

35 Nash to Milne, 30 Mar. 1825, *ibid.*

36 Nash to Milne, 29 Feb. 1826, *ibid.* A. Saunders, *Regents Park: a Study of the Development from 1086 to the Present Day* (1969), pp. 122–7.

37 Milne to Wilkins, 6 May 1826, *ibid.*

38 Nash to Milne, 13 June 1826, in CRES 2/768. Burton to Milne, 21 June 1826, in CRES 2/1737.

39 Treasury to Commissioners of Woods, 25 Aug. 1826, in CRES 2/1737.

40 Nash to Milne, 29 Feb. 1826, in CRES 2/1737.

41 CRES 2/1738. *London Survey*, xix, pp. 116–17, Pls 87–97.

42 *Elmes*, p. 313.

43 *APSD.*, s.v. 'Thomson, James'.

44 In CRES 2/1738, however, is a plan signed 'F. G. Green 1828'.

45 I am indebted to the late C. H. Bell for communicating his inquiries into the history of the Hospital and for extracts from letters written by Ambrose Poynter on which this paragraph is based.

46 *DNB.*, s.v. 'Scoles, J. J.'. *London Survey*, xix, pp. 98–9, Pls. 53–4.

47 CRES 2/786.

48   *Builder*, 1861, p. 848.

49   *5th Report CWFLR*, p. 11.

50   CRES 2/768.

51   MPE 9/12.

52   F. C. J. Hearnshaw, *The Centenary History of King's College, London* (1929), pp. 58–61.

53   *6th Report CWFLR*, p. 74. CRES 2/742.

54   *6th Report CWFLR*, p. 74.

55   A. Saunders, *op. cit.*, pp. 130–3.

56   MPE 911.

57   CRES 2/778.

58   Contrary to the legend, probably indestructible, that they were occupied by kept women.

59   *Survey of London*, xxi (1949), pp. 153–8, pls 87–99.

60   *1829 Report*, p. 119. *4th Report CWFLR*, p. 56. Chabanne, Marquis de, *On Conducting Air by Forced Ventilation* [1819], appendix with plan and section. I am indebted to Mr Andrew Saint for this reference.

10   REGENT STREET, CHARING CROSS, THE STRAND

1   'All the working designs and details are made by the builders, who are not very scrupulous in deviating from their designs, and departing from architectural rules, or of not consulting them at all; and this is the source from which come the architectural defects in the details of the elevations in the New Street.' *1828 Report*, p. 73.

2   Here and in what follows the dates of buildings and names of builders are extracted from the *Reports of the Commissioners*. Plans of all buildings in the street are given in the 21 volumes of Deeds of Purchase in the Public Record Office (LR 1/255, etc.). Drawn and engraved views are to be found in various collections and are too numerous for individual reference. The best selection of reproductions, including the whole of the John Tallis series (1845 ed.) is in H. Hobhouse, *A History of Regent Street* (1795). A photographic survey of the street in 1910 is in the National Monuments Record.

3   A coloured drawing is listed in *Sale Cat.* (1835). Plan, LR 1/259, f. 237.

4   A coloured drawing is listed in *Sale Cat.* (1835). Measured drawing and photographs in *Architect and Building News*, 5 Jan. 1934.

5   Plans and elevation by Repton in RIBA.

6   *Britton and Pugin*, i, pp. 102–6. Drawings in RIBA.

7   Son of Sir Charles Blicke, a surgeon, who died in 1815, leaving a large fortune. The house cost about £12,000. Shide Ledger, ff. 185–6. Plan, LR 1/269, f. 223.

8   Plans, LR 1/259, ff. 156–9 and 175–6.

9   *Britton and Pugin*, ii, pp. 287–9. The iron gates to the forecourt are illustrated in L. N. Cottingham, *The Smith and Founder's Director* (1824), pl. 29.

10   *Elmes*, p. 149.

11   D. Watkin, *Thomas Hope* (1968), p. 230.

12   Nash's account with Evans is in Shide Ledger, f. 216.

13   *Tour in England, Ireland and France by a German Prince* (1832), iv, pp. 85–6.

14   CRES 26/6, p. 11.

15   Article in *DNB*.

16   CRES 26/134.

17   *Builder*, vi (1848), p. 548. *Illustrated London News*, 1848, p. 280.

18   The first allusion is in a letter from Nash to the Commissioners dated 7 September 1813 (CRES 26/17) relative to the curve at the north end of the street leading to Portland Place. 'Individuality and variety of design and separation of the buildings by the intervention of trees may make this the most interesting part of the New Street and produce the same effect to the eye as the High Street of Oxford so generally admired.' In his first proposal for the Quadrant (WFLR, *2nd Report*, 1816) he describes it as 'a bending street, resembling in that respect, the High-Street at Oxford.'

19   D. Watkin, *C. R. Cockerell* (1974), pp. 136–45.

20   *1828 Report*, p. 73.

21   *Elmes*, p. 137.

22   *Ibid.*, pp. 111–12.

23   J. Elmes, *Annals of the Fine Arts*, V (1820), p. 196. Plan, LR 1/265, f. 115; 272, f. 190.

24   *Survey of London*, xxix, pp. 237, 241.

25   56 Geo. III, cap. 128.

26 *1829 Report*, p. 127.

27 CRES 26/5, p. 222. *Britton and Pugin*, i, pp. 262–72.

28 1 and 2 Geo. IV (1821), cap. 52.

29 All the above details are from *1829 Report*.

30 Whitley, *Art in England, 1821–37* (1930), pp. 51–3. *Elmes*, p. 298.

31 *King's Works*. vi, p. 303.

32 *Britton and Pugin*, ii, pp. 219–23.

33 *5th Report*, CWFLR, p. 12.

34 CRES 26/15, p. 438.

35 *King's Works*, vi, p. 463.

36 *Athenaeum*, No. 221 (21 Jan. 1832), p. 70. *Gent's Mag.*, ci (1831), pp. 204–5; *Architectural Review*, March 1979, pp. 150–160.

37 *5th Report*, WFLR, p. 12.

38 *Ibid.*, pp. 12–13.

II   SCENES IN THE ISLE OF WIGHT

1 Probably for the 1st ed. of W. Cooke, *A New Picture of the Isle of Wight* (2nd ed. 1813). For other engraved views see Peacock, *Polite Repository*, Nov. 1800; R. Ackermann, *Repository of the Arts,* vii (1826), p. 249; *Barber's Picturesque Views of the Isle of Wight* (n.d., c. 1834). Other engraved views are reproduced in *Davis (1960)*, pl. 41 and *Davis (1966)*, pl. 39. A photographic record of the house in a state of dereliction was made by G. B. Mason in 1949 for the National Monuments Record.

2 B.M., Add. MS. 43, 228, f. 74.

3 *The Farington Diary* (ed. J. Greig), viii (1928), p. 143.

4 *Ibid.*, p. 301.

5 *Ibid.*, p. 268.

6 Windsor, RA, 33980.

7 B. Ferrey, *Recollections of A. W. N. Pugin* (1861), pp. 4–5. H. Twiss, *Life of Eldon* (1846), p. 555.

8 Entry in a contemporary logbook, contributed by Miss K. E. Roberton, Isle of Wight.

9 *The Farington Diary*, as above, p. 142.

10 Pennethorne papers.

11 Farington typescript, p. 7490.

12 T. Brettell, *Topographical and Historical Guide to the Isle of Wight* (1840), p. 134.

13 Farington typescript, p. 7853.

14 D. Watkin, *C. R. Cockerell* (1974), p. 68.

15 *The Journal of Mrs. Arbuthnot 1820–32* (ed. Francis Bamford and the Duke of Wellington, 1950), i, p. 334.

16 Article, 'Curtis, Sir W.' in *DNB*. Nash designed stables for him (Repton sketch-book, RIBA).

17 George Ward (1752–1829) was an important figure in Nash's circle at least from 1812, when he participated in the Regents Canal project. In his will (PRO, PROB 11/1755) he left £100 each to 'my much esteemed friend Mr. Nash', to 'his good wife Mrs. Nash', to 'Miss Anne Pennithorne' [*sic*] and to 'my valued friend Lord George Seymour'. He is buried at West Cowes. His son, George Henry Ward (1786–1849), was also a friend of Nash. Other associations with the family are mentioned in Chapter 13.

18 M. D. George, *Catalogue of Political and Personal Satires . . . in the British Museum*, ix (1949), No. 13854.

19 Faringt on Typescript, pp. 8077, 8079.

20 Genealogy in Pennethorne papers, showing descent of Mrs. Nash from John Gregory (b. 1682).

21 *The Farington Diary*, as above, p. 302.

22 L. James, *A Forgotten Genius: Sewell of St. Columba's and Radley* (1945), p. 29. I am indebted to Mr Roger Fulford for this reference.

23 Diary of Ann Pennethorne, 13 Feb. 1851.

24 *DNB.*, article 'Pennethorne, Sir J.'.

25 Communicated to the author in conversation by the late R. K. Liddon, 1933.

26 Pennethorne Hughes, 'The Last State Architect', *C. Life*, 22 Feb. 1952.

27 *Pigot and Co's National Commercial Directory* (1835), p. 669. Information kindly supplied by Worcester Public Library.

28 Bodleian Library, MS. Finch d. 21.

29 *The Farington Diary*, p. 268.

30 *Ibid.* p. 302.

31 Cwmgwili MS. 433.

32 *Victoria County Histories: Hants.*, p. 273.
33 *Davis (1966)*, pl. 41, reproduces a drawing by G. S. Repton.
34 *Barber's Picturesque Illustrations of the Isle of Wight*, p. 44.

35 *Ibid.*, Nash's drawings for the building, in a red morocco binding, are in the care of the Borough Surveyor.
36 Sketch-plan and elevation in *Summerson* (1935), p. 157. This lodge adjoins the churchyard.

12 THE KINGS PALACE

1 Farington Typescript, pp. 7846, 7853.
2 Soane Corres., 2, xii, G(2).
3 *King's Works*, vi, p. 647.
4 Soane Corres., 2, xii, G(2).
5 Soane Museum, Inv. No. 82.
6 Soane Museum, Inv. No. 123.
7 Soane Museum, Inv. No. 93.
8 Soane Corres., 1, iii, N. Printed, with omissions, in *Bolton* (1927), pp. 351–3.
9 Soane Corres., 1, iii, N. *Bolton* (1927), p. 355.
10 WORKS 4/22, p. 33; 4/23, pp. 81, 307; 4/24, p. 365. O. Morshead, *George IV and Royal Lodge* (1965), p. 16.
11 D. Linstrum, *Sir Jeffry Wyatville, Architect to the King* (1972).
12 *King's Works*, vi, pp. 381–3.
13 *The Penny Cyclopedia* (1833 etc.), *s.v.* 'Windsor Castle'.
14 6 Geo. IV, cap. 77.
15 *1831 Report*, p. 271.
16 *King's Works*, vi, p. 278.
17 *Ibid.*, pp. 267–8.
18 *Creevey Papers* (ed. Maxwell, 1905), ii, p. 156.
19 *1828 Report*, p. 61.
20 *Ibid.*
21 *King's Works*, vi, pp. 294–6.

22 *1831 Report*, pp. 270–1.
23 *King's Works*, vi, pp. 297–9.
24 3 Geo. IV, cap. 7.
25 *1828 Report*, p. 66.
26 The temple is shown on a drawing of the terraces in MPE 891, No. 16.
27 *1828 Report*, p. 63.
28 P. 79, *ante*.
29 *1833 Report*, pp. 51 and 54.
30 MPE 43.
31 *Ibid.* Nash's covering letter, sent with the book, is among the unnumbered papers in CRES 2/533.
32 *London Survey*, xxix, pp. 386 ff.
33 D. Stroud, *Capability Brown* (1975), pl. 54a.
34 *1828 Report*, p. 63.
35 *Parl. Debs.*, xxi (N.S.), pp. 1320, 1578.
36 *1829 Report*, p. 25.
37 *Statement* (1829).
38 *Parl. Debs.*, xxi (N.S.), p. 1818.
39 *Statement* (1829).
40 Wellington, *Despatches*, 2nd ser. (1873), V, p. 616.
41 *Ibid.*
42 A. Aspinall (ed.), *The Letters of King George IV, 1812–30* (1838), no. 1563.

13 THE CLOUDED YEARS: THE END

1 St George, Hanover Square, Rate Books, Westminster City Library.
2 Lytton, Earl of, *Life of Edward Bulwer, first Lord Lytton* (1913), i, pp. 245–7.
3 E. Bulwer, *Paul Clifford* (1830), i, Ch. X.
4 A letter from Lawrence to the Principal of Jesus College, 11 Oct. 1827, in the college archives, shows that the portrait cost £449 10s.
5 This portrait is in the possession of Major

Allan J. Cameron of Lochiel, together with a letter from Knighton to Nash (4 March 1824), conveying the King's permission, a letter from Nash to Lawrence (20 December 1824), asking for 'a bit of the pavilion seen through a window or sticking out of a portfolio' to be introduced and Lawrence's reply dated 18 Feb. 1825.
6 *1831 Report*, p. 172.

Notes

7 I am indebted to Mr Robert Stanley-Morgan for sending me a transcript of this letter which he has since published in *Architectural Review*, December 1965, pp. 452–3.

8 *1831 Report, loc. cit.*

9 *1831 Report*, pp. 187–8.

10 *Ibid.*, p. 190.

11 *Ibid.*, pp. 190–2.

12 *Ibid.*, pp. 46 ff.

13 *Ibid.*, p. 226. *King's Works*, vi, pp. 275–6.

14 *1831 Report*, p. 285.

15 *Ibid.*, pp. 3–7.

16 *King's Works*, vi, pp. 277–8.

17 *Ibid.*, pp. 280–92.

18 *Ibid.*, p. 293. H. Clifford Smith, *Buckingham Palace* (1931), pp. 174–6.

19 *The Creevey Papers* (ed. H. Maxwell, 1905), p. 493.

20 *King's Works*, vi, p. 269. M. D. George, *Catalogue of Political and Personal Satires in the British Museum*, ix (1944), Nos 15668–15676.

21 Quoted in R. Huish, *Memoirs of George IV* (1830), p. 132 n.

22 *Parl. Debs.*, 3rd. ser., iv, 1447–1450.

23 *Fraser's Magazine, for Town and Country*, No. 4 (May 1830), pp. 379–388.

24 W. Knighton, *Memoirs* (ed. D. Knighton, 1838), p. 54. WORKS 4/26. p. 406.

25 One of several designs listed in *Sale Cat., 1835*. Two of them are in the Soane Museum, including the one from which the Picton monument derives. The drawing is by Frederick Mackenzie.

26 *Carm. Antiq. Soc. Trans.*, xxi, p. 39. W. Spurrell, *Carmarthen and its Neighbourhood* (2nd ed., 1879), p. 54 gives a woodcut and a water-colour is in the National Library of Wales (Mansel Franklin Collection, Prints, etc., No. 27). A bas-relief from the monument is preserved in the Carmarthen County Museum.

27 Nash's diaries for 1832 and 1835, the only survivors, were kindly placed at my disposal by their owner, Mr Peter Laing, a direct descendant of Sir James Pennethorne. Both are written in *Simpson's Gentleman's Almanack and Pocket Journal* for the appropriate year. The Penne-thorne diary was, in 1934, in the possession of Mr J. Pennethorne of Richmond, who kindly

allowed me to make extracts. I am not aware of its present whereabouts.

28 1818–91. Article in G. Grove, *Dict. of Music.* (ed. E. Blom, 1954).

29 J. C. Herries, was at that date President of the Board of Trade. Thomas Pemberton, later Baron Kingsdown, was a famous barrister. Vaughan and Lyon were, of course, the partners in Edwards and Lyon. There were two brothers named Pollock, both well-known KCs.

30 The letter is printed in full in *Davis (1966)*.

31 *The Farington Diary* (ed. J. Greig, 1928), viii, p. 275.

32 R. C. Papers, Book iv.

33 What follows is largely based on a letter from Nash to Vere, Sapt, Banbury and Co., dated East Cowes Castle, 25 July 1834, and now in the archives of the National Westminster Bank.

34 Communicated to me verbally by the late Mr R. K. Liddon in 1933.

35 PRO, PROB 11/1830, f. 249.

36 PRO, PROB 11/1851, f. 507.

37 The will contains an alternative disposition, in the event of Mrs Nash's predeceasing her husband, as follows: G. H. Ward and James Pennethorne (executors), £300 each; James Morgan, J. W. Lyon, Emma Lyon, Mrs Elizabeth Martin (sister-in-law), £200 each; children of Elizabeth Martin, £100 each; Sarah Edwards Vaughan (widow of John Edwards Vaughan) and Jessey Lee Lee, her daughter, £500 each; Ann Pennethorne, £10,000; Grace Parker (sister-in-law), annuity of £500; all real estate to Nash Vaughan Edwards Vaughan. We may suspect that this disposition reflects a previous will.

38 For Booth see article in *DNB*.

39 A local tradition, communicated to me in 1933 by the Rev. R. S. Moxon.

40 Information kindly supplied by Messrs Christie, Manson and Woods.

41 A priced catalogue is in the Soane Museum (Pamphlet 43).

42 Extract from the correspondence of Cecilia Parke, daughter of Lord Wensleydale, com-municated to me by the late Lady Ridley.

43 *The Times*, Dec. 1841, p. 6, col. f.

44 *Annual Register*, 1835, p. 221.

45 See articles in *DNB* on Theodore Hook, the

Rev. James Hook and his son, Walter Farquhar Hook. The Rector and his son (his father's curate) were dining with Nash when Farington visited him in 1821.

46 *John Bull*, 18 May 1835, p. 156. Reprinted in *The Annual Biography and Obituary*, xx (1836), pp. 449–50.
47 *Builder*, xv (1857), pp. 287–8.

Index

Index